Withdrawn

CLOUDEHILL

A YEAR IN THE GARDEN

CLOUDEHILL

A YEAR IN THE GARDEN

Jeremy Francis

Principal photography by Claire Takacs

images
Publishing

Published in Australia in 2010 by
The Images Publishing Group Pty Ltd
ABN 89 059 734 431
6 Bastow Place, Mulgrave, Victoria 3170, Australia
Tel: +61 3 9561 5544 Fax: +61 3 9561 4860
books@imagespublishing.com
www.imagespublishing.com

Copyright © The Images Publishing Group Pty Ltd 2010
The Images Publishing Group Reference Number: 910

National Library of Australia Cataloguing-in-Publication entry:

Author: Francis, Jeremy.
Title: Cloudehill : a year in the garden / by Jeremy Francis; principal photography by Claire Takacs.

Edition: 1st ed.

ISBN: 9781864703771 (hbk.)

Notes: Includes bibliographical references and index.

Subjects: Francis, Jeremy.
                 Farmers–Australia–Biography.
                 Gardens–Victoria–Olinda–Pictorial works.
                 Cloudehill (Olinda, Victoria)–Pictorial works.

Other Authors/Contributors: Takacs, Claire.

Dewey Number: 630.9945

Edited by Robyn Beaver

Designed by The Graphic Image Studio Pty Ltd, Mulgrave, Australia
www.tgis.com.au

Pre-publishing services by United Graphic Pte Ltd, Singapore
Printed on 150 gsm Quatro Silk Matt by Everbest Printing Co. Ltd., in Hong Kong/China

IMAGES has included on its website a page for special notices in relation to this and our other publications. Please visit www.imagespublishing.com.

CONTENTS

FOREWORD

I first met Jeremy Francis in the late 1980s when he came over to Victoria from Western Australia and talked to me about his dream of making a seriously good garden. I like nothing better than talking about gardens, gardeners and gardening and Jeremy's enthusiasm was infectious. A long, warm and rewarding friendship developed from that original meeting. Mind you, I had no idea just how grand Jeremy's plans were until I saw the terraces being cut into the hillside at Cloudehill and the massive retaining walls started.

This was gardening on an awesome scale. I hoped that the Francis family fortune would hold out until the job was finished. Hold out it did, just. The garden was finished inasmuch as any garden is ever finished. Cloudehill has become one of the great Australian gardens, certainly the most original and beautiful made in the last few of decades.

I visit the garden regularly and yet each time it astonishes me. It is part Italianate, part Arts and Crafts, part van Sweden, part wild gardening, part woodland gardening and part meadow gardening. All these elements are combined in a thrillingly logical way. Each part of the garden is as important as the next. It pays to take time to wander around. There's just as much purpose to the smallest detail as the largest architectural feature.

Anyone who gardens in more than a perfunctory way knows just how hard it is to make anything half-way decent. Germans and Danes use the term master gardener to describe someone who, over many years, has learnt the complex, difficult skill of gardening. While it isn't a phrase commonly used in Australia, it perfectly describes Jeremy Francis.

The story of Cloudehill isn't the only story to be found in this fascinating book. It is also a family memoir spanning most of the 20th century. Jeremy Francis wasn't born into horticulture but into agriculture. His father was a successful Western Australian sheep and wheat farmer and Jeremy was brought up on the family farm and spent most of his early working life farming.

Travelling through rural Australia you will often pass derelict farm buildings surrounded by senescent trees planted by some long-dead gardener. These old farms have long been bought by more fortunate or wealthier neighbours and amalgamated into ever-larger holdings. In time the old buildings and trees will disappear and there will be no trace left of the lives, dreams and struggles of the people who once lived there. There is something incredibly sad about this process. The author's grandparents, uncles and aunts once lived in some of these now-deserted farmhouses and this book gives us a glimpse into their lives.

The book chronicles in much more detail a childhood spent in the country, the early working years farming and the deep love his parents had for each other. If, like me, you enjoy reading about other people's lives you will enjoy this part of the book.

In the end though, this is the story of the making of a gardener and the making of the Cloudehill garden. Anyone with even the remotest interest in gardening should read this book. It is a real book written by one of the finest gardeners of our age.

David Glenn
Lambley Nursery, Ascot

PREFACE

This is primarily a book about gardening, interspersed with brief diary entries, originally written between June 2004 and the end of May 2005; it is the story of Cloudehill, what it is and how it came to be. Part way through the first twelve month's writing, events overtook me and in response the project expanded. The text was added to, tidied up, interlayered with other material; most was written in snatches between gardening, running a retail nursery, talking to customers, or on occasional evenings. This, I guess, contributes to the book's somewhat episodic nature.

The writing is part diary of the gardening year, part brief family history, part an examination of the links between farming – those elements of agriculture that involve fundamentally altering the landscape – and conventional garden landscaping. I try to make the point that an average farmer's aesthetic influence on the landscape is, at every level, more heartfelt and serious than for most ordinary gardeners.

As the writing unfolded, themes spiralled away as enticing stories were stumbled upon. My parents can be blamed for this, to a degree; they were never great ones for family background. As an illustration: in August 2008, an aunt asked if I was aware that my mother's grandfather, Charles McGowan, died as a result of an Aboriginal spearing. It happened, she said, when he and his 15-year-old-son, my great-grandfather, were out sandalwood cutting in the country between Williams and Narrogin in Western Australia in the last years of the 19th century. Charles was not immediately killed; he survived the bullock dray journey of several days back to

Thompson Brook but he died shortly after they arrived home. Now, one might think this tale should figure somewhere in the family annals but I'd not heard a whisper. It was as though my parents' marriage in 1951 was a turning point of such moment in their lives that nothing earlier mattered. Certainly, little was spoken of and my brother and I seemed to know not to ask. Several years into retirement, at the family's urging, my father got around to penning some foolscap pages of reminiscences. More vivid details in following pages draw heavily on Cam's little memoir. Still, there was plenty of opportunity left for playing detective.

There are many people I must thank. Foremost, my father, Cam, for his interest and support those first months, likewise my sister, Jenny Clairs. In the Lakes District in 2007: Cameron Mudge and Vicki and Aubrey McPhee; at Moulyinning: Karl and Marny West; Mogumber and Moora: Paul and Robyn Linke, Simon and Claire Forrester, Tom, Kaye and Stewart Kelly, Don and Moira McKinley, and Wendy Mckinley, also that stupendous pilot and great sport Bob Conn; in Perth: Sally and Wade Dodson, Sue McPhee and Margaret Wilson; in the Dandenongs: the Woolrich family in general, especially Sylvia McElroy, also David Glenn and Criss Canning, Arnold and Don Teese, Ethyl Genet and her family; also landscapers and gardeners Simon Donald, Richard Dooley, Craig Shalders, Wes McIntosh and numerous others who have helped, physically, with the garden over what is now 18 years, culminating in the inestimable Geoffrey Barnes; finally, my own family, Benjamin and Alys, and especially my nerve-wracked wife, Valerie, for patience beyond all right and expectation.

Jeremy Francis

PART ONE

7 June 2004, late morning

Today is a still, silvery, early winter day; two weeks left to the solstice. Banks of mist move silently, almost imperceptibly, without direction. Low cloud opens to clear sky, the mountain momentarily radiant, then the blue fades swiftly to shadow and white. Dense lead-grey fog slides from under neighbouring mountain ash, envelopes the garden for a while, then slowly rises and thins to a luminous silver sheet hanging entangled through the trees. It is cold, 5 degrees Celsius and almost midday. Several times these past hours I have found myself standing, watching the sky.

Gertrude Jekyll, the garden writer of late Victorian and Edwardian England, famously pondered which trees to remove from her Munstead Wood garden on a similar morning. Detail today is generally hazy, barely visible; only Cloudehill's bones are clear: walls and trees and hedges. Smaller plants are lost in mist so a good time for rethinking structure, for decisions. The mists of West Surrey in the winter of 1898 were likely similar to the mist we have today. Miss Jekyll wrote in Wood and Garden *of deliberating with her axeman over trees to fell, to more crisply define her Scots pine copses. Thin mist concentrated her eye to the task in hand. Mind you, with losses of several big trees in storms these past winters there is no reason to think of my removing things; it is good to just stroll and see the light through the clouds.*

The garden in winter has its own rewards: the down-beat architecture of brown hedges and bare trees, and the joy of weather. Better, though, than silent mornings with sun and mist are days with wind and weather systems, roaring days with nearby mountain ash, young Eucalyptus regnans, all 45 to 60 metres high, swaying vertiginously and twisting skeins of grey purple cloud moving at speed just out of their reach. With a good thick jacket I can walk for hours, or at least until squalls pour over the ridge with that hissing, chaotic surf roar from the big gums to the west. Sheltering in a garden pavilion I watch cloud tumbling through the trees, an eddying grey mass falling vertically into the garden, spilling across the lawn, obliterating rows of skeletal English beech.

The hous is krynkeled two & fro,
And hath so queynte weyis for to go
For it is shapyn as the mase is wrought.

Chaucer, *The Legend of Ariadne*

THE MOGUMBER HILLS

I have always enjoyed winter. As a child and for 30 years I lived on a wheat and sheep farm a little inland from the central west coast of Western Australia – a place enjoying fiercely hot, perfectly dry summers and moist, mild, green, idyllic winters. 'Merrie-Lea' covered some 3000 acres a few miles north of Mogumber. Comprising a small stone post office, tiny pub, bulk grain silos beside the railway and just two or three houses, Mogumber is famous, notorious even now, for the Moore River Settlement (the 'Methodist Mission' we always called it), a few minutes' drive off to the west. This was a place where the 'Stolen Generation' were sent. Thousands of Aboriginal children, taken from their families from all over Western Australia, lived out their childhoods here. In the middle of a couple of thousand acres of banksia sandhill country, the Settlement amounted to corrugated iron barracks and spartan classrooms scattered under pine trees beside a string of river pools. Mogumber was one of several diminutive towns whose lovely names preserve voices of those same people: Wanamal, Gillingarra, Koojan – all have dwindled to a few abandoned buildings. The city of Perth was around two hours' drive south through the orange

Merrie-Lea from 'Pat Kelly's hill'. River gums lining the Moore River with the railway and road beyond, Merrie-Lea homestead half way up its little hill left of centre, Babillion ridge on the skyline upper left, Darling Escarpment flowing from left to right down to some of our cropping paddocks and the Dandaragan sandplain, extreme upper right, leading towards the Moore River Settlement.

groves and vineyards of Bindoon and Bullsbrook; the nearest place with stock and station agents and grocery shopping was Moora, half an hour to the north and 20 minutes to the east, the four square red brick buildings of the Benedictine Monastery of New Norcia arose with unexpected grandeur each side of the Great Northern Highway.

Merrie-Lea was ruggedly handsome and its predictable winter rains and generally fertile soils made it reliably productive. The farm faced west with the northern branch of the Moore River flowing down the valley in front of us. Our best cropping paddocks bounded the river flats along the low western edge of the property. Merrie-Lea's spine was a range of rock-strewn hills that rose sharply above our wheat crops as a series of broken ridges. The Moora road snaked beside the river flats in long lazy curves along our west boundary with the Perth–Geraldton railway close to the road. The rattle of freight trains laden with grain echoed between the hills at odd hours, even shook the house on still nights. It was a comfortable sound though, and never entirely wakened me.

The Merrie-Lea hills formed part of the high western edge of the Darling Escarpment and from our east boundary successive ridges of the Darling Ranges could be seen dropping away to the horizon. Beyond the last grey ridge, the eastern branch of the Moore River formed a broad valley as it flowed past New Norcia. Further east, the open paddocks of the central wheat belt stretched across wide shallow valleys of the Victoria Plains. Then came the Wongan Hills and further the uncertain wheat lands of Mukinbudin and Kalannie and Southern Cross, then immense paddocks with thin wheat crops before the first of the pastoral leases: station country. The big map on the wall of the Gillingarra primary school showed sparsely settled pastoral lands, arid goldfields and empty deserts for thousands of miles across Australia. Green reappeared as a meandering strip following the Pacific Ocean shoreline. The cities and towns and farmlands of those distant parts seemed like a far away foreign country to all of us, sitting in that classroom, the people unimaginably different.

Mogumber farms depended on their soil. River flats consisted of excellent silt loams washed from upstream red earth areas. Riverside paddocks grew dense swards of clover and ryegrass and the ochre loam paddocks sloping gently up to Merrie-Lea's steep hills were capable of growing some of Western Australia's best cereal crops. However, farms on the far bank of the Moore River, barely a mile from our house, were made on banksia sand. To the west, Merrie-Lea overlooked a very different geological region, the Dandaragan Plateau or, as we called it, the sandplain. We looked at the efforts of people farming their pale sandy blocks with misgiving.

Top: From the razorback across the gully dam paddock towards the Sherwood hills
Above: From the Sherwood ridge back towards the house hill

The impoverished, endlessly deep sands of the Dandaragan Plateau, with its tattered grey banksia scrub, flowed out from the escarpment hills for more than 20 miles before stepping down further to low sandy heathlands. Heathland met the sea in shifting sand hills and wind-blown dunes edged the white-sand beaches of the Indian Ocean nearly 50 miles to our west.

Wind is the constant of the central west coast of WA. Apart from polar regions, meteorologists regard it as close to the windiest place on earth. In winter, westerlies roar across the coast every few days while in summer, fiercely hot, bone dry, sirocco-like winds pour off the Australian landmass out over the Indian Ocean. The winds were so relentless that when estimating the amount of water our farm windmills might pump, rather than allowing the four to eight hours wind each day usual to the rest of Australia, we could presume 16 to 20 hours for Merrie-Lea. Close to the coast, the sea winds force exposed trees over to the ground, stretching off to the east. A little inland, sea winds and winds from the land counterbalance, more-or-less upright trees buffeted from the west for the winter months and throughout the long summers by never-ending cycles of ferociously hot easterlies. Winds blow from both directions in spring; the only time with little wind is that waiting season of every year, autumn.

Merrie-Lea's homestead was near the top of a small hill, around half a mile in from the front road. It overlooked our wheat paddocks, the encircling hills and the sandplain over the river. A typical farmhouse of the area – fibro and weatherboard with a corrugated tin roof painted green – it was large, rambling and awkward. Windows lined the north and west walls to enjoy the best views and so allowed plenty of sunshine in; the warmer months of the year could be stifling.

I have always supposed my mother Jan came from generations of women experienced at making something out of not much. My parents began married life with makeshift packing-case furniture and odds and ends given them by friends. Still, Jan was never one to be complacent with her lot and, with every satisfactory wheat harvest or wool clip, another room was carpeted or a sideboard added. But it happened slowly, season by season and walking around the Merrie-Lea homestead was eventually unsettling. Enthusiasms arose and waned and the vivid paint colours, inspired by early 1960s American *Vogue* magazines, would 15 years later provide the backdrop to curtains and furniture that might be more at home in a Gloucestershire vicarage. Rooms had wallpaper at odds with the next and in defiance of farm life and our dusty soils my mother laid thick creamy white carpets over the pine floorboards. Need I add though, all was kept fastidiously?

Jan was always tidy-minded, nothing was left lying around in the house and our car was carefully washed before shopping trips to Moora. Her hair was permanently immaculate at the expense of a four-hour round trip to Perth to see one especially entrusted hairdresser she visited fortnightly for nearly 30 years. In later years Jan became ever more exacting, took to covering kitchen benches with greaseproof paper before working on them and, on completing each task, removing and disposing of paper and crumbs, the benches then scrubbed until gleaming; ready for next time.

In early 1959, soon after my parents bought Merrie-Lea and moved onto the farm, my father Campbell made a rose garden for my mother. Soil around the house was riddled with shaly rock so Cam excavated truckloads of loam from the edge of a stream back in the hills and carted this in for the roses. The loam was pushed into a diamond-shaped bed with a front-end loader and 20 hybrid tea roses arranged in a nice diamond. They grew and flowered happily enough in Mogumber's dry air and sunshine except, after a run of low rainfall winters in the 1970s, the water supply from the front windmill dried up. For a summer or two we carted truckloads of water for the garden but dry times between the waterings lengthened and the roses shrivelled and died away.

The house site was chosen for its views and convenience to the road; certainly not for the soil – atrocious rocky stuff. Digging a hole anywhere near the house was the work of an hour at least, with heavy crowbar and strong-handled shovel. Still, previous owners had made an attempt at a garden: a patch of dusty couch grass grew below the sunroom, sheltered by a windbreak of grape vines trained along fence wire. A purple leaf plum and lilly-pilly shaded the kitchen from the western sun, though after 30 years battling in that rock they were still shrubs. Despite its liking for difficult soils, even the Cape lilac by the pantry corner struggled. On the other hand, revelling in a spot near the back door, a bougainvillea spilled prodigious masses of furnace-red flowers across the path. A jacaranda and Monterey pine, two lemons and an apricot, and several assorted gum trees lined the rabbit netting fence around the house, with a peppercorn tree due east to slow down the wind. These trees, with pelargoniums and pigfaces in narrow beds under the weatherboard walls were all selected to tolerate months of summer drought without water. The windmill in the front paddock pumped a trickle at best into the concrete tank on top of the hill. We shared this water with a flock of sheep – little was left for plants.

Jan and Cam, dressed up for a big night out in the late 1980s

My parents, Janet and Campbell, were known to everyone always as 'Jan and Cam'. They fell in love in the early war years and married close on ten years later in 1951. For both, this involved heartbreak and renunciation. My mother left her first

Left to right:
Fine examples of the ubiquitous blackboys –
Xanthorrhoea preissii – referred to as grass trees
nowadays; One of our many winter streams, the
slope dominated by sheoaks – *Casuarina*;
A typical white gum, or wandoo. Older wandoos
all retained a few dead branches in their crowns,
reminders of bad seasons from 20 and 50 years
earlier.

the hills. To drive off these twisting tracks risked becoming trapped in a chaotic maze of rock. Between the rocks rearing from the earth, subterranean clover pasture grew luxuriantly and supported substantial numbers of merino sheep. Half my childhood and teenage years, much of my life I guess, seems to have been spent in moving flocks from paddock to paddock through those bony hills, always on foot, always with the help of two or three sheep dogs.

Several streams flowing east to west over the eons had eased their way down through our north–south hills on their way to the Moore River. In my memory, their valleys were extraordinarily like an unfolding series of Japanese gardens. Winter rains beaded gullies with pools threaded between tiny waterfalls every few steps, the old rocks tumbled sideways, polished smooth. Stony pools were full of tadpoles that Michael and I would catch with our hands, and splashing water glittered with polished quartz. On maps, the largest of our streams was the 'Diggers Hill Gully'; we examined rocks tirelessly for gold and yellow mica glinting out of translucent quartz pebbles teased us deliciously. Close-cropped rye grass and clover pasture grew down to the water through stands of tammar and sheoak, their fine, needle-like leaves sounding low and melodious in winter squalls. Otherwise trees were nearly all eucalypts – gum trees – which as a child I thought were the only trees in the world: red gums and white gums, sugar gums and manna gums, river gums and powder barks. On clay soils, stands of salmon gum grew with slippery smooth bark, dappled pink and grey, while rough black barked and flat-topped York gums preferred ridgelines. High gravelly soils were home to several species of suckering mallee and on the loose 'sand plain' soils out to our west, black butts were everywhere. Our father talked of gimlets in the outer wheat lands far away to the east on a bush block he helped clear as a youngster. Gimlets were the loveliest of trees, he told us, with wonderful twisting trunks and narrow blue-grey leaves and gleaming bark in astonishing colours – rose mahoganys and sandy silvers – and wood so tough as to make the keenest axe ring and bounce. Two species of casaurina, or 'sheoak', grew throughout the Mogumber district and perhaps 50 species of acacia – wattles. They were usually small shrubs but one reached 20 or 30 feet; these were simply 'jam' trees. In winter and spring, the flowering of innumerable wattles splashed the hills with perfumed gold.

Exploring the Digger's Hill Gully stream that first winter in 1959, beside a pool carved from living rock by a little waterfall and almost hidden by great slabs of granite all grey-green with lichen, Michael and I found a little paper bark tree. The melaleuca grew from a narrow crack and was dwarfed into a dramatically contorted shrub. Although dense stands of swamp paperbarks grew beside the Moore River under tall river gums, this was one of just a handful on Merrie-Lea. The tree was barely high enough to keep its tiny grey leaves above the reach of hungry sheep. For my brother and me, this place became a storybook world. The stream was a mighty river, the big rocks precipitous mountains, their crevices never-ending caves. The stream dropping a few feet from a ledge was a cataract and the twisted, wizened paperbark was a jungle and an echoing fir-tree forest. Michael and I played out elaborate and intense stories with small toys and these endless games went on through all those green winters.

The rock pool, 2007. Just the shattered stump of the melaleuca remains, in the lower right hand section of the photo. The tree snapped off by a cloudburst of water moving down the valley, I guess.

The first Europeans to the area were a small community of families known as the 'Scotch Shepherds': the Macphersons, MacIntoshes, Davidsons, Drummonds and Fergusons. The Scots explored the Mogumber hills, on the lookout for sheep grazing, as early as 1841, just 12 years after the founding of Perth by Captain Stirling in 1829. They rode out from Western Australia's first agricultural settlement, some 80 miles to the southeast of Mogumber, what is now Toodyay. With fresh spring growth, the shepherds walked their flocks from the Avon Valley onto the Victoria Plains and down the valley bottoms of Mogumber and Gillingarra and Koojan, searching for grazing close to the permanent sweet water pools along the east and north branches of the Moore River. One of their favoured camping sites was the 'Jilgil' pool, lying in the Moore River a few minutes' walk from where Merrie-Lea's northern boundary would eventually be. Another was the 'Mount Mary' pool, in the big valley below our southern boundary. The shepherds were walking through an Aboriginal 'firestick' landscape tens of thousands of years in the making. Throughout their country, the Yuad and Yamatgi people used small, cool fires to create a patchwork of open woodlands; regrowth after burns encouraged good numbers of game: kangaroos, emus, wallabies and goannas; this opening out of the bush also made for easy hunting. Autumn burns every few years would have had the Mogumber hills looking lush. On arrival to much of southwest Western Australia, white settlers found they could gallop their horses through open stands of eucalyptus; however, in higher rainfall districts such as Mogumber and Gillingarra, the suppression of firestick agriculture led to the bush filling with taller, more vigorous shrubs that were frequently armed with spines and prickles. I suspect the grazing flocks of the Scots slowed this inevitable deterioration only marginally.

That original vegetation posed considerable danger to the shepherds. Colonies of 'crinkle-leaf' and 'york road' poison have always grown around Mogumber and 120 years later were still to be found in our hill paddocks and along road verges. Both are extremely toxic. I have seen sheep die in agony within minutes of swallowing a single mouthful of york road poison bush. I'm sure the shepherds led their flocks rather than walking behind. Deciding which of the multitude of plants were killing their stock cannot have been easy and constant vigilance would have been crucial. Curiously, through the eons, indigenous wildlife has become immune to the toxins of the Mogumber flora and kangaroos browse york road poison without consequence.

The Scotch shepherds walked their sheep through the Mogumber hills for nearly 40 years until, ironically, they were succeeded by shepherds associated with Bishop Dom Salvado's Benedictine monastery of New Norcia. Here was a most energetic and ambitious ecclesiastical gentleman. With dreams of establishing a pastoral mission servicing the spiritual needs of the indigenous people, in 1846 Dom Salvado and his fellow priest Dom Serra founded the Benedictine community near the banks of the east branch of the Moore River. With the long traditions and learning of the Benedictine order at his back and his friendship with the Spanish royal family to strengthen his arm, Dom Salvado swept the raw Scots from their hills and river pools with ease. He lobbied the colonial authorities with such effect that by 1885 he'd amassed grazing rights to some 960,000 acres. The New Norcia community's holdings stretched from Bindoon in the south to the Irwin River in the north, from the flood plains of the northern Moore River to the Wongan Hills in the east, with droving tracks radiating throughout from New Norcia. However, the good bishop's giant pastoral mission collapsed within a handful of years. Grazing rights to much of the monks' land were revoked with the arrival of the railway in 1892 and the Mogumber hills surveyed into farms.

Irish families who followed the Spanish monks to New Norcia: the Kellys, Halligans, Lanigans, Marrs, Clunes and Norwoods, along with a few Scots who had been biding their time, took up the new farms and began pulling down the big old gum trees along the river flats. Two generations later, as a boy in early 1959, I remember first seeing the Gillingarra and Mogumber hills, low-lying paddocks long cleared and well pastured, foothills still only part-cleared and hilltops covered in almost impenetrable bush in its summer livery of soiled olive and khaki.

In the Mediterranean-like climate of the district – mild winter rains followed by heat and drought of a six-month-long summer – the Merrie-Lea streams only flowed for a few weeks in July and August. Warmer September days brought capeweed into bloom to form paddock-wide sheets of buttery yellow and with this flowering our precious streams slowed to puddles and vanished between the rocks. In early November the first east wind of the summer came out of the southeast and day by day swung to true east and northeast until its long sweeping path took it deep over the baking inland. The wind in turn baked us, dried out our farm, turned our green to gold and brown – and summer.

November was the end of our growing season, the end of our green months; a kind of dying. However, during the last weeks of spring – September and October – road verges and uncleared hilltops erupted with a tremendous show of wildflowers: green and red kangaroo paws, red and gold cat's paws, sometimes black and green kangaroo paws. In shady soils in moist valleys we might see green hoods and spider

Spring wildflowers near Mogumber, 2007

orchids while gold and crimson donkey orchids and blue enamel orchids enjoyed dry slopes. Yellow flowering hibbertia grew best on sunny road verges, often near lechenaultia with little clouds of sky-blue starry flowers. For those few warm moist days the detail and intricacy of the flowering of the bush was everywhere. Callistemons and dampieras, dryandras and grevilleas, hakeas and isopogons filled every gully, every slope and every hilltop. Last to bloom, in a way signifying the months to come, were lanky smoke bushes with a haze of oyster-grey flowers. Then flowers died away with the grass turning yellow and brown. Warm November winds pushed long rolling waves through our fields of wheat and barley, softening their emerald to grey-green, to ochre-yellow and rusty gold.

In the winter of 1845, Johnston Drummond was speared by an Aboriginal by the name of Kabinger. This was not another of those anonymous killings of the time, part and parcel of white encroachment into the bush; the two men actually knew each other rather well. Drummond was leading an exploratory party onto the Victoria Plains and in his party were several native guides including Kabinger's wife, his sister and brother-in-law. Kabinger's wife joined the expedition despite her husband's strenuous objections, leaving Kabinger on his own in the Avon Valley. After days of brooding Kabinger set off, tracked the expedition down and the spearing ensued. Some time later Kabinger's brother-in-law passed word of the killing to John Drummond, the acting Police Inspector for the district, who also just happened to be Johnston Drummond's brother. In a blind fury, John Drummond hunted Kabinger down and shot and killed him on the spot. When news of the murders reached Hutt, the governor of the colony in Perth, he ordered Drummond to face a board of enquiry. Drummond promptly went bush. He evaded capture, curiously, by hiding out with Kabinger's family who kindly took him in and concealed him from the authorities. They hid him without rancor and for so long that, when he eventually walked back out of the bush to visit his ailing mother on Hawthornden (the Drummond family's farm near Toodyay), she no longer knew him. Half-naked, sun blackened, with years' growth of dark hair and a long beard, his mother took Drummond for just another wild black man.

Easterly winds filled up our summers five to ten days at a time, sometimes more. Wind generally blew for three-quarters of every day; often for all but an hour perhaps in the early evenings. Mornings were worst, the windmills shuddering and leaves ripped from gum trees and spinning through the air. I sat at my desk in the one-classroom, one-teacher Gillingarra School, watching dust swirl off the bare gravel playground. Each day was hotter than the last and afternoons especially became wretched. This was years before air conditioning and our classroom was ridiculously hot. We kids wiped sweat from our palms, wrote a little, wiped sweat away again, yearning for the school bus to take us home.

Once home, Michael and I would beg a snack from the pantry before picking our way in sweaty, sandalled feet over the stinging pebbles down the track to the gully dam. An earth wall was thrown across the Diggers Hill Gully stream near where it emerged from the hills. The dam held a good-sized pool from each winter and was just ten minutes' walk from our house. It was big enough for our canoe and made an excellent swimming hole. We leapt and crashed into the weedy and muddy water alive with tiny fish and gilgies, little freshwater crayfish, and often the surface was hotter than bathwater yet freezing deep down. Pathways kicked across the dam, when we crossed back, could easily be felt as a tepid strip of mixed up water.

A South African gladiolus cropping up in the Mogumber/Gillingarra bush in 2007, which I don't remember ever seeing in the 1970s or 80s

The Moore River, October 2007, site of the Jilgil Pool, now an ephemeral, shallow salt stream. Pat Kelly's hill is behind.

Looking upstream

River gums

Moore River Pools

Mike and I also swam in nearby river pools, the deep shady pools to each side of the Mogumber railway bridge and sometimes the Jilgil Pool itself. We swam with care to avoid the broken trunks of fallen river gums and sharp roots of paper barks, invisible under murky river waters. We never dared dive in without exploring first. Still, despite the obvious dangers and acrid odours as we disturbed mud, swimming and canoeing in those rivers was the best part of every summer. Yet the tang of salt was obvious, even then, and the water now is crystal clear, suspended sediment forced out of solution by rising levels of salt. Salt has killed the river life and even the pools have vanished. To reduce the regular flooding of the mid 1960s, authorities de-snagged the river with bulldozers to eliminate impediments to water flow. With no tree roots to stabilise banks and plenty of disturbed soil, within months the Jilgil Pool filled with silt.

Wind! Good for windmills, making them spin and clatter through the summers, pumping water in gulping splashes into concrete tanks. Sheep sheltered under trees to sleep through the heat of the day. In the late afternoon one thirsty sheep would stand and stretch and idly wander towards the water. Eventually another, spotting the first, stirred itself and followed. They walked a little, then trotted, then the entire flock took notice and were quickly up on their feet, some trotting, most running, all in single file along the narrow sheep pads. Reaching the trough they heaved in a milling huddle, butting and jabbing their hooves into each other in their determination to drink the coolest water splashing from the float valve. If the tank was overflowing, sheep delighted in licking the water that slipped down the outer surface of the concrete wall. Then they wandered off to explore for the burrs of subterranean clover, secreted a little into the ground. Sheep pawed at the hard, dry ground with their sharp hooves to unearth the bristly burrs and wind caught the disturbed soil, dust lifted into the air and sailed away. On windy days the horizon was grey with dust.

Remembering the wind – the rattling hush of gum trees on any summer's day, like a wave spending itself over sand and the melancholic drone of the fine-leafed tammar scrub. A tight fence wire, vibrating in a soft eternal hum and the more complicated humming of telephone lines suspended from our house eaves in an enormous swoop down into the valley; from inside the house the wind over the wires sounded an interminable minimalist symphony. Very early morning, waking to the rhythmic metallic screech of a distant windmill set spinning by the east wind rising, the sound punctuated by a loose sheet of corrugated iron flapping percussively where a peppercorn tree brushed one corner of the shearing shed. Somehow the tree was never cut back properly or the iron fastened down effectively. And I recall one 'cocky gate', its mesh stretched between short lengths of pipe suspended vertically, hovering in the wind, held tight by loops of wire around the wooden gateposts. One end of the gate was water pipe with wire netting threaded through some 12 holes. The holes were held at precisely the right angle to the wind and the distance between holes was ideal to make the thing a flute. Two or three breathy notes played always, the wind's changing speed and direction caught in the melody; the music of the east wind so different, so different from the southwesterlies, the sea winds.

Day by day the wind swung from east to northeast to north and at the longed-for end to a heat wave, it would swing suddenly to the west. This generally happened mid-afternoon, often after days of battering easterlies culminating in a blistering northerly roaring away all morning, pushing temperatures a long way past 100 degrees. Around noon the wind slowed, became fitful and died. The heat was notably more savage now for the calm – too hot for ordinary work, too hot for anything really but slow jobs in lots of shade. And then we waited; waited and listened. Eventually, sometimes after three hours, sometimes six, a hushed roar from gum trees lining the river signalled *the change*. Then the first swirling gusts were on us – the southwesterly, the sea breeze, the 'Fremantle Doctor'. The change came straight from the Indian Ocean, just over the horizon from us, yet even this was hot for a time, while some of that inland heat blew back over us. No matter, coming from the sea, the wind must soon cool. By evening the thermometer might fall by 30 degrees, so windows around the house were thrown open to

The Gillingarra School, circa 1960. Jeff Needham presiding.

allow perhaps a week's accumulated heat to blow away. The following days were a joy: relaxing, refreshing; good days for working, cool nights for sleeping. Soon enough, the east wind would return, always within two or three days, occasionally after just hours of respite. A new cycle of wind arrived from out of the stillness as a teasing gust in the late evening or around midnight, falling away to leave one wondering a bit. The following eddies always strengthened though and the old sugar gum outside my bedroom was soon thrashing, timbers of the house creaking and the tin roof shifting, crackling, bracing to the roaring, pummelling, never-ending easterly.

The Gillingarra school colours were blue and gold. Sports days would see us Gillingarra kids, all 20 or so of us, marching out onto the Moora footy oval in our lechenaultia-blue shorts and our wattle-yellow t-shirts along with the children from some 15 other little schools in every combination of colours. Away we would go, running and triple jumping and tunnel balling, and lining up for our ribbons and certificates at the end of the day. Gillingarra School has long closed and only a couple of those schools still exist. The small inner wheat belt towns along the Darling Ranges are all reduced to a few empty buildings and remaining farmers accept that their children will be on a bus for hours every school day.

I find myself thinking about the choice of blue and gold for the Gillingarra sports uniforms. In retrospect, the combination was apposite. Yellows dominated the flowering bush from the cooler months into spring and flooded through the landscape with the ripening of pastures and wheat crops. The blue, of course, was that mindless never-ending sky, those summers with no hint of a cloud for weeks at a time, that colossal dome claustrophobic with wind-blown, eye-scalding azure.

Summers dragged on and on. Some time in February, perhaps March, the easterlies quietened, the days became calmer and Cam now became concerned that the windmills no longer had sufficient wind to pump desperately needed water. Dams were dry or, worse, just muddy puddles and dangerous for sheep. In their eagerness

Gillingarra landscape by Ian Marr

to reach the remaining water, sheep walked out through the muddy shallows of dams, their stiletto hooves allowing them to sink into the mud and the underlying slope often tipped them sideways. Deep mud could trap sheep, sometimes for days until, doing our inspections in the old farm ute, us kids balancing on the back like surfboard riders, we found them, heaved them from the sucking mud and set them tottering weakly across the paddock, watched them career off sideways and fall onto their muddy, heavy side. And we would pick them up again and again, propping them upright, jogging beside them as they gained strength and confidence, figuring out eventually for themselves how to stay upright, walk and run without falling down.

By autumn the earth was always bare, paddocks eaten back to the red-grey pebbly soil and the bony ribbons of cerise-purple rock entirely exposed along the ridges. There was never a scrap of grass remaining and stock needed to be hand fed. Cam drove the utility through the clamorous flocks in tight circles while I, balanced atop a pitching stack of oaten hay loaded six layers high, heaved bales one by one to the sheep. This was made trickier by our border collie, Reilly, who, in his delight at the animals crowding around, leapt frantically from bale to bale. He always aimed to sit on the highest bale, usually the next to be thrown to the stock. The milling sheep ran crazily at the vehicle, roaring all the while and I yelled and yelled to Riley to shift himself. As loads were carted away we looked to the dwindling haystack wondering: How long might it last? When might the season break? When might it rain?

To provide more pasture for stock, season by season Cam cleared the last vegetation off the Merrie-Lea hilltops. Along our east boundary bulldozers knocked down and windrowed the mallee trees and prickly scrub into long piles and in autumn, with no danger of burn-off fires escaping, the dry debris was set alight. Faded scrub and broken trees erupted with pops and hissing shrieks, acrid smoke tumbling into the blue. Occasionally, slow westward autumn winds rolled the smoke over the hills and past our house. Listening to the ABC 'Argonauts Club' on our family's crackly valve wireless at the very end of the afternoon, Michael and I would notice this thin smoke as an aromatic, almost delicate, perfume. Thinking back 50 years, every element of those hills seemed to be in that peppery fragrance.

24 June 2004, early evening

It is darkening quickly as I walk around the garden. A moderate wind is disturbing the trees and the air is full of cloud. Our ridgeline is in mist and overhead the sky is deep mauve-grey. Mist is right through the garden. To the steady hush of trees in the wind I pick my way along wet paths. Steps are indistinct and the garden is entirely without colour, only shadows and the faint outline of shadows.

SOILS

Above the hills, Merrie-Lea levelled out into a high plateau, like the backdrop in a cowboy movie. The soil was different too, 'buckshot gravel' country; sheets of orange and red pebbles, almost perfectly round but more the size of marbles than buckshot. On steep slopes under the plateau's broken edge these pebbles were very like marbles. As kids we could skid on a slope of pebbles the colour of congealed blood, spin them over and leave a pale orange wake behind us. When we were older, we heard of bauxite mining to the south and came to understand these pebbles actually were bauxite, but low grade, non-commercial, full of iron, which allowed the upper surfaces of the creamy orange aluminium ore pebbles to turn rust-red with the weathering of sun and rain.

Unlike our cropping paddocks, higher soils along our east boundary were poor. In the 1970s while testing paddocks for mineral deficiencies I found that the buckshot gravel contained excessive levels of aluminium and iron; they were hopelessly deficient in the vital trace element manganese, and, as with all our soils, lacked phosphorus and nitrogen. Nitrogen levels could be expected to rise as legumes such

A nice example of a white gum, after a major setback painstakingly re-establishing itself. Tenacious trees, the eucalypts.

as clover became established but we needed to add phosphorus and manganese as artificial fertiliser. The two were expensive, still, there was no alternative but to spread the mix over our hilltops in order to grow pasture after the scrub was bulldozed.

The irony of this was the extraordinary diversity of the original vegetation. I remember, one spring in the 1960s, walking into an area of virgin bush immediately below our plateau, counting herbs and shrubs in flower. Within a few steps I had a tally of some 50 species, with other plants to bloom and others going to seed. The vegetation was different in the narrow valley below me, likewise on the hill above. Beyond, the mauve-khaki hills of the horizon grew plants that varied tremendously from those of our own hills. It was bewildering. How could this unappetising gravel provide sustenance for such a display? Few plants enjoyed a common name and when summer winds put a stop to their flowering nearly all fell back to spiny, small-leafed or leafless shrubs of uniform khaki-green. Each cycle of wind faded their oily green to autumnal coppery brown until, by February, entire hillsides were dried out, ready to burn, ready to erupt with any flicker of lightning from a dry, rainless, useless thunderstorm.

Due to the overwhelming variety of plant life, Mogumber and Gillingarra must be among the few places on earth where even those with not the slightest interest in botany used Latin rather than common names for plants, at least in a casually generic way. Everyone talked of banksias and lechenaultias and verticordias and dryandra. Trees, it is true, generally did have common names, in fact several were referred to by both white and blackfella names: red gums or marris, white gums or wandoos. I struggle to remember common names applied to any more than a handful of the innumerable shrubs though. Toxic plants certainly: 'york road' poison and 'crinkle leaf', and a few others. The only name for a non-toxic shrub growing in those hills leaping to mind is 'kerosene bush', so useful for stuffing into a heap of logs to set a match to.

Autumn was the best time for fertilising pasture. This was done with a tractor and superspreader trailer on reasonably level cropping paddocks but a light aircraft was used to spread superphosphate over our rocky hills. Merrie-Lea was unusually hilly and, despite the heavy expense, more than half the farm was fertilised from the air. Around 200 tons of fertiliser was spread each year at roughly half a ton per flight, resulting in many trips to and fro for the pilot. For years Bob Conn was contracted to do this tedious and tricky job. Bob was very experienced with farm airstrips and thought ours handy due to its site high on our east boundary plateau. He never needed to climb with his aircraft loaded – the heavy flying was all downhill. But, until we re-aligned it, I guess the original strip was a little short.

Flowers on top of Pat Kelly's hill, spring 2007. Reasonably open vegetation and quite likely the best example remaining of the bush between Mogumber and Gillingarra.

To demonstrate the problem, one autumn day in the 1970s Bob suggested that I join him. Because of the fierce thermals, flying in a light aircraft over our hills was always an adventure. With some hesitation I climbed into the co-pilot seat and strapped myself in. The loader operator raced to the aircraft, swung the loader nozzle over the aircraft's hopper and dropped the superphosphate in (less a bag to compensate for my extra weight). Bob opened the throttle and acrid dust smeared the windscreen as the aircraft rolled onto the strip. Throttle wide open, motor yowling, we leisurely gathered speed. Halfway along we were still moving, but slowly, and the laden plane only gained speed enough to bounce its way off the ground startlingly close to the scrub overhanging the fenceline at the end of the strip. In fact, the scrub seemed way above us as we came near and I remember noticing I was gripping the seat with white-knuckle desperation – with a bank of vital switches in front, the edge of the seat seemed the one safe place to hang on to. The engine now shrieking, Bob nudged one of the controls and with a faint metallic scrape from underneath, the aircraft nose lifted ever so slightly, the mallee scrub fell below the windshield – just – obviously a whisker below the undercarriage and we were out sailing over the steep rock-strewn ravine beyond the end of the strip, the ground suddenly way, way below and the next ridge easily cleared as we lurched and banked and bumped giddily towards the paddock to be fertilised. Three minutes later I climbed out of the cockpit, still shaking uncontrollably.

Following the aircraft in my ute on Bob's next run, as he neared the fence, sure enough, a puff of fertiliser appeared from below the aircraft. Clearly, another last-minute reduction in weight was required to clear that scrub. And at the end of the strip I found perhaps 30 bags, nearly three tons of fertiliser, discarded over the final yards of the by now very heavily fertilised airstrip. I drove home and returned immediately with lopping saw and wire cutters.

I gave this to my father to read and although he could see the funny side, he was more indignant than amused. Three tons of super – that was serious money! And it didn't matter that it happened 30 years ago. That wasted fertiliser was no laughing matter.

*   *   *

Some time later, Bob was spraying one of our wheat crops for wild radish. At least 200 big white gums – wandoos – were scattered through the paddock so Bob was continually banking around or climbing over trees as he made his low-level runs from one side to the other. I was acting as marker for him, standing to the windward side of each run and moving over so many paces at the end of each pass, hoping the wind kept up strength and did not allow weedicide to drift back over me. As it turned out, this was no problem. Half-

way through the job the wind gathered pace, trees were whipping about and conditions were making Bob's runs between the white gums rather perilous. There was no two-way radio so I wasn't able to discuss the matter with Bob; I was wondering what to do when, overhead, I noticed a rock drop from the aircraft and land fairly close to where I was standing. Pacing to the next run I picked it up to find a note, attached with a piece of string, reading something like, 'The wind's a bit strong, how about we knock off and try again tomorrow?' I have wondered from that day to this how does one write a message, tie it to a rock (that just happens to be available), open the cockpit and hurl the thing out; all the while piloting an aircraft between trees, over trees, around trees, always a few feet from the ground – and with a fairly vicious cross-wind adding considerable interest to the occasion.

A couple of years later I was helping one day, tipping a couple of buckets of a new subterranean clover seed into each hopper's worth of super. There was tonne or so of seed to be spread over a 200-acre paddock, to improve the pasture and raise the stocking rate. Bob was spreading late that season, mid-April, I guess. The day began with a faint white haze to the west. Hourly the haze thickened and the wind began to move in from the north. This was good, the airstrip ran north–south and a north wind made it easier for Bob to lift the aircraft off the ground.

The day was promising, perhaps rain on the way, the first for months. By midday, the sky to the west was white, shading to inky grey at the extreme horizon. From our vantage point on top of the hills I could see cloud way out over the Indian Ocean. (As children, we always thought, on a clear day, we could see the ocean itself from our air strip. That sliver of level grey-blue between the very last hilltops, miles and miles and miles to our west, surely that was the sea?) Cloud smeared the horizon and the sky over Merrie-Lea was erupting in spectacular plumes of cirrus; I do not think I have ever seen a sky like it. A vigorous cold front had lined up against the coast, heaving layer upon layer of turbulent cloud before it. Immediately above us a feathery spear of cirrus was flung from the west to beyond the eastern horizon; a bleached fishbone against the blue, ribs flowing to each side. I knew it was high, ice crystals rather than water vapour, up at least 30,000 feet. Looking north and south, there were similar plumes spaced across the sky. Over the extreme northern and southern horizons the plumes meshed to white. I tried to count them through the afternoon, the wind rising, tried to imagine how far I could see. The cirrus was all the same height of course, the cloud pattern uniform north and south and east, plumes perhaps 25 miles apart. I could count eight cirrus plumes, perhaps 12 in each direction, so supposed I could see cloud across maybe 500 miles of sky: enormous cloud shoals moving east, stretching from over the Southern Ocean to beyond the northern wheatbelt.

Road verge weeds. South African gazanias settling in across the road from the now-abandoned Gillingarra School.

Bob could see too. He was keen to finish the job, taking off with particular urgency and flying back and, directly over the fertiliser dump, throttling hard back, allowing the aircraft to almost free fall, coming in like a helicopter. After moments of plummeting he was gunning the motor to reach just sufficient speed to touch down safely. Within yards and seconds he was beside the loader, the operator dropping the next load in the hopper and instantly roaring off along the strip.

By evening, the last fertiliser was out and the entire sky was black. And then rain. Steady rain all through the night. Tapping and pattering and drumming in wave after wave after wave. That most glorious of sounds on our tin roof, the easiest of sounds to sleep to. According to my father, my grandfather always claimed the two best sounds in the world were horses chewing oats and rain on canvas; for me though, rain on a corrugated iron roof after a long dry summer, the house reverberating to its deliciously sibilant swash, part waking to windblown eddies, then fading, inescapably, to sleep.

The next morning we drove around the farm checking dams for water levels. The first rains on the bare hills always made for excellent run off and were the best chance of filling dams to last the following summer. Checking the ten or twelve dams was always *the* grand ritual of every autumn for our family. Rainfall was rarely even from the north of the farm to the south, so runoff was impossible to estimate. We might find dams one-third full, perhaps half full, on notable occasions brimming – with just one rain. Finding a dam overflowing was like winning the lottery, and everywhere the earth was dark with moisture, wonderfully aromatic, seemingly up to growing anything after that grand opening soak. Just four or five days later the first green blush appeared, initially on slopes of just the right gradient for emerging leaves to catch the light. Over following days, the entire farm turned green – as green a green as the mind can imagine. And half a week later sheep were trotting around happily, chasing the fresh pick. By then Cam and I were on the tractors ploughing, folding the green under the rich brown earth, preparing the bottom paddocks for the new season's wheat crop.

ANTECEDENTS

8 July 2004

I was visiting South Perth and talking to Cam about his farming days this week. He is 84 and long retired. I was asking why he and my mother chose our particular farm back in 1958. I told him that, looking at aerial photographs, the neighbouring farms

My grandfather, Mark Allan Francis, circa 1906

all had gentler slopes and more substantial areas of arable soil than ours. "You did look at a few other blocks I suppose? Why on earth did we end up with all the hill and rock?" He smiled a bit and shook his head, "It was a nice-looking place. I thought you and your brother would enjoy it".

I could see the choice of property came to puzzle even him in later years. Surrounding farms were obviously easier to work. As a friend remarked, "When it rained 40 days and 40 nights, it was raining rocks on Merrie-Lea". Yet the decision epitomised my father's thoughts on the land. Merrie-Lea may not have been easy to farm but was clearly the most dramatic and handsomest place for miles.

My father was born in 1919 in South Australia and lived his first years on a farm near Loxton, just north of the Murray. His father, my grandfather, Mark Allan Francis, was born in Cave Vale in South Australia in 1870 and married Emily May Field of Mt Gambier around 1910. In the mid 1920s, the Loxton farm was sold and Mark and Emily and their three children moved to inner Adelaide. The sale proceeds were quickly lost in my grandfather's attempt to establish a retail business. Following this setback, Mark, leaving his family behind, moved to Western Australia where he travelled through agricultural districts selling farm machinery for a couple of years. When Crown land was thrown open at Holt Rock in 1928, he applied successfully for a block and sent for his wife and children. So it was that in the first days of that not-so-promising year – 1929 – Emily May, with Cam and his two older sisters, Dorothy and Ruth, travelled to the Lakes District on the eastern edge of the WA wheat belt, hard up against the Rabbit Proof Fence, to start over again.

Holt Rock is the northernmost of the Lake King, Lake Camm and Lake Varley settlements, with Lake Biddy, Newdegate and Lake Grace away to the west and Perth more than 300 road miles away. The Lakes District settlements were hours of travel out from previous farming communities; an experimental endeavour to find just how far into this low-rainfall country wheat would grow – settled with the thought that, 'rain might follow the plough'. No such thing happened of course, and only the narrow, westernmost strip of the vast area Perth authorities hoped to see under wheat was ever cleared – only those acres sheltered by the Rabbit Proof Fence.

The alluring name of the area is misleading, perhaps coined as a joke; the lakes of the Lakes District are and always have been salt lakes, dry for most of each year. Here, my grandfather took up a 1200-acre selection of bush. With little money remaining after moving from Adelaide, the family set about turning their patch of wilderness into a farm with no more, perhaps, than could be loaded onto a wheelbarrow or two. They commenced work with no car or truck, no vehicle for the many hours' drive to the nearest town, no tractor or machinery, not even a horse for a couple of years. Just about the only tool they possessed to turn the scrub and timber into a farm was the axe. As my father recently mused, the most curious thing about this splendid adventure was that my grandfather, exploring his selection, doubtless did so with the thought in mind he was just 12 months shy of 60 years old.

Cam has vivid memories of the journey from Adelaide to Holt Rock as a nine-year-old: Emily May's anguish at selling their heirloom jarrah dining table for ten pounds because they had no money to take it with them; enjoying a bath overflowing with hot sea water while steaming across the Great Australian Bight on the SS *Karoola* (the biggest deepest bath he would see for a long time); meeting elderly relatives in Perth; the long journey to the new farm and the final stage from Lake Biddy riding on the open tray of an early model International truck. Because the truck was already heavily loaded with supplies and a team of clearing contractors heading off to work for one of the wealthier settlers, his mother and sisters stayed behind in Lake Biddy. My grandfather rode in the cab with Mr Commons, the owner/driver, while Cam roughed it on the back with the navvies. They set off after lunch and, travelling slowly on the unmade bush track, finally arrived around two in the morning. Cam, fast asleep, was woken by one of the men saying, "Welcome to your new home". My father remembers the night was very still and brilliant with a full moon. The surrounding salmon gums were enormous shafts of silver rising, cathedral-like, to lacy clouds of foliage. The rounded outline of the big rock loomed clearly above the trees in the moonlight to the south. Their new home was a long narrow tent covered in broom bush thatch. It was the first time Cam had seen his father in two years and to celebrate the occasion the two shared a tin of pilchards. Cam does not remember what special feast was saved for the arrival of his mother and teenage sisters with Mr Commons on his next trip.

Pioneering at Holt Rock in the 1930s was like living a story by Banjo Patterson or Henry Lawson. After two years under canvas the family moved into a little shack made from salvaged corrugated iron with hessian dividing walls and termite mounds spread out and rammed smooth for a floor. It was nine years before a conventional house was built – a mud brick and corrugated iron affair. Supplies were naturally difficult to obtain and very expensive, and in those depression times my father remembers frequent meals of rabbit served with boiled wheat; the rabbits supplied by Cam himself from his extensive trap run. Water for the household was collected daily from a seepage at the base of the big rock a few minutes' walk away. The tiny seepage made just two kerosene tins full each day, never more; it was

The immemorial salmon gums of Holt Rock. Growing slowly in near-desert conditions, I imagine they looked much the same in 1929.

Wildflowers on a Lake District road verge, 2007

another of my father's jobs to collect this vital water and carry it back to camp. This was used for drinking, cooking, washing, some left in a tin basin for bathing, everyone using the same water in turn, from cleanest to dirtiest – Cam usually last – and the murky dregs tipped onto tomato bushes. The first couple of years Cam remembers doing correspondence lessons each morning and helping out the rest of the day. After that though, when my father turned 12, my grandfather gave Campbell a two-and-a-half-pound *plumb axe* and school lessons were largely forgotten in favour of a full day's clearing.

There was a shop nearby for a couple of years, until it occurred to the owner that he was never going to make it rich in Holt Rock. It was not a conventional shop, more a tiny shed with flour and tea and molasses, the bare essentials, stashed in boxes against the walls. Cam tells the nearest thing to lollies and sweets the storekeeper kept were dates. The dates came as masses of fruit pressed into big cubes; the lump of fruit left sitting at one end of the plank counter, under a tea towel to keep flies off. The little store was within easy walk of the family camp and when Cam was sent on errands to buy flour or sugar or milk powder, he always contrived to stand close to the dates and as the shopkeeper put his order together could quickly pinch a few from under the tea towel. As a nine-year-old this was an immensely scary thing to do, even though in umpteen visits he was never caught. Years later it occurred to my father that the elderly Jewish storekeeper saw it as part of running his shop to allow small, very hungry children to steal his dates.

Larger Holt Rock eucalypts had mellifluous names such as morrel, yorrel, boree, salmon gum, gimlet; but the country was dominated by low mallee scrub. Species of mallee sucker with numerous whippy stems from massive root systems, or *lignotubers*, they needed to be grubbed or burnt out of the ground before a wheat crop could be planted. In my family's instance, this was done by hand. As paddocks were cleared, settlers could apply for a loan to the Agricultural Bank, to be granted according to the size of the paddock. An inspector from the bank, Frank Collet, a tall, rather languid bloke (according to my father), came to measure each paddock and 25 shillings of government money could be borrowed for every acre cleared. Frank rode from one end to the other and from side to side of the paddock in question, counting each pace of his horse as a yard. This horse was immensely tall, Cam remembers, and he and his family were positive the long strides of the inspector's horse meant the acreage was always considerably underestimated, though it did not do to complain.

Cam tells how a first-time farmer neighbour found the business of grubbing mallee roots too exhausting and dispiriting to be borne. He took time off, carefully exploring his 1200 acres and, to his delight, hidden away he found an area bare of trees. Over the remainder of the summer he enlarged the clearing and that autumn borrowed a team of horses, a plough and a drill to put in his first wheat crop. Weeks into winter he began to wonder why the expensive 'seed' wheat was not germinating. He came to my grandfather to ask advice and they both went to have a look. My grandfather found the crop was sown in a salt pan such that the little bit of clearing and some winter rain would turn it into a little salt lake. Indeed, the depression was already filling with water. In bewilderment the new chum gave up farming forthwith and come spring was back at taxi driving. My father always recounts the story with an air of such pained candour that I have to believe him.

Mallee scrub, Holt Rock

With the proceeds of their first crop the family bought a chestnut gelding called Star. They immediately found Star's forte was the ability to gallop while hobbled. He galloped out of the unfenced paddock and was a fair part of the way home to Burracoppin, 150 miles away, before they tracked him down, "still hobbled and going strong". A little later, with the aid of a bank loan, four more horses, a drill and a plough were purchased from a dealer in Newdegate. Cam drove Star, pulling a cart, into town to bring back the horses and supplies and remembers the round trip took about a week on the sandy bush tracks.

The isolation of the district is also evident in something my father first spoke of around the time of his 80th birthday. In early 1935 my grandmother told Cam and the rest of the family that she was returning to South Australia to see her family. Weeks later, news of two telegrams for my grandfather came from the Lake Biddy post office. Arrangements were made and Cam, accompanying his father in a recently purchased little truck, met the postmaster half way. In the middle of the open road the telegrams were handed over. The first was to say my grandmother was very ill; the second, that she had died of cancer. With nothing to be done my grandfather and Cam turned the truck around and drove back to the farm. For days following, Cam says, a music hall ditty lodged infuriatingly in his head: "It was a cough that carried her off, a coffin they carried her off in".

The depression years were followed by the Second World War and Cam volunteered for a stint in the RAAF. He returned to the farm in April 1945 in time for the ploughing, enabling my grandfather to retire. My grandfather died four years later, in 1949, while fishing off the jetty at Mandurah, on the coast south of Perth. The story goes he was lucky enough to land a monster kingfish just seconds before a heart attack killed him.

My grandmother, Emily May (Field), circa 1900

Cam, circa 1941

Cam and Ben, May 1982

I know very little about my father's grandfather, Mark Francis, only that he was born in Edwardstown in South Australia in 1841, married Mary Jane Clegg, (1849–1931), and died in 1882 near Mount Gambier. His widow, Mary Jane, moved to Western Australia and eventually died at Mount Lawly, in Perth. Mark's father, Edward Francis, my great-great grandfather, was born in Burnhill Green in Staffordshire, England in 1800. Originally a small-time farmer and labourer, he lost his livelihood, I suspect, in the land enclosures of the time. He moved to Stalbridge, in Dorset, looking for work and there married Sarah Clark. However, Thomas Hardy country proved no better than Staffordshire for steady farm employment and in 1839, Edward and Sarah and their six children sailed to South Australia. According to family lore, local villagers paid for their passage. This is probably correct. To ameliorate hardship amongst rural poor, many schemes were established in mid-19th century England, sponsoring emigrants to all corners of the empire. Edward and his family set sail on a six- to ten-month voyage to the very rim of the world with the thought in mind, I guess, of no chance of ever securing sufficient money for the return journey. So in this way my great-great grandfather was the first of four generations to farm the Australian bush, all of them with axe in hand. I don't know if he prospered but have doubts. Edward died 30 years later and was buried, according to family legend, in the inauspiciously entitled 'Humbug Scrub'.

I do not count myself in this tally of generations. By the time I was farming, clearing Merrie-Lea was finished and the axe stayed on the woodheap.

*   *   *

When my father joined up (in the days of dogfights over the English Channel and the fields of Kent), like everyone signing on with the RAAF he was hoping to be a spitfire pilot. He was gladly received, then told there was no spare aircraft for that batch of recruits and absolutely not for those lacking formal education past age 12; however, the RAAF were short of instrument repairmen. In disgust, he tried transferring to a bomb disposal course, thinking this expertise should at least earn him a trip to London but found, with wartime's perverse logic, that only men past 35 years were being recruited to dispose of unexploded ordinance. So, Cam settled down unhappily to a war behind the lines at Burdekin in the Northern Territory, repairing altimeters and navigational gear. It was such rotten luck he was never a fighter pilot – boy, did he look the part! Then in 1946 he could have moved to Hollywood and become a matinee idol – he'd have had any number of leading ladies queued up and patiently waiting. Three days ago I came across a photograph from 1982 of Cam, holding my newborn son, Benjamin. My father was just in from the paddocks at the end of an afternoon and, in this photo, he was 62 at the time, he still looks like the more handsome younger brother of, perhaps Clark Gable, or maybe Cary Grant. Jan was also attractive in her day. Sadly, their looks have entirely skipped the subsequent generation.

CLOVER DOWNS

In 1973, an adjoining farm of some 2200 acres was purchased and eventually Clover Downs became the predominant property on which I worked. Although there were several hundred yards of mutual boundary in one corner, Clover Downs and Merrie-Lea were completely different. Clover Downs was almost entirely arable, with gentle hills and very little rock. It comprised the upper part of one valley system with a stream running diagonally from the northeast to the southwest and a second valley with its stream flowing parallel to the first, close to the northwest corner. The same corner rose swiftly above the stream to become an extension of Merrie-Lea's bauxite plateau and, hundreds of feet higher, provided a magnificent view across our new farm.

Because it was located within two valleys with just a gentle rise between and boundaries almost exactly following outer ridges, there was an inward looking aspect to Clover Downs' geography. Looking down from the plateau evoked thoughts of stumbling across a hidden, cloistered place; certainly in marked contrast to Merrie-Lea with its many high vantage points and long views to every horizon. Clover Downs' soils were fertile except for a belt of deep gritty sand across the centre which, in effect, was a below-ground reservoir. Some 400 acres of sand soaked up winter rains like blotting paper – there was never a sign of runoff. Rainfall sank into the sand, springs bubbled out of intersecting valleys and, to our delight, in a district of seasonal drought and bone-dry gullies for months on end, we were now the proud owners of more than two miles of perennial streams. They were often brackish, occasionally rather salty but in two places substantial flows of deliciously sweet water oozed from the sand right through the driest summer.

Despite its streams, Clover Downs looked most unhappy when we took possession. Ghostly eucalypts stood in their hundreds across several paddocks, ring-barked years earlier and left to die. Fences were slack, often lying tangled on the ground and pastures hopelessly weedy, seemingly not fertilised for years. Even the streams were in trouble. Because sheep had constant access, they destroyed germinating plants and, in summer, heavy evaporation from the resulting bare soil allowed a thick crust of salt to form areas of 'scald'. This made any chance of regeneration doubly impossible. Even worse, winter rains saturated one large area of bare sand and the slope was shifting, eroding, falling away as one stood and watched. An entire hillside was inching its way down into a valley, loose sand washing through a neighbouring farm and along to clog culverts under the railway line next to the Moora road. Worse still, a flash flood from a summer storm washed over the partially blocked culverts, right over the railway line, damaging the embankment and resulting in the derailment of a Perth–Geraldton train. Soil scientists and engineers from several government departments were immediately despatched.

The upshot was that months after we purchased Clover Downs, the four farms along our valley formed a Soil Conservation Group. This was one of three groups established by the WA Agriculture Department at the time as an experiment to gauge farmer interest in soil reclamation. Within a couple of years, the positive response led to the establishment of many such groups throughout the WA wheat belt, from where the concept was taken to other states and the name changed to Landcare.

Cam once mentioned to me how he came by his driver's licence. After years working with one or two early tractors and long periods on the road driving the farm truck – and, I might add, at the end of delivering an entire wheat harvest to the Newdegate rail head – he thought to drop in to the police station and ask about a licence. The copper on duty glanced at the little Bedford on the side of the road and regarded Cam with silence for a long moment. Shaking his head, he replied, "Mate! I've been watching you drive that thing every day for six weeks. I suppose you have been behind the wheel since you were knee high to a grasshopper". And with a sigh, "How about we go across to the pub and you can buy me a beer while I sort out the paperwork".

Those years were interesting but exhausting. Our advisors recommended we fence salt-affected areas to prevent stock from grazing and establish salt-tolerant plants to bind the soil and lower the water table. To my surprise we were specifically warned against planting trees: they could actually worsen our problems. The crucial factor in the rate of erosion, it was explained, is the percussive impact of rain as it strikes bare soil. Large raindrops fall faster than small drops due to air resistance and, as common sense indicates, showers of heavy drops are more damaging to soil than gently falling drizzle. We were told trees can accelerate soil erosion as leaves catch drizzly rain and release it as big drops. It was emphasised, in the circumstances we faced, tree roots would do nothing to slow soil erosion. Clearly, topsoil gained no protection from underlying roots and a tree's thread-like feeder roots, growing in upper layers of soil, die and disintegrate when exposed to sunlight. Trees dropping a thick blanket of leaf litter definitely serve a useful purpose, but only while the cover stays in place. Mogumber winds easily blow leaves from under trees, and sheep and kangaroos disturb the debris under shady trees when digging comfy daytime sleeping holes. Finally, in districts such as Mogumber, trees compete much too effectively for sunlight and moisture to allow ground-covering plants to thrive – the soil within range of tree roots is always dangerously bare.

The solution to our erosion problem was to plant only ground-hugging, salt-tolerant perennials. Many grasses were suggested and several broadleaves. Every spring I hand-sowed a mix of some dozen grasses and salt-tolerant clovers and to my delight they germinated and grew. Over 15 years as I worked on these problem areas, scarred, salt-scalded valley bottoms turned from appalling eyesores to some of the most interesting landscapes of the entire farm. Generally each soil type was colonised by a different plant. One lush grass preferred areas saturated with fresh water while on drier, salt-free soil a wispy greyish-green grass came to dominate. In dry salty areas, a taller clumping grass with exquisitely fine sprays of seed heads thrived. In wet salty areas, a couch-like grass won the day. Strawberry clover, its cerise flowers coming in early summer, spread enthusiastically, stems rooting at every node and a yellow flowering dwarf pasture lotus arrived, I guess, quite fortuitously from neighbouring farms on the webbed feet of wild ducks. Gradually the two valleys filled with a dense array of plants, one or two species even colonising heavily salt-encrusted scalds as winter rains temporarily flushed salt away. From blistered sterile wastelands, the valleys turned to flowing patchworks of shimmering greens and grey-greens, soft beige and silver-mauves; the continuous carpet of plant life binding the hillside and eliminating soil movement. The two valleys together comprised some 200 acres. Sometimes I walked for hours, noticing season to season changes, exhilarating in the subtle logic of the swiftly changing patterns of growth and colour. In recent times landscape designers in Germany and elsewhere have torn up formal lawns in public parks, planting 'tall grass prairies' to achieve similar effects. I find myself reading articles on their work and wondering how the Clover Downs valleys must be now.

One morning around 2001 I noticed Cam, reflected from a bathroom mirror, combing his hair with a concerned, earnest look. Days earlier he'd commenced chemotherapy and, sure enough, his hair was soon falling out all over his pillow. He was 81 then, yet weeks later and the treatment over, his hair was back and as luxuriant and handsome as ever. It seems to me now that was the only time I have ever seen Cam showing a hint of conventional vanity. I was laughing and teasing him, partly out of surprise. Mind you, he had reason to be pleased with himself, I suppose; he had more hair than I, even then, and I was not 50.

Spring and summer I walked through our summer-land fields watching fawns and mushrooms and mauves bleaching with the sun and variations of texture from slope to slope. I was drawn to one place especially, where stock walked in through laneways to drink at several pools excavated out of saturated sand. The water encouraged a velvety grass to colonise and sheep grazed the shallow slope into a lawn of bowling-green consistency. The pools were small, a few yards across and at most 2 feet deep; grass growing into the water resulted in vertical and even undercut sides. No matter the season they always overflowed, water flowing through the sodden grass and becoming a little stream between the trees below. Each pool was pellucid, its sandy floor clearly visible and often sand could be seen moving, individual grains gyrating with water rising from below.

Visiting this spot, with its luxuriant greenery in the midst of dusty dry paddocks, was a joy. The springs also reminded me of a favourite passage from Herbert Read's symbolist fiction, *The Green Child*. Read has his protagonist return to his native village in the depths of England after years of travel to find a stream he knew as a boy flowing backwards. Bewildered, he follows the stream onto neighbouring moors to find the water dividing into rivulets that seem to feed an area of scattered pools. The traveller walks to the closest of these and notices its sandy bottom restlessly moving, every particle vibrating. Wading into the water he slips through the shimmering sand into an allegorical underworld. I could never walk past our pools without noticing patches of sandy floor gyrating and thinking of *The Green Child*. I imagine one day making a pond, its surface welling with rising water and its glittering floor forever shifting with the current.

For anyone from dry country, water springing from the earth is an extraordinarily moving thing. As children, Mike and I would follow winter streams up the Merrie-Lea hillsides, searching for the tiniest oozing seepage forming their source. And high on the list of things I would like to do some day is to see the *qanats* of Iran, made millennia ago in the times of the Persian empires. Underground streams were tapped by deep wells dug into lower slopes of rainy mountains. Wells were connected by networks of subterranean channels, tunnels, gathering water to a single main channel which directed it out, flowing deep underground all the way, to fruit and vegetable gardens, tens, sometimes hundreds of kilometres away. The heroic courage and incredible effort required to excavate the qanats, all by hand,

A hint of a rivulet in the Merrie-Lea hills

with minimal, if any, timber for shoring, made water flowing into the gardens precious beyond imagination – every drop to be used with consideration. Imagine stone-walled gardens in desert surrounds, fierce sun, dusty earth and rock, filled with the sound of water. These are the oldest of gardens, likely the inspiration for that first of all gardens: Eden.

The rabbit-proof fences are a bizarre monument to the European settlement of Western Australia. The original, Number One Fence in particular is extraordinary, running from an Antarctic storm-riven beach of the Southern Ocean, north along the eastern edge of the wheatbelt, further through the best part of 1000 miles of semi-arid pastoral country and skirting the Great Sandy Desert, it plunges towards the Timor Sea, deep within the tropics. However, it was a forlorn hope that a mere fence might prevent the tidal wave of rabbits, introduced into Australia in Victoria, from washing across South Australia and the Nullarbor Plain into the WA wheat lands. Within months and weeks of the barrier going up rabbits simply melted through. In desperation, more fences were thrown up, one very near our first farm at Moulyinning, again with imperceptible effect on the advance of the plague.

However, the fence did prevent larger native animals, kangaroos and emus, from moving out of the pastoral zones into farmlands during droughts. In these drought years, farmers might see numbers of kangaroos and immense flocks of emus beating a broad track back and forth beside the fence, desperate for the water and feed beyond. Wild dogs and foxes and feral cats and the rabbits treated the fence as a joke. But the plague of rabbits flooding over the southwest was not entirely bad, especially through the 1930s, as my father can attest. Cam supplied just about all the meat his family saw for years. He set out some 70 traps daily, providing sufficient meat for five people and two dogs, plus pelts good for a bit of pocket money. On the other hand, one can eat only so much rabbit happily – Cam cannot abide it nowadays. Retired in the 1980s with funds to enjoy eating at an exclusive Perth restaurant specialising in game, I remember my father's appalled face when, perusing the menu, he spotted a north African dish of rabbit relaxing on a bed of couscous and was not at all surprised to hear him plump for beer-battered dhufish.

This photo of Cam as a teenager in the 1930s has 'Catch of the Day' written on the rear. Note the homemade gimlet ladder leaning against the shanty.

Perhaps the symbolism of the fence is its notable attribute; the sense of keeping plagues from the east out and civilisation in – and its sheer geography is impressive. The fence was the vital guide used by three Aboriginal children in their trek from the Moore River Settlement back to their home and family at Jigalong in the Great Sandy Desert back in the 1930s, the story made famous by the book Follow the Rabbit-Proof Fence *and subsequent film. Jenny Harris, a friend of my wife, Valerie, made me aware of the tale in 1983. Jenny was appointed to the nursing outpost at Jigalong the previous year and met two of story's protagonists – Molly and Daisy –*

by then elderly ladies who giggled and laughed their way through their story of walking out of Moore River with their cousin Gracie as 14 and 10 and 8 year olds, paddling for miles through river pools to escape the resident black tracker (used in lieu of locks and bars to hold the children), foraging their way east past wheat belt homesteads for hundreds of miles through to the fence, then following the rabbit netting north for the final leg – many hundreds miles of desert and near desert in one of the world's more dangerously hot climates, and always on watch for government trackers. I remember thinking that the children possibly walked over our farm in the first hours of that 1600-kilometre long walk; also how curious it was that I was hearing the story, surely one of the wondrous treks of all time, from Jenny Harris despite having lived right next door to the mission most of my life.

Beyond seasonal farming chores, another project of those years was the reduction of stormwater erosion, especially on our cropping paddocks. Summer thunderstorms could lash bare paddocks and move thousands of tonnes of topsoil into streams and farm dams in minutes, the water turning to liquid chocolate in its rush down the slopes. A dam might entirely fill with mud after one bad storm and paddocks left scarred by gutters converging into gullies requiring days with a front-end loader to repair. Events of this severity occurred several times in the 1970s. I found them more shattering than bushfires; vegetation regenerates in a few years whereas topsoil requires millennia to form, especially the thin, ancient soils of WA.

Originally, as with most Mogumber farms, our paddocks were divided by fences set out in a north–south, east–west grid; fences were constructed with no thought as to the topography of the countryside, frequently running up and down slopes. Ploughing operations near fences left gutters that gathered and directed runoff from heavy rain straight down hillsides. Naturally, water flowing quickly over loose soil frequently resulted in erosion. The easiest way to eliminate this was to plough across slopes, never up and down; to make such ploughing practical all subdividing fences were pulled down and moved to contour lines following levels as closely as possible across hillsides. Each year for some 15 years a minimum of 4 kilometres of new fenceline was budgeted for; in the years I was farming around 90 kilometres of fenceline were erected. Paddocks were further divided into level strips by contour drains surveyed by a WA Agricultural Department officer and excavated by a road grader. Perhaps 40 kilometres of contour drains were constructed to trap runoff water and direct it as gently as possible across slopes held securely behind a half-metre-high earth bank.

There was immense pleasure in these efforts to alleviate some of nature's destructiveness. Contour drains diverted immense volumes of stormwater gently to streams and, if possible, also to dams. Extra water captured in dams was always good, especially in dry seasons, but that was just one reason for satisfaction; the work also fundamentally changed the character of the landscape. Each season I concentrated on a particular part of the farm, pulling down fence lines from their old grid configuration and re-erecting them to curve and weave across the hillsides, and also constructing drains in similar patterns following contour lines over slopes. In autumn, newly configured paddocks were ploughed in preparation for seeding the wheat. Rather than the old solid rectangles, pasture was ploughed into curving corduroy-like strips, draped elegantly between contour drains and fence lines and exposing the topography of the hillsides with revelatory precision. At the end of ploughing I would choose an adjacent hilltop and enjoy the view. It was as though a Filipino mountainside might be terraced, not over innumerable generations, but a day or two of ploughing; perhaps a lowish and very gently sloping mountain side. Years later I came across a magazine article featuring a Scottish garden made by Maggie Keswick and Charles Jencks, their design inspired by Chaos Theory. A valley and stream were shown made into folding and enfolding strips of sloping and terraced grass, twisting around teardrop lakes. Seeing photographs of this extraordinary garden evoked precisely that feeling when, on the farm, I'd drive to the best vantage point to see what the previous 12 months' work might bring to light.

INCIDENTS (RAMMED EARTH)

Wet winters of the early and mid 1960s were the years black swans came to Mogumber. The stream flowing from Clover Downs through the neighbouring farm, Studleigh, became clogged by collapsing sandbanks near where it dropped into the Moore River. Trapped water spilled out over several hundred acres of river flats to form a shallow lake, and with the water came the swans.

Great flocks of black swans congregated every year on the Wannamal lakes to our south together with thousands of ducks and water birds of every type. The swans were quick to spot the new lake and 30 or 40 took up residence. Shallow water made it easy for them to rummage through flooded topsoil for tasty morsels and it was an appropriate depth for nest building. The swan nests were huge affairs, conical piles of weeds and rubble, perhaps 6 feet across and rising a good 2 feet clear of knee-deep water. The swans constructed a couple of dozen nests, carefully spaced out over the lake. Mike and I were keen, albeit very amateurish, naturalists in those days and we persuaded our father to drop us off with our canoe to explore. We paddled over to the nests with the swans circling suspiciously but found only a couple with eggs. The remainder were empty, abandoned.

Splendid fairy wren

Scarlet robin

Western yellow robin, or forest robin

Months later, I was talking of our little adventure to Peter Toms, an Aboriginal neighbour who lived with his family in a house on one edge of the new lake. As soon as I mentioned the swans' nests Peter told me how splendidly tasty all those eggs had been. I was startled into bewildered silence. I was around 12 at the time. I remember Cam smartly changed the subject and saved the day.

* * *

Low scrub on Merrie-Lea was home to many handsome smaller birds such as western honeyeaters and matchbox rattling willy wagtails. Family groups of splendid blue wrens regularly shrilled and chattered from the 'prickly moses' wattle along the edges of our wheat paddocks and Mike and I occasionally spotted their cousins, the equally lovely white winged blue wren. Scarlet robins and red-capped robins enjoyed areas of taller cover and both these species, with jet-black backs, white underbellies and blood-red breasts, put English robins to shame. Occasionally we might see the forest robin with his chartreuse grey-green back and yellow breast popping out almost to handshaking proximity to greet us, always keen to check out newcomers to his little corner of dense bush and taller trees. Migratory rainbow birds, or bee eaters, arrived whistling sweetly to their flockmates in late spring; extraordinary creatures, all greens and blues and chestnut bellies, the underside of their wings flashing ochre yellow with each wing beat, elegant forked tails and a black mask strapped over their face. Rainbow birds swirled and skimmed after insects and were agile enough to snatch honey bees out of the air. Bees were taken to a perch and bashed until safe to swallow. Rainbow birds loved open paddocks and areas of firm sand for their nest burrows and as we herded stock past they launched themselves from the dry grass with an unnerving whirring swish.

Once while droving cattle Jan and Cam found a baby bird disturbed from its nest and flopping on the ground in the dust kicked up by the herd. Amazingly, it was unhurt but that seemed the least of its troubles. An unlovely little pink blob, just a hint of 'pin' feathers protruding from its naked skin, its avoidance of a trampling by a herd of cattle was something of a mixed blessing. Jan and Cam were not even sure what the creature might be but thought perhaps it was a rainbow bird that had, for some odd reason, crawled from its burrow. Knowing how Mike and I felt about such things, they brought it home and we thought we might have a go at feeding it. We crushed milk arrowroot biscuits into milk and eggs and dabbed the oozy mix into the creature's gaping bill. Somehow the bird survived this atrocious diet and within days its feathers grew; to our delight it became a sacred kingfisher – perhaps the most exquisite of all local birds with iridescent blue-green back, creamy yellow breast and a black mask over its face similar to a rainbow bird's. Within weeks it had climbed to the side of its shoebox and, launching itself tentatively into the air, was soon swooping around the house. Mother found the thought of a kingfisher darting over her hard-won carpets too much and the bird was banished to our concrete-floored bathroom where it perched on the towel rail and could safely splot onto newspaper placed strategically underneath. As we walked into the room it would fly from the rail and land cheerily on our shoulders.

Weeks later, my sister Jenny and her family came to visit for Christmas. It just happens that Jenny has a horror of everything feathery, a phobia for birds, and the little kingfisher, handsome as it might be, was a thing of considerable dread. While Jenny showered, our kingfisher was banished to the sunroom, several rooms away. This arrangement held for a time but the inevitable day came when the sunroom door was left ajar and the kingfisher flashed through, zipped along the hallway and did a hard left into the bathroom. That yearning for water felt by kingfishers through the ages urged our little bird up over the shower curtain – and there was a magnificent waterfall, even a generous perch in the middle of it. Now this strikes as a curiously Hitchcockian scenario. Indeed, two of that gentleman's films come to mind in conveying my sister's response to a kingfisher landing on her as she washed soap from her eyes that summer morning. Our little bird was equal to the moment though, hanging on gamely while Jenny screamed bloody murder. I think Michael rescued the kingfisher from Jenny, rescued Jenny from the kingfisher, and it was back in its shoebox and en route to a bird sanctuary in Perth before the day was out.

Rainbow bee-eater

Sacred kingfisher

Around the early 1980s we were visited by a botanist from King's Park, the magnificent botanic gardens of central Perth, researching the Mogumber bell, *Darwinia carnea*. That its family is named for Erasmus Darwin, Charles's grandfather (also, curiously, an advocate of evolution), suggests a darwinia is no ordinary plant. Darwinias are all small shrubs with intricate foliage and showy, bell-shaped flowers. *Darwinia carnea* produces elegant pale apple-green bells, which are persistent as its 'flowers' are formed from long lasting bracts rather than petals. A handful of darwinia species occupy a few acres each of mountaintop of either the Stirling or Porongurup ranges along the south coast of WA. Nearly all darwinias live in these moist, coolish parts indicating they evolved when Australia's climate was much milder. The Mogumber Bell is the one anomalous member of the family. I am not convinced Mogumber has ever enjoyed cool summers, even when Australia was within paddling distance of Antarctica.

Darwinia carnea has always been extraordinarily rare. When first discovered, a mere handful of plants were found growing among stunted white gums and powder barks on the bauxite plateau forming the extreme northwest corner of Clover Downs. Years later, cuttings were taken for propagation purposes and, to the botanist's concern on the day, only one plant of that original colony remained. Astonishingly, a decision was taken not to inform the then owner where precisely this lone plant might be, and yet he was sternly lectured on the importance of safeguarding the general area. In effect, stock were to be removed from the paddock permanently. The owner, reluctant to close off a 150-acre paddock, suggested fencing off just the plant, but the botanists refused point blank. The exasperated farmer promptly put his largest flock of sheep in to graze and on the next occasion someone went hunting for *Darwinia carnea* there were none to be found.

I listened to this tale with amazement and suggested we take another look. The hill was densely covered in eucalypts and a rare dryandra but, sadly, no darwinias. However, cuttings had been taken from that last plant, so cutting-grown progeny did exist and were thriving in King's Park. Surely we could re-introduce some back to the hilltop? But because the cuttings all came from one plant, and *Darwinia carnea* is self-infertile, cutting-grown specimens could never produce seed.

Darwinia carnea

The botanist did volunteer to bring a few plants the following spring to at least make an attempt to re-establish a population in its old location. I fenced off some acres and that August we planted some 200 cuttings of *Darwinia carnea*. We were thinking that, if seed from original plants remained lurking within our little nature reserve, some might eventually germinate and, with sheep excluded, seedlings could thrive and eventually bloom with the chance of fertilising flowers on the specimens we were planting. The futility of all this became obvious weeks later when a plague of wingless grasshoppers moved onto the hill and ate our newly planted darwinias into nothingness. Every spring following this, Valerie and I searched, hoping to find germinating mogumber bells in our fenced-off plot, sadly with no success. There is a happy ending to this tale of woe however: several years after selling Clover Downs I was delighted to hear of a new colony of *Darwinia carnea* found on a hilltop several kilometres southeast of Mogumber. After 20 years believing the plant was, in practice, extinct, there is now an excellent chance of re-establishing the Mogumber bell back onto its original gravelly hill.

My first year back on the farm after five years at boarding school, 1969, just happened to be a drought year after decades of reliable and above-average rainfall; the autumn rains failed and winter rains did not fall until weeks into June. We still harvested reasonable crops the following summer due to our living on the 'wet side of the wheat belt'. Cereals prefer dryish soils; in a winter of above-average and even average rainfall, wheat frequently struggles in the wet and boggy paddocks of Mogumber. The thin rains of 1969 held out long enough for the wheat and oats to scrape through and our harvest was acceptable. Sheep, on the other hand, had a terrible time.

Merino ewes dropped lambs onto bare paddocks through April. We had sufficient hay for four or five weeks, but not enough to feed more than 8000 sheep for three entire months. By the end of May we were desperately selling stock at give away prices and buying in bewilderingly expensive hay. Most paddocks were also short of water.

A haunting memory from that time is of Cam and me feeding our big mob of ewes in our southwest paddock. There was plenty of water from its very reliable windmill but the paddock was dust bare. Ewes, with ribcages bursting through their skins, tottered away from newly born lambs, chasing the utility whenever we appeared, desperately fighting for the rubbishy hay I threw to them. We knew the ewes would not go back to their lambs – the bonding process was incomplete and the lambs had no chance of survival. Every day, hundreds of lambs gathered by the windmill and stood bleating for their mothers. Each day we would see them and know it was not really the same flock as the previous day, the lambs could only live a few hours. We bottle fed many but had neither time nor resources to save the hundreds of abandoned young of those weeks. More than a thousand lambs and several hundred ewes were lost that autumn.

Jan and Cam retired in 1983, and part of Merrie-Lea was sold to finance their move to an apartment in South Perth. Around that time, my wife Valerie joined me on the farm and our first project together was to build a house on Clover Downs. The low sandy hill forming the main recharge site for our two areas of *summer-land* seemed an ideal spot. Perennial pasture greened much of the valley to the west and this was framed by surrounding hills and the jagged spine of the Darling Escarpment to the southwest and northwest. Directly west was a long sloping view to the sandplain and that faint suggestion of Indian Ocean. The house was to have rammed earth walls, a silvery pewter corrugated iron roof and its interior resplendent with beams of mahogany red jarrah. The beams were to be dressed from hefty pieces of timber reclaimed from the demolition of an old Perth hospital. However, 100 years' worth of hospital regulation paint proved impossible to sandpaper off and I decided to try to resurface them with an adze borrowed from our next door neighbour, Ross Forrester.

As well as our neighbouring farm, Ross also owned Yarlaweela, a pastoral station of around a million acres, near Meekatharra in the centre of Western Australia. Ross was a lovely neighbour, the proverbial gentleman in every way, but I did notice him hesitate when I asked to borrow his family heirloom adze and try it out. I thought this may be due to its razor-sharp edge – Ross shaved a patch of hair from his arm to prove the point. An adze carelessly allowed to bounce off very old jarrah and into one's leg would certainly leave one minus a leg, he told me. But later, and out of earshot, Ross's wife Shirley explained there were other reasons for Ross's hesitation.

It seemed the mid-19th century pioneers of Western Australian stations took with them not much more than the bare essentials: always an axe, a rifle and an adze; these three items were vital. It was said, according to Shirley, looking me straight in the eye, that, "A true station man would rather lend his wife than his rifle or his axe or his adze". I counted myself more than privileged and went to work. The antique adze did a superb job, giving the beams a rumpled appearance that looked very telling against the smooth, salmon-honey rammed earth. I always kept a very firm grip on the adze handle throughout those weeks of chipping away and after dressing some three dozen beams, all 4–5 metres long, thankfully all my limbs remained intact.

The Forresters were quintessentially station people with that relaxed and practical attitude of those living in the true bush. I once was listening to a Perth ABC radio presenter conducting a telephone interview with Ross and Shirley's son, Geoffrey, who was describing the consequences of a huge cyclone that had roared through the Meekatharra area days earlier. After torrential rain, both the Gascoyne and Murchison rivers were in heavy flood, kilometres of fence line had been washed away and many head of sheep and cattle were drowned and swept downstream. Geoff himself had just completed a flight in his light aircraft delivering food to motorists stranded along hundreds of kilometres of outback roads. As Geoff spoke, the presenter, imagining that he was stumbling onto a major news story, became increasingly excited. "It sounds a disaster, would you yourself describe it that way, Geoff?" "Hell no", Geoff replied, clearly aghast at the question and thinking of umpteen previous years with negligible rain, "this country needed a good drink".

*   *   *

Shirley and Ross were both born and raised on stations; in Ross' case, Yarlaweela, in Shirley's, the famous Mount Augustus Station, named for its monolithic rock (which happens to be substantially bigger than Uluru). As children, both played with Aboriginal kids more than whites and grew up speaking the language of the community living on their respective stations. Among his many outback skills, Ross excelled at tracking.

In the 1970s at the Landall picnic races (one of inland Australia's half-dozen historic race meetings), a child visiting from Perth walked away from his family and into the bush. Ross volunteered to lead the search party. Fortunately, the missing child wandered across a road and was picked up by a passing car just as Ross's party were leaving camp and the search was called off. However, there could easily have been a tragedy; the child was rescued 20 kilometres along the road under extremely fortuitous circumstances. I asked Ross later how he intended mounting the search. He explained that the initial tracks leading into the bush would need to be located first, and from there it was a matter of speed. Scrub around

Landall was thin mallee, with a small tree every 25 to 35 metres – anyone walking 200 to 300 metres away was out of sight. The terrain was gently undulating, with pebbly rises between slightly sandy broad valleys. Ross explained that once tracks were found, the tracker must sprint in their general direction over the first pebbly rise to a low, sandy area, perhaps 2 or more kilometres on, then walk at right angles, using the sand to quickly relocate the tracks and refigure their direction, then run over the next rise to the next valley, find the tracks again and so on. There was danger, naturally, in ignoring the actual tracks for most of the time and running about guessing their direction, yet it was pointless walking steadily along locating every footprint; this was way too slow, at the end of his search Ross and his friends would inevitably find a corpse. Ross told me that while running, it was crucial for the tracker to put himself into the mind of the child. Were they attempting to head north, perhaps another direction, or walking towards a hill, or deliberately zigzagging? Then the thing was to run, run like the wind, with this indicating the best place to relocate the tracks in the next valley.

As one part of our house was to be two storeys, steps were required; I had this neat idea for building a spiral staircase. Internal walls were to be made from glorious wood-fired bricks sourced from a kiln deep in the southwest jarrah forests. The bricks complemented the rammed earth external walls nicely and I hoped they might also make the wall of the staircase. Two young bricklayers were recommended and, after the earth walls were up, the boys arrived to commence work. It took only a couple of days to complete most of the internal brick walls, leaving the spiral staircase as the final job to tackle. The boys stopped to have a look at the plans and chalked a three-quarter circle onto the concrete slab floor, representing a tightly curving brick wall. Each tread of the staircase was to be fastened to the inner surface of a three-quarter brick cylinder and notched into an old gum tree telegraph pole at the centre. It was straightforward really; the boys were to lay a three-quarter cylinder, 2 metres wide and 5 metres high. And the wall was to be one brick through. "Should be an interesting job," they said, "we might charge by the hour from here", (rather than so much per 1000 bricks).

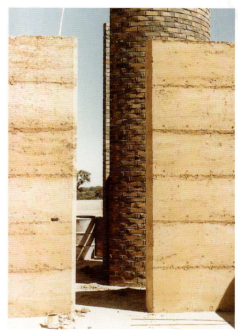

Coming back half a day later I found not a brick had been laid. "We set out the first course," one of the boys volunteered, "and found either the internal mud gap too tight or the external gap too wide, so we are knocking corners off." To my amazement, there was a stack of bricks, all with one corner neatly broken off with a trowel. The boys commenced laying bricks with the missing corner to the inside and the internal mud gaps matched the external mud gaps precisely. The brick cylinder arose before my eyes, a thing of beauty. Indeed, such beauty it was a shame to eventually turn this astonishing brick cylinder, rising from the monolithic

Our rammed earth house under construction

49

One of my 12-foot diameter windmills, more than twice the size of a conventional farm windmill

rammed-earth walls, into something so prosaic as an ordinary house. I could see my builder was awestruck, quite bowled over by their job. After all, not one string line was used, every brick was laid to several measurements of a spirit level, yet the brickies took only two days to build the cylinder despite half a day spent shaping bricks. I thought I must at least congratulate them. "No fuss," they replied, "no fuss at all – it's been almost as much fun as putting up that lighthouse over on the coast 18 months back." The boys even laid an extra wall in the kitchen and they were off back to Perth halfway through Friday, less than five days' work in all.

The house was eventually finished and in those last years on the farm we made a garden. Having chosen the site for convenient water, I now found the soil ran through my fingers like beach sand. There was a soft red colour to it that hinted at nutrients; however, digging trenches for footings, the further down, the paler and coarser it became until, a metre down, it was loose, rounded gravel. What sort of hill was this?

We did, however, have plenty of water. Two windmills were erected to pump from shallow wells sunk into springs, one to the east and one to the west. The extra large windmills had ample strength to pump thousands of litres daily into a 90,000-litre concrete tank on top of the hill. From there, an electric pump pressurised the water to the house, garden and stock troughs. The windmills, pumping around the clock in our around-the-clock wind, pumped much more water than the garden and stock required. The tank overflowed most of summer and all of winter. Surplus water fell through the gravelly subsoil and, I imagined, formed a big mound on top of the original watertable. In effect, the interior of the hill could serve as a colossal reservoir to guarantee water supplies through low rainfall years. Eventually, as the extra groundwater oozed to the sides of the hill, an increase in the flow of the springs could be expected and an extension to the green *summer-land* pasture, but that was something to look forward to years hence.

Insects dominated the Mogumber hills. Bush flies in summer were a constant conscious and unconscious presence. Anyone walking out past a fly-screen door quickly gathered a buzzing cloud of hundreds of them. Individually, they were inoffensive. They were small and did not bite or sting, but simply settled in the corners of one's eyes and nose. To avoid inhaling them we pursed our lips and waved them from our eyes in a gesture that continued from the first weeks of spring until the heat waves of February and March put an end to them.

Night-time insects homing in on any glimmer of light in summer were almost as irritating. For some reason, pasture around our rammed-earth house was ideal habitat for umpteen species of tiny moth. Our first summer there, to prevent them swarming into and overwhelming the house, we fell into the habit of quickly turning nearly all internal lights out after our evening meal and switching on several big external lights to divert their attention. The paving below these would be stained by tens of thousands of tiny desiccated carcasses in the morning.

Termites were also ubiquitous. Soft pink termite mounds littered hillside and bush areas, so that any timber left touching the earth never lasted long. On one occasion, the ceiling of our shearers' quarters came crashing down just as the shearers arrived, ceiling joists turned to dangling runnels of splinters in the few months since our pest controller previously visited. And spiders, plenty of those too, the infamous, highly venomous redbacks under every flat surface, and monster wolf spiders and huntsmen and daddy long legs and jewel spiders and jumping spiders. I remember a grove of sheoaks in the Brecon paddock, trees strung one to the next with ropey cobwebs often many paces across. It seems individual webs were maintained for years at a stretch by teams of little spiders. The curious thing was, these distinctive webs were only to be found in this one grove of trees, nowhere else. They were always there, year after year, right in the way of any mob of sheep to be moved down to the mill paddock and an utter nuisance. I wonder what an entomologist might have made of them?

Ants were everywhere also; under each stone there seemed a different species. Their variety was phenomenal; we accepted this for ages without comment or discussion – they were only ants after all. I paid more attention in the 1980s after hearing of an entrepreneur hoping to establish a tourism business. His idea was to invite entomologically minded visitors from all over the world to visit southwest WA to see its ants. Apparently a substantial percentage of the world's species of ants called Western Australia home. Then again, as a reason to travel from the US or Europe, ants are not quite up with the massed wildebeest and zebra on the Serengeti and I cannot say I have since noticed any enthusiasm for his venture.

There were a few common, everyday species of ant. Little black sugar ants, for instance, which crept into our pantry exploring cake tins for mother's prize sponge cakes and scones, and Sergeant's ants, monstrous things, an inch and a half long, with scimitar jaws for ripping into flesh and leaving poison behind with at least the kick of a European wasp. Another ant to be seen everywhere was the meat ant. Dark red and black, medium size, and although stingless, they were very aggressive and equipped with a ferocious bite. Their nests were big, occasionally huge. One occupied half a tennis court's worth of hillside, capable of spewing forth dark swarms of ants to hurl themselves gallantly at any intruder. The damage they could do to any incapacitated animal was appalling; in her final illness and mind wandering, my mother spoke of dreams – nightmares – in which she was helpless and immobile within reach of meat ants.

We also had big centipedes and tiny scorpions and all the usual biting insects; but of all these creatures, blowflies were the worst. Humid springs allowed population levels to soar. September and October were often devoted to keeping sheep free of them. Merinos feeding on capeweed pastures in particular became prone to scouring and their rear ends became ideal nesting sites for blowflies. We did everything we could to prevent this, crutching them (removing wool from around their tails just before spring), jetting (saturating the same area with an organophosphate – which, as I now know, wasn't doing me any good at all, and was only effective for the sheep for a few days), dipping (the same chemical applied over the entire animal as a shower bath some days after shearing, with me dripping in toxic chemicals for weeks), and mulsing (removing folds of skin around the rear end with shears; a horrible operation but less cruel by far than fly strike).

Of all those years, the spring of 1974 was the most difficult, more so because I was looking after the farm alone for several months. The season stayed mild and moist week after week and the flies became so bad I dared not bring mobs to the yards to treat stricken animals. This only increased their exposure to egg-laden flies hovering around the shearing shed. Fortunately, I had good dogs that year – Mr Chu was in particularly fine form. So sheep were mustered and moved quickly to a corner of a paddock; the three dogs, Chu, Rick and Mintie, then spread out and could sit and relax and hold them steady. Mr Chu's job was catching each animal. Easy really – he simply homed in on the putrid stench of the maggots and seized the animal by a mouthful of wool. I came in behind to catch the victim by its muzzle – one handed of course, with shears and strike treatment powder in the other. Wool was then clipped away from the infestation with hand shears, the writhing mass of maggots scooped out of the wound as far as possible and powder applied from a puffer pack impregnated with the same organophosphate, resulting in my breathing it in, for hours and weeks and months on end. Every three days mobs were checked and always 20 or 30 animals needed treating. As spring progressed, wounds on the sheep grew increasingly more appalling: great fistfulls of flesh eaten away, deep layers of muscle, sinews and tendons, and occasionally bones, exposed. Their suffering was unimaginable. I came across a badly flystruck sheep near a dam and, not having sufficient treatment powder with me, returned 15 minutes later to find the animal had wandered into the shallows of the dam in the meantime, lain down, body upright, lowered its head and drowned itself, in a few inches of water. Most pitiful of all were the old ewes, hanging on to life with heroic grit despite terrible wounds, for the sake of their lambs, I suppose. Wethers let go much more quickly. And rams needed daily checking if I was not to lose the lot of them. Despite frantic efforts, as many as 400 sheep died, perhaps more. After weeks of dealing with it, I could not get sight or smell of the maggots out of my head. My mind was bloated with their gaping loathsome wounds, maggots wriggling, the stink of them; exposed flesh pockmarked and tunnelled, clouded grey and blue and green. Blowfly maggots invaded reveries and infested my dreams every night.

A GARDEN AND ITS INSPIRATION

That first summer I excavated three areas close to the house to a depth of some 25 centimetres and levelled them to plant lawn. Cool grass in summer for children's feet, I feel, is essential in warm-climate gardens. I made these lawns as level as possible within the gentle surrounding slope to suggest of pools of water. Several massive angular rocks were let into the highest section of bank above the main lawn and trees were planted for shade and as windbreaks. The trees were selected to let sufficient light through their canopies to allow me to experiment with ornamental grasses and perennials in the dappled shade below, keeping in mind most perennials could never survive a Mogumber summer fully exposed to the sun. I planted several honey locusts, *Gleditsia triacanthos* 'Sunburst', one or two *G.* 'Rubylaces', a little grove of *Sapium sebiferum*, or Chinese tallow trees (one of the few trees with reliable colour in our mild autumns), and several fruit trees including a couple of quinces with large soft green leaves nestled around their pale sugary pink flowers. The under-planting consisted of anything I hoped might survive. Daylilies were happy, and sedums and other succulents. Chrysanthemums did well, likewise autumn flowering asters, although the latter often tried to flower in mid-summer then staggered along for the rest of the season. Those ornamental grasses then available all thrived; however I was soon to discover that the herbaceous perennials suited to Mogumber formed a meagre field of study. Any number of plants ordered from nurseries in the Blue Mountains and cool parts of Victoria and forest glens in Tasmania and planted on a gentle day in spring faded instantly to a dry wisp of nothing on the first warm windy day of summer. There again, Mediterranean sub-shrubs such as lavenders and artemisias were at home and roses grew splendidly.

I found a Perth nurseryman selling old roses: rugosas, hybrid musks, bourbons, gallicas, and experimented with these. Rugosas produced lovely flowers in October but summer blooms were regularly scorched. But they were worth persevering with as the autumn flowers were particularly good and their leaves turned brassy yellow and crimson in winter while spangled with reddening hips. Autumn flowers of hybrid musks were produced in gigantic panicles, their perfume drifting across the garden and into the paddock, and other old roses were worth growing as long as their blooming did not coincide with an early heatwave.

I came to know the nurseryman quite well and after a time he accorded me the special privilege of telling me how he propagated his plants. After much experimentation, West Australian nurserymen have found roses do well in Perth's deep sand only

Top to bottom: *Pennisetum villosum* edging the path; pergola with ornamental grape vine; *Pennisetum setaceum* to the right and the variegated pampas grass, *Cortaderia selloana* 'Silver Comet'

when budded onto *Rosa fortuniana* root stock. In fact, an understanding was reached by these nurserymen that roses must be put onto this root stock in WA. This, I should point out, is exactly the reverse to just about everywhere else where roses are expected to do best in clay. It happens, though, *R. fortuniana* has roots adapted to delving into sand and plants grafted onto this stock in Perth are some of the finest to be seen. Unfortunately, I was told, budding onto fortuniana is no easy matter. Perversely, the buds will not take unless the task is performed during hot weather, in fact, very hot weather. On warm days when the temperature is in the low 30s, the take is barely passable; on high 30s days perhaps acceptable. However, budding onto fortuniana during a heat wave, when temperatures are in the 40s, or even better, the high 40s, results in the cultivar buds clamping to root stock stems with barnacle-like tenacity. *R. fortuniana's* growth habit also bore consideration. In my friend's field, fortuniana root stock protruded from the ground as a bare stem to around 30 centimetres, then branched sideways into a mass of twigs armed with long razor-sharp prickles. Plants in each row were spaced 45 centimetres apart with a 1.2-metre gap between rows; lateral growth formed a continuous, briar-patch-like canopy. My friend was on his belly below this for most of each day and, with his head twisted sideways and one ear brushing the ground, with luck there was just sufficient wriggle room to make each 'T' incision, slip a cultivar bud into the cut, bind the wound and snake along to the next plant. Naturally, if air temperature was in the 40s, the ground temperature was hotter, enough to blister bare flesh not already slashed and bloody from those re-curved (backward facing), exquisitely sharp prickles. However, I must say his roses grew magnificently.

17 July 2004

Found myself leafing through old photograph albums last night, books I had not looked at in several years. There's always that slightly masochistic thrill looking through 20-year-old photos, the feeling of Marvell's 'time's winged chariot hurrying near'. Did I really have that much hair 17 years back? But largely I was looking for photos taken during two visits to England, the first in 1981 and the second in 1988.

In August and September 1981, Valerie and I visited her family near Herne Bay in Kent. It was a particularly lovely summer, plenty of sunshine and rain when required. We hired a little car and on our first free day skirted around Canterbury and drove over the North Downs through the medieval village of Chilham. To an Australian used to broad roads and gentle curves, the narrow twisting lanes of the Kentish countryside gave pause for consideration. They were useful to encourage one to most enjoy the countryside perhaps, and certainly the orchards and hedgerows were heavy with fruit and the tiny fields thick with wheat. From Chilham we drove into the Kentish Weald and a patter of villages, Smarden, Pluckley and Biddenden. Still only mid-morning and I remember first sighting Sissinghurst's tower across farm fields with mist still thinning and burning in the sun.

After reading books and studying photographs I imagined there should be some familiarity to walking through those gardens, yet the next few hours were revelatory. Sissinghurst seemed impossibly perfect. Thin mist lent the garden a soft-focus mood and also served to intensify colour. Entering the first courtyard the purple border instantly caught our eye – mauve and vermilion clematis draped in great swags over enormous silver thistles behind cerise bergamonts and steel-blue sea hollies, then buddleias erupting in midnight purple. My photographs of the cottage garden show *Cosmos astrosanguineus*, the chocolate perfumed cosmos, with little dancing flowers the colour of congealed blood. And further, a bank of rusty apricot arctotis against a Tudor brick wall. How could this be – arctotis blooming in August? On the farm they flowered in spring and perhaps a few blooms in autumn. And the *Cosmos astrosanguineus* – I had read of it in one of my reference books but had never seen it before. Crocosmias were everywhere, with their curving spikes of terracotta and apricot gold – they looked as though they should grow in Australia but I had not seen them. The ingenuity of the intersecting vistas left Valerie and I shaking our heads and laughing. And then, by accident, we saved the white garden for last and that was good; the elegance of green and white and silver overflowing crisp box edging and a view out into a field of wheat settling me gently to earth.

A week later we were exploring the Cotswolds and pages in my album are filled with stone villages: Bourton-on-the-Water, Chipping Campden, Stow-on-the-Wold and Broadway. We stayed at a bed-and-breakfast in Chipping Campden and enjoyed an evening meal of Gloucestershire sausage at the Eight Bells pub, with old farmers drinking ale and a sheep dog asleep on the floor. The following morning we drove northeast through the broken countryside and hedge-cloistered lanes to Hidcote. It seemed the entrance to Hidcote then lacked something of the Tudor grandeur of Sissinghurst. We tagged along with a group of visitors through a courtyard that, I'm sure, was never meant to be the way to the garden. The main axis we found by happenstance, but from there, again, Hidcote was beyond criticism. Perennial plantings lapped the glorious Lebanese cedar in a froth of lemon and pink and crimson, and a broad grass path drew us irresistibly between the famous red borders to the twin summer houses flanking the steps. We climbed the steps and strolled through the hornbeam clipped *palissade a l'Italienne* and out between tall wrought iron gates hanging above that long, long view: the Vale of Evesham and England at one's feet.

Several memories are vivid from that morning. As with Sissinghurst, the playfulness of the architecture was striking. A visitor wandered past with a telephoto lens attached to a somewhat battered camera body. Climbing the steps he drew level with the twin pavilions, spotted the surprise cross axis opening through the left-hand pavilion and swung his camera up and snapped a photo in one swift action as though all might suddenly vanish, like a celebrity into the crowd or a tennis player returning the ball. He lowered his camera, smiling a little ruefully to himself.

Everything seemed grown to perfection that day: fuchsias in full sun, an astonishing sight for anyone from a hot climate, and phlox and penstemons and sedums, plants I had read of and wondered about for years. Hedge clipping was almost complete, edges crisp, paths raked, sunshine filling the old swimming pool mysteriously – that day seemed the crescendo of all those weeks travelling. Later, back in Australia, thinking of both Sissinghurst and Hidcote, and other gardens: Tintinhull, Stourhead, Montacute, Wisley and Great Dixter, it seemed Hidcote's red borders were the most memorable thing of all. The repeated clumps of the old orange double daylily, *Hemerocallis* 'Kwanso Flore Pleno', were at their best with brick red geums and orange dahlias and beetroot lobelias, and sheets of coppery foliage behind, and the old *Pinus mugo* leaning hugely from one side.

Perhaps, of the regions of England, I felt a tiny bit more at home in the Cotswolds. This had to do with the history of the area. England rode on the sheep's back from medieval times to almost the industrial revolution. The Cotswolds hills, in particular, provided prime grazing for sheep whose fleeces supplied the bulk of the English wool industry and wool made up most of England's exports for generations. Cash from cloth merchants of Antwerp and Bruges built the magnificent 'wool churches' and manor houses to be seen throughout the Cotswolds; that Australian farmers, and we ourselves, had picked up and carried on the baton was something I took a touch of pleasure in.

*　　*　　*

Shearing was one of the two or three great annual events on the farm calendar. We shore in June–July during my first years farming. Later, we moved the main shearing to February and March, as wool shorn in summer is stronger and sells for a premium. However, shearing in February was tough work for us, the shed hands, and particularly for the shearers. Sheep also hated it. Daylight in summer is their sleeping time and sheep waiting their turn to be stripped of their fleece would stand and doze in the catching pens, oblivious to the noise and insults to the dignity of their companions out on the 'board'.

The actual process of shearing is almost ballet. A muscular form of dance perhaps, but watching a 'gun' shearer is awe inspiring, his work an exercise in energy and elegance. Shearing is the toughest job I know. Manhandling and shearing 200 sheep over eight hours in a corrugated iron shed, with outside temperatures in the 40s and temperatures within higher still is not for the faint-hearted, demanding levels of fitness an average Olympian would envy.

Through the 1980s I wondered about the perennials we had seen in England. I experimented with every plant that might succeed at Mogumber from mail order nurseries all over Australia and eventually began to wonder why no one was listing *Sedum* 'Autumn Joy' or some of the crocosmias or any ornamental grasses. In 1988 we took the chance to travel again and with Valerie's family generously offering their homes as a base, we again allowed time to visit gardens, this time though with our two children, Benjamin and Alys. So steadied by a baby stroller and back packs, we hired a little Renault and set out. We revisited Hidcote and Sissinghurst and this time attempted to see something of the Jekyll–Lutyens gardens. My interest in the work of Gertrude Jekyll dates back to the mid 1970s and by 1988 I had accumulated most of her seminal books. As it happened, our touring involved three days in Surrey with nothing to show but several photos of the façade of Tigbourne Court. The many Jekyll gardens of the area, including her own, Munstead Wood, were stiff with 'No Trespassing' and 'Beware Dangerous Dogs' signs. However, in Somerset we saw Hestercombe and Barrington Court. Barrington Court was superb that season and the Lutyens part of Hestercombe was almost entirely restored.

That summer I could not resist collecting a few of those wish-list perennials tantalising me everywhere we went, so during the last days of our visit we did a huge nursery crawl. From Lambrook Manor in Somerset we drove to Beth Chatto's in Essex, then Blooms in Norfolk, dropping into the nursery attached to Wisley halfway around the M25. We found Graham Trevor, a specialist in Mediterranean plants with his business near Sandwich. He was conveniently just around the corner from Herne Bay. Graham generously offered to mind our plants and we returned to him with several carloads of treasures including *Sedum* 'Autumn Joy', *Crocosmia* 'Lucifer', *C.* 'Emily McKenzie', and Beth Chatto's form of *C. masoniorum* with its right-side-up orange flowers. We purchased *Buddleia* 'Pink Delight' and *B.* 'Black Knight' from Blooms, along with *Achillea* 'Moonshine' and *A.* 'Coronation Gold', and many Kniphofias and Tradescantias.

Details of grasses, top to bottom: *Cortaderia selloana* 'Silver Comet'; *Miscanthus sinensis* 'Sarabande'; *Miscanthus sinensis* 'Gracillimus' and *Calamagrostis x acutiflora* 'Overdam'

While visiting Kew Gardens at this time I noticed several varieties of *Miscanthus sinensis* with German names all new to me. According to the gardeners in charge of the ornamental grass beds, they were bred by Ernst Pagels, of Leer in Germany. The following day we drove back to Great Dixter to see if Christopher Lloyd knew anything of Ernst Pagels. Christopher sold me a handsome *Yucca gloriosa* 'Nobilis' (I felt I must include this in my collection if only for its name), and suggested we speak to Beth Chatto to advise on new miscanthus varieties. Also, Rougham Hall near Bury St Edmonds was recommended as a nursery that could help with other grasses. So back around the M25 to Cambridgeshire and Essex and yet more flying visits to inspirational nurseries and back to Herne Bay. Best of all, Beth Chatto provided contact details for Ernst Pagels and it was a simple matter to obtain his catalogue and make a selection.

On our final day, Graham Trevor instructed me how to bare root our plants and pack them into cardboard boxes between layers of slightly damp newspaper, then sit on them, squeezing them tight for that very long flight home. And he included some of his own treasures, including a chocolate cosmos propagated from a plant given him by the Sissinghurst gardeners no less. From Herne Bay, I took the train journey across to Heathrow followed by 28 hours sitting in a jumbo jet before staggering through arrivals in Perth puzzling how to reply to the custom officer's query, "Anything to declare?"

Despite 40 hours without sleep I went straight to the quarantine station to help with potting up following fumigation procedures and watched as my plants were wheeled into an insect-proof glasshouse. As it eventuated, with the enthusiastic attention of a young quarantine official thoroughly intrigued with all these strange plants, of some 140 perennials put into the glasshouse around 120 were released, happy and healthy, three months later.

The grasses were another story. Strict regulations regulate the importation of grasses to reduce the risk of foreign grass-specific viruses being introduced into Australia. Of some 120 grass viruses around the world, around 45 are on the 'not to be admitted under any circumstances' list. Naturally, identifying these among the others is no easy matter and my grass specimens disappeared into quarantine and stayed for years. Some were released after three years, some six years, two after 11 years. And a number of lovely plants were never released. Around 20 of the original three dozen came through testing procedures. These included such famous plants as *Calamagrostis x acutiflora* 'Karl Foerster' and its variegated form, *Calamagrostis x acutiflora* 'Overdam'. Of Ernst Pagels' miscanthus selections, *M.* 'Graziella' and *M.* 'Flamingo' were declared clean, also *M.* 'Sarabande' from Kurt Bluemal in America. A couple of pennisetums were released: *Pennisetum alopecuroides* 'Woodside', an old sterile form selected for its flowering in cool climates and also *P.* 'Hamelin', a dwarf sterile form. Overall the exercise was worthwhile, but to my intense regret we lost the exquisitely variegated *Miscanthus sinensis* 'Morning Light' and several of Ernst Pagels' plants: *M.* 'Malepartus', *M.* 'Rotsilber' and *M.* 'Kaskade'.

During the 1970s, several springs in Merrie-Lea's lower-lying paddocks failed; springs we relied on for watering sheep dried to dusty holes surrounded by our wheat. This was disappointing but not surprising – the wettest years of the 70s were more than dryish, well below average rainfall and these intermingled through rolling seasons of serious drought. What did surprise my family was that, simultaneously, new springs were erupting from the slopes around our eastern plateau. Nearly all appeared high up, just under the plateau's rocky edge and every one of them was choked with salt. We were amazed, also appalled as it was impossible to prevent the salt from washing into our streams and dams. How this could happen was a mystery until, in the 1980s, I attended WA Agricultural Department seminars on salt and soil reclamation.

Salt is stored in soils all through the southwest of WA and its source, we learnt with astonishment, is the rain. It seems rainfall is never pristine little drops falling innocently from the heavens – minute traces of dissolved minerals are present in every shower. Actual levels of dissolved salt varies, coastal districts have saltier rainfall than inland areas for instance. As luck would have it, Western Australian rain is exceptionally salty. Storms in the southern Indian Ocean are ferocious enough to sweep quantities of salt into weather systems and cold fronts making landfall deposit this onto farmland at around one kilogram per hectare annually. A handful or two of salt sprinkled across an acre once every 12 months may seem ridiculously trivial, but given tens of thousands and tens of millions of years this adds up to thousands of tonnes of salt raining down on every hectare of the landscape. What, then, becomes of it?

Some rainfall is taken in by plants, some flows to streams and a little evaporates. Most rain however, soaks into the soil and its burden of salt is stripped away and accumulates over the millennia in subsoil overlying impermeable bedrock. The rate at which salt is deposited varies from low in free-draining, sandy subsoils to bewilderingly high in clay. In some tight clay areas of southwest WA, in just that 20- to 30-metre layer between the surface and bedrock, more than several thousand tonnes of salt are stored within each and every hectare. The salt deposited in an entire valley system in these parts does not bear contemplation: vast underground stockpiles in the millions of tonnes. Yet Europeans exploring these salt-infested landscapes found springs brimming with sweet water, and rivers fresh and just right for the drinking – how could this be so?

Not all salt is left behind as rainfall moves through the subsoil. In fact, most never settles. Salt is flushed along underground streams in 'groundwater' oozing its way to emerge as a spring, feeding a river perhaps. Steady movement of groundwater through 'preferred pathways' never allows its accompanying salt to accumulate; salt is flushed away and springs have similar salinity levels to the original rainfall – in other words, so minute as to be undetectable. Certainly, the Yuad people and the Scotch shepherds knew the Moore as a fresh water river and the reason for this was the very steadiness of the flow of groundwater from season to season and millennium to millennium. However, underground streams generally flow below strata infested with salt deposited over the previous several interglacial periods. A sudden increase in flow will cause groundwater to flood up through the subsoil. Pockets of stored salt are submerged; these dissolve and become mobile. The larger the increase in underground water, the more salt exposed to movement.

Unfortunately, it so happens that the clearing of native vegetation sets exactly this disastrous process in train. Groundwater levels rise precipitously as bush is removed because deep-rooted trees and shrubs take up and transpire vast volumes of underground water, especially in summer, while winter growing crops and pastures, both with shallow roots, transpire barely a drop. Cam's clearing of the 1960s allowed huge volumes of groundwater to accumulate in our high country (even during those desperately dry winters of the 70s) causing the watertable to rise, saturate upper layers of subsoil, dissolve pockets of salt and spill out of our hillsides along with its insidious cargo.

So, ancient salt deposits sitting high in the landscape were now mobile, but why did those briny springs appear so close to the top of our hills? Why did they not emerge in our valleys where they might have been easier to control? Because, we discovered, a 'pulse' of water from heavy rainfall moves rapidly down through subsoil to the water table, often within hours, then sideways through open gritty soils at only metres annually and through dense clay at barely centimetres each year. In other words, there is a marked tendency for groundwater to 'pile up' vertically through subsoil and the watertable is often much closer to the surface than one might imagine, particularly in clay areas. It was just our bad luck that the subsoil under our airstrip plateau was ideal for storing salt, that the added groundwater inevitably turned to brine, and was bound to flow along extremely high preferred pathways to be excreted immediately under the edge of our plateau.

If nothing is done, the rate of recharge to discharge of salt will settle down of its own accord. Salt leaving the landscape in rivers flowing to the sea will naturally come to match the salt arriving in rainfall. Balance will be restored by the flushing away of the stockpiles

of mobile salt and, with it gone, Merrie-Lea streams and the Moore River will turn fresh
once more. This will happen at nature's own sweet pace; possibly before the next ice age,
but probably not, and certainly not in the space of human lifetimes, remembering how
many millions of tonnes must be flushed from every valley to rid the subsoil of its mobile
salt. Thus the race is on in the Mogumber hills and farmland throughout Australia to
lower watertables to levels of 200 years ago by planting recharge areas of the landscape
with deep-rooted thirsty trees.

THE LAKES

In 1986 I was introduced to a stonemason who offered to teach me how to lay a stone wall. There were nice things to gardening on a farm. We did have a front-end loader and a tip truck to play with and a good 600 hectares of hillside covered in rock. Occasionally this broke up into geometric pieces with good crisp edges. Unfortunately, edges were not often at 90 degrees, usually either 60 or 120 degrees. Much of the stone looked like three-dimensional parallelograms, making it very tricky to lay. However the colours were wonderful: soft grey-browns and chestnuts and pinks.

I suppose my interest in garden walls came as a child, seeing a stone wall around my grandparents' house on their Lake Camm farm. While living at Moulyinning, my family and I used to visit my mother's family regularly. The districts of Lake King, Lake Camm, Varley and Holt Rock adjoin each other along the edges of an extinct river. The slightly richer silt soils of the old flood plain are easily seen in the earliest of the farms meandering in a north–south strip through these parts. The river has long turned to a string of shallow lakes that have been salt for thousands of years. My mother's family pioneered Lake Camm when the district was thrown open to selection in 1928.

Visiting Lake Camm we took the seemingly endless dead-straight road due east from Lake Grace and Newdegate to Lake King. I suspect whoever surveyed this road found a map showing Lake Grace and Lake King, pencilled in a line between the two with a ruler and then told his construction engineer to get on with it. Still, there is something that tugs at the imagination driving on a road constructed as a compass bearing: a hint of the surreal and uncanny. Vast valley floors stretched on and on with the slightest of rises between. As we at long last breasted a high point, the next umpteen miles of road would swing into view, ramrod straight, leading to the tiniest gap in the low trees on the most distant horizon. Faint rises, miles further, were smudged by mirages that danced and flickered and vanished as we approached and

towns became smaller until they were no more than a general store, a corrugated iron community hall and a footy oval away in the bush. Certainly bush dominated in the 1950s, broken by occasional roughly cleared paddocks, perhaps a few sheep picking their way through stubble and wild turnip tumbleweed. The olive-green scrub slowly turned khaki from winter to summer and the only other features were the salt lakes. The road passed through periodic bands of lakes and in a couple of places was but a causeway over grey salt flats. Covered in winter with thin steely water, the lakes dried quickly in spring and on any warm summer's day far shores shimmered in a tangled haze of mirages. To look across salt flats towards the light those days was to peer into the pulsing heart of the sun itself.

By the mid 1950s my grandparents were retired on a small farm in the midst of wheat farms, mainly owned by uncles with houses bursting with cousins. Uncle Ronnie and Aunty Barbara were to the north, Uncle Hec and Aunty Eid's place to the west overlooking Lake Camm, and Uncle Brick and Aunty Margaret off towards *the fence* on the far side of the road. My grandparents' concrete breeze-block house was painted cream with a silvery corrugated iron roof. Its little garden was surrounded by a low stone wall. I imagine this was the only garden wall for hundreds of miles, and one of a handful of gardens. The house stood near the top of a rise with an almost hilly landscape surrounding, by the standards of the eastern wheat belt. That's how I remember it from near 50 years back, but chatting on the phone last weekend, my father tells me that the highest part of the farm was all of 20 feet above the lowest and this over a couple of miles. Several acres of a continuous rock capped the rise with my grandparents' house a few paces to the south. For young children, this immense low rock was a strange and magical place. Undulating, it occasionally reared into miniature cliffs while elsewhere, hollows in winter became substantial pools filled with tadpoles. In summer, uppermost layers expanded in the sun to crack away from the parent rock in great exfoliating sheets. These broke further into blocks and, during his retirement, my grandfather collected enough to build his wall.

We parked our car under sheoaks, pushed open a creaky wooden gate and walked the few steps through the garden into the kitchen. Let into grandfather's wall near the gate was an outside toilet, its high stone walls neatly mortared. The freestanding garden wall to each side of the toilet was also carefully put together but as he worked his way around the house my grandfather used less and less cement to the point where, I suppose, in places it immediately fell down. Thus, the house was sheltered by a handsome stone wall to the west and north, the east side was part standing, to the south was a mere tumbled down bank of rock.

My mother's family were McPhees. They sailed from Scotland to the Victorian gold rushes in the mid-19th century and as a young man my grandfather worked as a timber getter in Gippsland. He moved to southwest WA around the turn of the last century and, after a spell in the jarrah forests, turned to farming, finally settling on a 1200-acre bush block at Lake Camm. To commemorate his early years in the east and thinking, I guess, of Lake Camm, just a little walk away, my grandfather named his farm for Ballarat's beautiful lake, Wendourie. He was a notorious soap-box firebrand, the story goes, as an official of the Forestry Workers Union in his salad days but with age grandfather had lost all signs of liveliness. After years clearing his farm he was diagnosed with *axeman's heart* and a doctor recommended he avoid further physical exertion. I think of him in the mid-1950s pottering around, carving ash trays out of mallee roots, or, on special occasions he might make toffee in a frying pan for visiting grandchildren. Michael and I would watch the bubbling mix turn and harden and cool; the solid disc was smashed with a hammer and we were given great translucent splinters to eat in the garden.

Every week a mail truck stopped by the front gate and tooted and grandfather pushed his wheelbarrow perhaps a mile down the drive to fetch the mail bag back. My grandmother then separated the mail for the various families into piles and put the five library books she was sent each week from Perth onto a shelf by the telephone. She would have these read in plenty of time to include with the many letters and outgoing paid accounts in the following week's pickup. The garden was my grandmother's. As my grandfather retreated into himself my grandmother took over the running of the house, of the farm, of all the families and their respective farms. My grandmother had fiery red hair inherited from every part of Scotland. She was known to all in the Lakes District as *Mrs Mac*, likewise a fair number from the Great Southern. My Nan was also a familiar face to anyone and everyone selling perfumes and chocolates and little luxuries in the fair city of Perth. The narrow space between the house and the garden wall was filled with her flowers: sunflowers and poppies, stocks and sweet peas; and I especially remember her snapdragons.

With grandfather's wall as inspiration, over spare days during the winter of 1986 I collected rock, enough, I hoped, to keep a stonemason busy for a few days. That spring, the mason, his offsider, a farm worker and I began building a wall to my garden. It was to be single faced, backed onto formwork and averaging around a metre high. The face of each rock was laid to a string line and the mortar raked back one centimetre. Because of their eccentric shapes, stones were inclined to pop out like watermelon pips. Many required propping steady while the mortar cured but despite

this, we built some 30 metres of wall over three days. To encircle the garden a further 90 metres of wall remained, largely a job for me, on my own. Every so often I took a day or two off to lay some more. The final stone was placed in September 1989 and the result was good: a patchwork of greys and coppery crimsons, honey and soft orange-browns; the wall certainly made an excellent backdrop to my perennials.

Perversely, weeks later and with the garden at last a little boast-worthy, we were selling the farm. For reasons accumulating over a couple of years it seemed time for a change of direction. My rehabilitation plans for Clover Downs were largely complete and attempts to expand by purchasing a nearby property were proving fruitless. And experiments growing herbaceous perennials were becoming increasingly ambitious, tinged always with exasperation at the endless list of plants I dare not even try in the sand and heat of my Clover Downs garden. Perhaps the final reason, the most banal, was a visiting real estate agent casually mentioning what the farms might be worth. We were astonished and thought, "In that case, let's sell".

Around 1962, Gillingarra School was invited to field a football team to play the Aboriginal kids of the Moore River Settlement, the Methodist Mission. At that time there were some 200 kids forcibly taken from their families living at the Mission. Gillingarra really didn't have sufficient children for an Australian Rules footy team – 18 players ideally with two or three reserves as well – but we mustered something of a team and travelled out into the sand hills beside the river in our VW bus to face the opposition. Oh boy, were we trounced!

The mission fielded a full team plus a few ring-ins to bolster the Gillingarra side, but to no avail. Little kids raced and wheeled and skipped around us, through us, over the top of us, laughing and yelling their lungs out in strange languages and versions of English we could not begin to fathom. We were clobbered! I don't remember touching the ball! Very few Gillingarra kids did. Apart from Johnny Halligan, who was very tall and contested every ruck, tapping the ball towards one of the hopelessly outnumbered white kids who instantly disappeared under the welter, the ball would pop out and whistle towards the goal posts with Aboriginal kids chortling and hallooing it along. No one bothered to keep count of goals scored against us and we didn't come close to scoring a point. We climbed back into our bus wide-eyed, silent, bruised and battered. We only ever played them once.

About that same time, I remember going along to a performance of the Mikado in the Mogumber hall, put on by the same children from the mission; a pretty ambitious undertaking for primary school kids. A makeshift orchestra struck up with drums, triangles and castanets, and several girls playing recorders tunefully enough for the local farmer audience to follow those complicated Gilbert and Sullivan tunes. The boy, perhaps 11 or 12, who played the male lead sailed through all his tricky songs with such sangfroid that even now I wonder what became of him. I clearly remember Cam and Jan remarking on him later and Pastor Clarke replying the child was the most promising he had seen in years and how well he might do in secondary college and university though no chance of it happening.

What is it that inspires a sea change decision in one's life? At the time an entire skein of threads seemed to have come together and seemed heading away in some new direction; the puzzle was the direction. Thoughts of selling our Mogumber farms to buy a larger property in what would have to be a different part of WA did not appeal for all sorts of reasons. That left my interest in plants and garden design. I found myself wondering – might it be possible to make a garden, along with nursery perhaps, and a restaurant maybe, with other accoutrements to gardening possibly, yet the garden as the focus to all of these? I was not aware of anyone attempting this anywhere but why should that stop me. The final question was where could such a thing succeed?

THE DANDENONGS

I had some time off farming in 1978–79, and travelled to Melbourne, taking a job for the spring and summer at the Royal Botanic Gardens. Apart from the fun of two entire seasons in those magnificent gardens my best memories were of weekends driving through the Dandenong Ranges. Roads winding through mountain ash and tree fern were reason enough for pleasure and everywhere gardens brimmed with extraordinary plants luxuriating in the volcanic soil. There was an exhibition of lilies in the National Rhododendron Gardens around Christmas time, long benches hidden under blooms and the perfume driving me repeatedly from the display hall. All of this suggested that a move to Victoria might be good. However, we also pondered Margaret River in the southwest tip of Western Australia. Margaret River has glorious coastline, vineyards, superb climate, plenty of rain and good numbers of visitors; we made many exploratory trips wondering. Then again, I thought I must do the Dandenongs justice and see the area once more to make comparisons.

The plants we brought back from England in 1988 were divided and pieces given to nurseries in several parts of Australia. We had done this with the thought that should I lose my specimens to Mogumber's ferocious summers, at least someone would have them somewhere and they need not be reimported. Many were sent to David Glenn of

Criss Canning

David Glenn

Lambley Nursery. At that time, Lambley was situated near Olinda, in the Dandenongs. On the strength of his undoubted local knowledge I asked David his opinion on making a garden in his vicinity featuring herbaceous perennials. David replied that the Dandenongs were ideal and must be first choice, so with no further hesitation I invited myself along for him to show me around and prove this conjecture.

Thus in the last days of November 1989 I left contractors harvesting our wheat crop, flew to Melbourne and on to the Dandenongs to meet David Glenn and Criss Canning. We met at Criss's front door, which, to my bemusement, opened into a log cabin. This was my introduction to some of the eccentricities of the Dandenongs. The cabin, dating to the earliest days of hills settlement, was built by Canadians to a traditional design but with massive Australian mountain ash logs. Its interior was like a dim wooden cave complete with creaky floor sloping some 30 centimetres towards the valley. The cabin was surrounded by gigantic, very shady trees and the few windows were rather small and filled with thick stained glass. Thus while being shown around by my charming hosts that morning I discovered the unnerving floor with my feet. For a moment though, the reason for my unsteadiness was uncertain; the invisible floor following the slope down the mountain was only one cause for bewilderment: Criss's log cabin was extraordinarily dark, yet also filled with colour. Slowly, I came to see that numerous shelves were packed with brilliantly glazed vases and the walls were covered with oil paintings; a couple of these were portraits but most were gorgeously painted flowers. It seemed nearly all the paintings were by Criss; she was, in fact, a professional artist. Criss had earlier worked at portraits and landscape themes, more recently devoting her time to still life. I was soon to find her glorious flower paintings were achieving much public acclaim and critical interest.

That morning we introduced ourselves over a pot of coffee. We sat around a table under an enormous vase spilling with flowers. To say I had never seen such a volume and variety of flowers in one vase before is the least of it; the display seemed positively beyond imagination, reminiscent of luxuriantly unseasonable paintings by Renaissance Dutch masters. The flowers were all from David's nursery across the valley. In fact, David's nursery and Criss's studio directly faced each other over a little stream.

Lambley Nursery was then entirely *in ground*; herbaceous perennials were planted in strips, in long beds divided by narrow earth paths. Plants were generally grown to flowering size and banks of green, silvery green, purple, pinks, yellows, reds and blues ran side-by-side across the slope to give an effect reminiscent of Monet's 'paint box' beds in his Giverny garden. For the purposes of flower arranging, David's entire nursery was available for picking. The several-acre paddock sloped into the afternoon sun with enormous mountain ash growing along the stream providing shelter to the west. Otherwise, old gardens filled with deciduous trees were backdrop. I walked through the flowers that glorious spring morning bewildered, entranced, astonished.

Exploring the hills with David later that day, I was already wondering where a garden might be made. That evening we sat down to trout fresh from a farm over Macclesfield way and talked flowers. We sampled red wine till three in the morning and I was woken first light (two minutes past five, I think) by an English blackbird calling from an attic window ledge mere inches from my ear. The blackbird chirruped and called and trilled and sang; indeed, so thrilling and lengthy was its celebration of daybreak that further sleep entirely escaped me.

I stayed three days with David and Criss. Mornings we explored nursery beds talking plants and evenings we enjoyed good food and pondered gardens. Each evening we ate under a new sheaf of David's flowers, with yet more flowers – Criss's – on the walls all around. We were late to bed every evening and mornings I woke to my blackbird heralding dawn. Arriving home, my head resounding with colour and song and lack of sleep, I suggested to Valerie that it might be much more fun to make a garden in the Dandenongs than the sandy vineyards of Margaret River.

28 July 2004

A still day, the sky without cloud for all but the past hour or two. A few hours' lull between two huge, violent weather systems. This morning is very cold and bright. Our ridgeline sheds frosty air down into the valley, but today there is ice here and there; the intensity of the light accentuated by the sun reflecting off a heavy layer of mist that formed overnight in the valley to our east. From the golf course along the road low cloud fills the valley across to Mt Donna Buang, the grey-mauve mass of the mountain rising some 900 metres out of silken mist. Around eleven o'clock, the weather systems seemed to jostle each other: a sporadic breeze blowing fragments of mist into the garden, the sunlight softening momentarily with each rush of air. After an hour or two the big depressions to the west and east settled, relaxed, for the wind has dropped completely. This afternoon has been still, mild and sunny.

JIM WOOLRICH

Within weeks the farms were sold and March 1990 we were on our way across the continent to Victoria. Belongings were loaded onto the Indian Pacific train for the journey to South Australia and we sat back to enjoy the ride. Waking the first

Perennials in their beds

morning and glancing out of the window, the train two or three hours east of Kalgoorlie, the rising sun illuminated a minimalist landscape of slim-stemmed eucalyptus some 6 metres high, their polished creamy brown bark and dark glossy leaves catching the low light. The only other vegetation were clumps of a steel-blue grass scattered between the trees; these elements and the bare oxide red soil.

We enjoyed that trip across the Nullarbor, certainly easier than driving. All went well on that long straight stretch, reputedly the longest straight of railway track in the world, punctuated occasionally with names of early prime ministers and state premiers: Forest, Reid, Deakin, Hughes, Cook, Barton; each a signpost and remnants of buildings surrounded by that dusty level plain – appropriate monuments to politicians, some might agree. After several hundred kilometres and a bit of a bend at the eastern end of the Nullarbor one of the crew noticed a vehicle slipping off the flat-bed wagon at the rear. The train stopped in the middle of the desert and the crew hauled the farm utility back on to the wagon and re-tied the ropes; *our* farm ute of course.

Arriving in the Dandenongs in autumn 1990 we rented a house and settled down to search for a few acres. Six months later, in late October, having walked much of the mountain, I had not the faintest glimmer of success. After door-knocking the length of the 'tourist road' running atop the western ridge of the hills, and exploring, despite extreme shadiness, numerous tiny lanes leading deep under mountain ash forest, I was becoming fairly desperate. Several acres of space to make a garden were not to be found easily, particularly somewhere visible from one of the two or three busier roads. In this mood, while visiting a garden, open as part of the Victorian Open Garden Scheme, I introduced myself to the owner, a rather dapper retired gentleman by the name of Keith Purves, and asked his advice. Keith suggested I talk to his neighbour Jim Woolrich who, he told me, was an authority on the Dandenongs. Jim, also retired, in fact 90 years old, had lived all his life in the hills. Keith explained that while Jim was hale and hearty, he was almost blind and naturally didn't get out much so would enjoy the visit. I was also warned not to ask about his own place – the little farm was very well known and coveted. Jim had been pestered for years and had no intention of budging, certainly not at his age.

Despite its prominent position, Jim's 5-acre block was not obvious. Larger than most blocks in the area, it was entirely hidden by a gigantic hedge made of ancient beech trees, Douglas firs, cedars, photinias and cherry laurel, all enmeshed with enormous swags of blackberry and ivy and sheets of viciously prickly holly seedlings below. To passersby, any glimpse of the acres within was out of the question.

Opposite, clockwise from top left: *Rhododendron arboreum* 'campbellii;' *Rhododendron arboreum* 'Bennett's Variety'; golden Irish yews among Japanese maples; hedge of rhododendrons behind buttercup meadow; *Rhododendron grande*; *Rhododendron* 'White Pearl' at end of New Zealand flax. The flax was pulled into strips and used as string to tie bunches of flowers. Clumps of flax were planted everywhere for this purpose.

Beyond the formidable hedge was another world. Any number of rhododendrons, azaleas, magnolias and cherries were flowering in that morning's sunshine. Narrow paths wound across the slope, plunged into blackberry thickets and out into tiny meadows alive with late spring daffodils. The garden stood high on its shoulder of the ridge; over the trees were the Warburton Ranges and beyond, the hazy blue Southern Alps. Near the top of the ridge was a little house, any semblance of paint long since vanished from its weatherboard walls and sheltered from mountain weather by a terracotta roof mottled silver by lichen. Giant camellias overhung the entrance path and, following several prolonged rings of a raucous bell, an elderly gentleman opened the door and peered approximately in my direction. Jim Woolrich stood less than five feet tall but seemed broad-shouldered enough to whip down a sizable tree if someone were to point him in the right direction and hand him an axe. He asked who I was, apologising as he did, "My eyes are not too good nowadays", and, squinting affably, invited me in. We settled in front of a small gas fire and I introduced myself and explained something of my quest. I found that Keith was right: Jim knew the topography and history of the hills back to the First World War and beyond. And he was right up to date with current gossip. Family and friends dropped in daily and, having been housebound for years, he was very happy to chat. I was to find that Jim's observations and ponderings were razor sharp.

Jim Woolrich's father, George, pioneered the original 10-acre block in the mid 1890s. Typical of selections thrown open at the time, it was covered in old-growth mountain ash, with wire grass scrambling up through tree fern undergrowth to 20 feet and more. Because this was a conditional purchase property, the Woolrichs were required to show they were making an income from the land before title could be granted. In other words, the land was to be cleared and planted with some appropriate crop or fruit tree. This would prove to be years of work. In fact, from the commencement of clearing in 1895–96, the family were only granted their title in 1908. Jim told me the native wire grass was extraordinarily abrasive, easily slicing bare flesh in the same way as pampas grass. Wire grass made it impossible to use horses, so trees were felled and sliced to manageable lengths with axes and cross cut saws, their mighty remains entirely manhandled. If the task of those pioneers needs underlining it's worth pondering the claims that a few mountain ash pulled down from nearby slopes were comparable in height to the tallest of the redwoods – 350, approaching 400 feet high – difficult to prove as once the mammoth trees were down, it seemed no one had any energy left to measure them.

The farm, circa 1908, taken from what is now Woolrich Road

Jim was born in 1899. I'm sure he was helping with clearing soon afterwards. An old photograph, taken around 1908, perhaps in celebration of the family receiving their hard-gained title, seems to show the bare 10 acres planted to cherries and raspberries; the remaining mountain ash growing as wind-blasted remnants along the road above the property.

Many pioneers failed to make it. Some walked off their blocks, some died, starved and exhausted, without ever becoming landholders. The worldwide depression of the 1890s coincided with the end of the gold in Victoria – these were terrible years, much worse than the 1930s. However, by 1920 Jim's older brother Ted had confidence enough to establish a nursery on the lower 5 acres of the property. In 1922 he imported the first ever kurume azaleas into Australia (following their release at the great San Francisco Exposition of that year by the famous 'Chinese' Wilson). By the late 1920s Ted was importing plants from England and Japan, and bulbs from Holland for *Rangeview*. Apart from a tiny business in Sassafras, which closed soon after opening, Rangeview was the first ornamental plant nursery to be established on any of the high ridgelines of the Dandenongs. It was quickly known throughout Melbourne for its cool-climate plants.

Later in the 1920s Jim established a flower farm on the top half of the property, growing ornamental foliage and flowers for Melbourne florists. He wooed and married his sweetheart, Bessie, and they moved into their newly built cottage in 1933. Two weeks later Bessie invited a friend up from Melbourne. Spring was at its height, the garden spangled with blooms and the girls walked around full of admiration. Jim overheard Bessie saying, "It's all due to the soil, it grows flowers but weeds won't grow at all!" Fifty years later he was still reminding her, and years after she was gone Jim was chuckling as he told the story.

Both Woolrich brothers prospered. As business grew, they purchased surrounding parcels of land and by the late 1930s they owned more than 70 acres, all under intensive hand cultivation. We found hoes, rakes and spades – hundreds of them – in tangled piles and in most instances entirely worn to nothing, the old handles slippery smooth, steel heads reduced to rusty fragments. Both Jim and Ted made a practice of employing Dutch immigrants as they arrived in Australia, especially in the years after the Second World War. The hardworking Dutch wasted no time earning sufficient money to purchase their own properties and establish their own businesses. Their children and grandchildren include many well-known figures in horticulture now and during our first years a few old-timers took the chance to pop in to see what might be happening on the old Woolrich block. Meeting them was a nice entrée into the industry for Valerie and me.

Trying to picture horticulture of the 1930s and 1950s is difficult, as little is left from that time. However, it seems the Great Depression encouraged enthusiasm for home gardening and by the late 1930s quite a few family-run businesses operated along the ridgelines. As the rhododendrons flowered, marquees were hired and displays of spring flowering plants were mounted on the Olinda football oval. I have been told these shows were astonishing, with the entire oval covered in flowering rhododendrons, azaleas and camellias and maples in fresh leaf. It has been suggested this event was one of the biggest in the world of those years, certainly the leading show of its kind in Australia.

Some older Olinda residents have memories of the Woolrichs from the 1950s and 1960s. Several have told of driving along the Olinda–Monbulk road to see Jim and Bessie carrying flowers from their paddock over the road to their packing shed. Bessie and Jim would have daffodil or tulip or rhododendron blooms heaped and spilling from a sling over their shoulders, hunched forward, almost on all fours, but always ready with a smile and a wave. If one had reason to look into the shed, the place was often a robber's cave of colour, benches overflowing with every cool-climate flower imaginable: kalmia, waratah, daphne, pieris and herbaceous peonies perhaps, and in summer, liliums and coppery piles of beech foliage.

Every summer, following weeks without rain and a hot north wind, the hills become prone to bushfires; flames licked along gullies for days in 1939 and 1962 was also a bad year. Toward the end of summer 1962, fire broke out on low ground to the north of the Dandenongs and was soon pouring embers into a pine plantation on the long slope immediately below the Woolrich's land. The pines caught and the ensuing conflagration overwhelmed thousands of acres. Fearing trouble, a number of friends and old employees gathered to defend the hilltop and all were in time for a grandstand view of a spectacular firestorm ripping through the pines with ferocity enough to lift a plume of flaming embers high into the air, coming down – still burning – miles away from the actual flames. Horrified police ordered everyone off the mountain and with the north wind driving the fire at a cracking pace up the slope towards them, most were only too happy to oblige. Ted and a couple of mates refused to budge, and even now stories circulate of his making the point plain by waving a pitchfork at disbelieving police. The coppers didn't hang around to argue their case, leaving Henk Koelewyn and Jim Simpson

Ted Woolrich, with his mother

the only ones to brave the day with Ted. Jim, clearly with experience of such moments, suggested they dig a pit and splash it with water and pull damp hessian over the top for protection from the heat and smoke. With just moments available to dig however, there was still barely shelter for two as the flames arrived. That left one of the three in the thick of it, dousing flames with buckets of water (so long as he could stand the heat and smoke), diving into the hole to cool down and get his breath back, the next taking his turn, leaping up to make space and take over the bucket. This slapstick routine continued for some 20 minutes while the fire front passed over. Remarkably, despite its weatherboard walls catching time after time – in flames 37 times, I am told – they managed to save Ted's house but had not a hope of stopping a wall of fire from raging through the nursery, leaving smouldering blackened wreckage.

Leo Koelewyn tells how his father spent much of the day battling to save what was saveable. By late afternoon, with the worst over, he thought to head back to check on his own place. Walking up to the road to where he earlier parked his car, Henk found his vehicle gone, removed by police to save it from the fire, leaving a long walk home along the ridge and down to Monbulk. This took hours. Thick black smoke made the road difficult to see and every two or three minutes he was forced into a ditch to fill his lungs with something like clear air. Leo remembers Henk arriving home late that afternoon, trousers in singed tatters, polyester shirt almost entirely melted, bare flesh blistered from flying embers, exhausted and shattered.

*   *   *

Talking 46 years later, Henk shook his head wonderingly and told me several times over that Jim Simpson saved all their lives that day. Not one of them would have survived the dense smoke or the incredible heat without the little bolt hole they so hastily excavated.

For Ted, the fire was devastating, a lifetime's effort swept away. Henk was one of several nurserymen to donate precious stock in acknowledgment of the brothers' earlier generosity. Gradually the rhododendrons, those mysterious and unlikely plants, re-sprouted from their blackened stumps and grew back. But Ted was now over 60 and his health not good. He died in 1968 and Iris sold the nursery to a part-time nurseryman who traded on the remains for a year or two before closing it down. The land and remaining plants were sold on to Keith Purves and John Turner in 1981 as a building block. Keith immediately set about turning the remnants of the nursery plantings, by now somewhat of a forest, into a woodland garden.

Jim Woolrich

Jim Woolrich carried on after the fire. His business allowed him to recover from the devastation, more so than his brother; he could fall back on collecting from the unburnt properties around the hills to keep his customers happy. However, in the mid 1970s Bessie became ill. Jim devoted several years to caring for her and ceased to maintain his garden from this time; other flower growers were occasionally allowed to pick from his plants. Bessie died in the early 1980s and from that time the garden gently went to sleep. A friend drove his tractor around for an hour or two each summer, slashing meadows and spraying blackberries. This level of maintenance was just sufficient to keep the worst weeds at bay but season by season, rhododendrons grew into tall tangled thickets, azaleas into little clouds of greenery and bluebells and grape hyacinths shifted out of their beds and waltzed across the meadow.

During 1990 and early 1991 I dropped in on Jim two or three times. In autumn 1991 I joined a landscape master class organised by Tony Mugg and led by the renowned landscape architect, Martha Schwartz. Martha was to oversee our group as we developed designs for projects suggested by participants. I needed a specimen project so asked Jim whether I might use his garden. He was intrigued, so for a couple of days I paced out the meadows and crawled under blackberries making a rough plan of the 5 acres. I asked Jim about a few of the notable trees. He told me 1928 was a special year for planting. Several of the bigger beeches were imported from England that year, from Fred Street's Nursery just west of London. Also two Japanese purple weeping maples, and an osakasuki maple and a nikko maple, among other plants, came in from the famous Yokohama Trading Company of Tokyo. All these were planted in Jim's garden to provide reliably named propagation material for his brother's nursery. As it happened, we were only talking for fifteen minutes; there were any number of plants we did not discuss: the glorious enkianthus scattered around the house for example, and the extraordinary collection of arboreum rhododendrons, many seemingly grown from seed. My questions arose from idle curiosity; I imagined one of the younger Woolrich clan would take over the place when the time came. As it eventuated, we worked on an inner urban project for Martha's workshop and my notes on Jim's garden were unused. Even so, those days with Martha were exhilarating and provided inspiration for years. Over the following months I looked over the scribbled plan made exploring Jim's old place and daydreamed.

In early September 1991, I received a phone call from Sylvia McElroy, Jim Woolrich's niece. She was visiting Jim regularly, bringing meals and helping with household chores – she was concerned for him. An operation for his glaucoma had proved unsuccessful and the stress of it had unsettled the old man. Sylvia had called several people asking if they could visit Jim on days she could not – I promised to do what I could.

A brisk morning later that week I called in on Jim. While we were chatting in the front room, both close to the gas fire, I noticed the sleet outside turning to snow. In response to my mentioning the flurry settling into the garden Jim jumped to his feet and went to the window. "I can't see it, I just can't see it," he exclaimed, exasperated. After saying something about his eyes, he went on, "But aren't the rhododendrons flowering well?" Although the garden was full of rhododendrons and many were blooming, he was actually facing towards an open part of the hillside. I mentioned this gently, saying perhaps his eyes were playing tricks. He turned back to his lounge chair, smiling ruefully, "Last week I could see daffodils growing out of the floor boards". The following week I again called by and the conversation turned to the ghent azaleas growing metres high along the lower edge of the bulb meadow. Jim spoke of a rare deciduous species, *Rhododendron schlippenbachii*, growing somewhere in the middle of the ghents and said that it should be flowering now. I walked down but could only see a tangle of bare azalea stems draped with ivy and honeysuckle. He was upset, sure the old schlippenbachii was dead. "I don't think so, Jim. I'm certain it flowered last spring." Days later I was back and went immediately to the azaleas. There was the schlippenbachii, a cloud of pale pink and perfume drifting along the slope. I walked up the hill with my news to find Sylvia just stepping out of the house. She told me Jim had died the previous day while preparing himself breakfast and had been found by a flower grower later that morning.

Several months later Sylvia rang to say that after long discussion, no one in the family was prepared to take the old place on. Might I be interested?

When I was very young we lived on a farm called 'Bletchley'. It was right beside the highway through the Great Southern, near the little town of Moulyinning, between Lake Grace and Dumbleyung. The Bletchley house had thick stone walls, a tin roof and verandahs all the way around. It was five big rooms, with a little pantry and bathroom off one end of the kitchen. There was a sleepout on the verandah with a canvas wall to keep the wind out. The laundry was behind the garage and the lavatory was way down in the garden. The old stone lavatory was a long walk from the house for a little bloke. And the worst of it was the trap door spiders living along the path. I was forever finding the beastly things, their little doors springing open as I poked a twig at them. I yelled and yelled and didn't dare move until Mum came running with a boiling kettle to pour down their holes.

I remember all one morning collecting a jam jar full of caterpillars from the yellow daisy flowers of the cape weed in spring and waking from my afternoon nap with the window flyscreen covered in black caterpillars, all crawling for the sun. Mum was so wild. Once I was walking through the trees to the shearing shed and as I walked under a big tree I looked to see a strange creature on a branch just above my head. It opened its huge eyes and stared at me and they were filled with ice; I screamed and my dad came running and, to make it worse, laughed and laughed at the mopoke owl ruffling its feathers and stretching its wings.

I was given a boat and it had a gun with a trigger that squirted water. I took the boat way off to a creek near the Moulyinning road. The creek still had water from the winter. I paddled in the water with my boat and when Meggy came close I squirted her with the gun. The water was so lovely and brown and so warm that I walked deeper and deeper and first my pants got wet and then my shirt and then I sat down and squirted and squirted my gun and Meggy was running round and around and barking like a mad thing.

One time Dad took me to a neighbour's place to see picture slides. We went the back way on the gravel tracks and it was raining and creeks were running over the road and it was slippery and muddy and dark. I sat right at the front for the pictures because I was the only kiddie there and there were lots of pictures of people I didn't know but right in the middle there was a paddock of yellow sunflowers and hundreds and hundreds of the biggest, yellowest sunflowers and right in the middle of one yellow sunflower – there was a bee. On the way home Dad told me I must stay awake because now there was lots of mist as well as water on the road and Mum wasn't with us to keep him awake and I sat in the front next to Dad and for ages I stayed awake until all of a sudden it was next morning. It was such a scary terrible thing to wake up in bed not knowing how my Dad got us home.

My mum sang a good night song to me every night as I went to bed. It was a song she made up specially for me. All the words went with the song, 'Lily Marlene'. I remember Mum's singing from as far back as I can remember.

My dog Meggy and me walked for miles and miles and miles in those big paddocks. We walked so far Mum always dressed me in red, just to be safe. One day we walked all the way to the mulberry tree that grew in the paddock by the road to Kukerin. The tree fell down in a huge big flood but kept right on growing and I could just climb its lying-down trunk and get the mulberries and throw them to Meggy. And once I was flying my kite and it was bumping along the ground and all the string turned into one monstrous knot. This happened right near our house on the bit of grass between us and the salt lake that was eating up our front paddock.

The author, aged not quite three, with younger brother Michael, Jan and Meggy

PART TWO
MAKING THE GARDEN

23 August 2004

A late winter's day, the first warm day since autumn. Mid-afternoon and the temperature touching 16 degrees Celsius, the sky cloudless all day except the early morning. Bending to wash my hands under the garden tap behind the office I notice the bank of self-seeded violets by their perfume, the foxy spicy scent of the box hedges making new growth has been obvious throughout the garden and a sweet moist pasture hay aroma hangs above the herbaceous borders as we work.

April 1992 was a perfect example of autumn in the Dandenongs. Still, dry days, an occasional overnight shower, but drier than any other season: the best time to begin a garden.

Several people helped out those first months. Simon Donald, a local landscaper specialising in dry stone walls, headed the civil engineering department. Many metres of walls were required to retain earth banks above and below the terrace we intended to excavate. Simon was also handy at bricklaying and was long experienced with moving ancient rhododendrons, camellias and maples. Simon brought with him Richard Dooley and Craig Shalders, both energetic and enthusiastic.

There were two immediate tasks. Numerous weed trees grew in the area we intended to work: holly, Himalayan dogwood, cherry laurel, a strange spiky prunus, English yew seedlings and frightening mounds of blackberries. All would need removal to give access to plants we hoped to rescue and relocate. There was also the business of excavating root balls around the two glorious Japanese purple weeping maples we intended to move. The maples were those Jim and I discussed 12 months earlier. Ted and Jim imported the trees from the Yokohama Trading Company in 1928, planted them on the outskirts of Jim's garden and they had been growing happily in the 64 years since. Neighbouring rhododendrons had spilled into their canopies and left gaps in their foliage but they were still awe inspiring, certainly the finest specimens I had seen.

Richard was given the job of trenching around each tree, then mining underneath. Trenches were eventually more than a metre deep and some 15 metres in circumference, the undermining operation on a similar scale. By the time Ric had the maples ready for burlapping and roping, he could climb under the overhang of the root balls and vanish from view. During this operation the trees went into glowing orange-red autumn colour, not too surprising perhaps, considering their drastically reduced root systems. After a few solid days digging, lining root balls with hessian and roping, Ric had the maples trussed and safe to move. The rest of us worked at removing blackberries and other weeds, and loading rubbish on to sometimes aromatic, sometimes pungent bonfires.

By the Tuesday after Easter we had the slope cleared and measured, with string lines in place all in time for the arrival of a drot, or trackless bulldozer. This versatile machine had sufficient power to do some serious work and its hinged front bucket was ideal for digging and lifting ancient, brittle rhododendrons. Also, the drot's skid tracks would not disturb our precious soil unduly. After years farming on exquisitely shallow soils, so thin that ploughs were set with immense care to avoid dragging subsoil onto the surface (subsoil was never more than 10 to 12 centimetres down on Merrie-Lea), it was breathtaking to see the drot's blade bite into deep loam. Topsoil across the excavation was a good 30 centimetres deep, dark chocolate in colour with an open fluffy texture. Soil particles were extremely fine. In reality, our so-called 'chocolate' volcanic loam is really a clay, but with none of the stickiness and density of ordinary clay. Left to its own devices, out in the forest for instance, it develops such an ideal structure that deep holes can be dug with naked fingertips and the heaviest rainfall drops through upper layers with never a sign of a puddle, so run off is negligible. The drot excavating into our hillside that day seemed to be slicing some sort of Bavarian confectionery. No pebbles could be seen; less than a wheelbarrow full of rocks was unearthed among the equivalent of truck loads of soil. This despite two outcrops of rock nearby, 'floaters' as locals called them, close-packed rocks of every size, up to several cubic metres to an individual boulder. These outcrops were both within a minute's walk, one to the west and the other east. I could only think George Woolrich had first pick of the parcels of land as they were made available 100 years back – and he had gone to much trouble exploring with a shovel before making their choice.

Below 50 centimetres, the soil paled to yellow-orange and eventually grey-yellow 2 to 3 metres down. It still looked comparatively good. I was told the yellow-orange subsoil quickly develops something of the colour and structure of chocolate topsoil with addition of organic matter. Still, it is vital not to disturb mountain soil when it is very wet. Driving machinery over saturated volcanic soil will make it collapse into something resembling plasticine. But I was to find that earthworm and micro-organism activity will repair this damage in as little as 10 to 15 years; I know from farming days that conventional soils require centuries and more to regain their structure after damage.

12 September 2004

Snow in the air early last night. Sleety rain intermingled with occasional damp flakes. This morning the garden is under a thin layer of sleet and snow. Rhododendron trusses filled with ice. Broken grey mist hangs through the trees, the temperature precisely zero.

A friend driving past around one o'clock in the morning says the snow was 12 centimetres deep. Children were throwing snowballs under streetlamps in Olinda. Warmer air moving through between three and four o'clock melted much of it. In 15 years there has been snow every winter. This is our first for the season yet it has been unusually cold these past months.

The main terrace took several days to excavate. It was crucial that it be wide enough for our double borders, however, the wider the terrace the higher the retaining walls required, both above and below. Walls above chest height are more expensive to build, and somewhat liable to tumble down again. The initial work thus involved a good deal of stress: how high would retaining walls need to be to create sufficient width for the terrace we required? The excavation was gradually carved out 11.5 metres wide and we found the exposed banks to be at most 1.5 metres high, generally less though, within safety limits and budget for the walls required to retain them. The 11.5-metre width would allow 1.5 metres for a hedge on the lower side of the terrace (opposite the retaining wall required on the high side), 2 metres for a generous central path (including brick edging), and the remaining 8 metres could thus divide into two borders, each 4 metres deep. I consulted my copy of Gertrude Jekyll's *Colour in the English Garden*. She made her Munstead Wood border 14 feet deep with a narrow access path behind and 2 feet of space for shrub plantings under her high sandstone backing walls. Four metres is almost 14 feet so I was satisfied; each border should have sufficient depth for several layers of plants from the front to the rear. Then the question became: how long could we make the various gardens?

Before commencing work I had surveyed the area and sketched out the central compartments I hoped for. However, the initial surveying was made rather approximate by the amount of vegetation across the site: a plantation of decrepit waratahs, some actually dead; rhododendrons, most movable; several small beech trees, dug and given to a neighbour; and any number of weeds, including awesome clumps of blackberries. Before we began work it was difficult to see 15 metres without vegetation interfering with the view; much of my planning was guesswork. Still, we could excavate the terrace to 11 or 12 metres wide over some 90 metres across the block, then for a further 36 metres it could narrow to just 3 metres as it passed between important trees. The terrace should thus be 126 metres long. My plan allowed for a plain 3-metre-wide crushed rock path over the final 36 metres with hedges a little over head-high at each side to hide the steepish slope near this boundary. Cloudehill generally slopes moderately to the east but falls away rapidly in the southeast corner; the southern half of the property has considerably more slope than the northern half. Excavating the 11.5-metre width was easy near the north boundary, trickier as we approached the south boundary.

We also had to thread the narrow section of our terrace between big historic trees. On the lower side grew two magnificent beech trees: a tri-colour beech, *Fagus sylvatica* 'Roseomarginata', and a fern leaf beech, *Fagus sylvatica* 'Heterophylla'. These, Jim told me, were part of the shipment of trees brought to Australia for propagation stock in 1928. On the top side of the excavation site was a magnificent *Magnolia kobus*. Kobus has floppy little uninteresting flowers and is rare in gardens for this reason. However, its blooming also happens to be extraordinarily generous. At the end of its season petals (more accurately *tepals* in the case of this dinosaur plant) fall inches deep. Viewed from a distance it is arguably the finest of all magnolias. We aimed our terrace a little closer to the kobus's trunk reasoning, no matter its glory in flower, its importance was outweighed by the historic significance of the two beeches and, besides, the magnolia could look dramatic hanging over the central path. There were heart-stopping moments as the drot sliced noisily through root systems of vital trees, but eventually we had our terrace. Topsoil was stored in impressive piles to each side and a slope of some 3 metres was left from one end to the other to provide drainage and places for steps. The northern end of the excavation was more than 2 metres deep; for safety's sake, a shelf was cut part way down to allow for a second wall to be stepped back into the vertical surface.

A lyrebird calling this morning. A male going through his repertoire. Magpie carolling sliding into rosella whistles, kookaburra chatter and a long whipbird crack. I wonder when I hear lyrebirds imitating whipbirds, a slow build to that piercing crack. There have been no whipbirds along this ridge for years. They are birds of stringybark bushland further down the mountain. Have there ever been whipbirds calling locally since George Woolrich commenced clearing in the 1890s? Have the lyrebirds passed on that very distinctive call, generation to generation, all by themselves for 100 years?

Glancing through a book on Hidcote I noticed the length of its main terrace similar to our excavation. It seemed an omen except, of course, we could never have the ethereal view from Hidcote's final gate – the Vale of Evesham and the mountains of Wales. On reflection, this was mildly exasperating. After all, Ted's old nursery was named *Range View*. Jim had spoken to me several times of its magnificent views. However, a solid screen of mountain ash had seeded and grown, had shot up to more than 60 metres high in a handful of years on our next-door neighbour's property. Much of the view Jim remembered of the Silvan Valley 400 metres below, rising tier by tier to the Gembrook Ranges on the skyline, had long since vanished behind our neighbour's forest. With this nuisance in mind, I planned Cloudehill to be self contained, with little structures at the ends of the main terrace facing each other; these could define the axis while masking the lack of any deep view of the immediate valley that one might hope for from a mountain garden. In the evenings, however, with the wind moving our neighbour's big ash trees, lights could be glimpsed way down in Silvan and I found myself envying Major Johnson for his clear hilltop site.

We then set about moving our two weeping maples. The drot excavated a ramp into one of Richard's trenches, thrust its bucket under the colossal burlapped root ball and the tree was roped firmly to the blade. The first maple was growing a short distance from its designated spot, so the move was straightforward. Relocating its partner required a detour out onto the Olinda Road and caused some sensation with passing traffic for a minute or two. Each tree was placed gently into position, ropes removed and topsoil heaped around the root balls. Then a quick trip to the pub for all concerned.

We then needed to make the earth banks on the high side of the excavation secure with retaining walls. These were to be *dry stone* walls, constructed entirely without mortar. Porous walls never allow water pressure to build behind them following heavy rain and are thus more stable than, for example, non-porous, watertight walls, walls made from brick or concrete blocks. Impermeable retaining walls tend to dam water up behind them and are prone to tipping over unless the weight of the water is eliminated with drainage. However, drains eventually clog with roots and rubbish; watertight retaining walls are never ideal. And good dry stone walls also happen to be cheaper to build.

Stone selected for building the walls was volcanic, collected from farmland west of Melbourne, largely around the appropriately named district of Stony Rises. This extraordinary part of Victoria was formed by a lava flow dating back a mere 10,000 years; more-or-less last weekend in geological terms. The landscape of Stony Rises is entirely volcanic: sheets of broken *honeycomb* rock overlaid with pockets of thin soil supporting occasional low eucalyptus, much bracken and scattered patches of pasture for dairy cows. The farmer was happy to have his stone removed. We collected truck loads; stumbling through bracken, making piles out of rocks of the right shape to pack into a wall. Curiously, the ideal rock for a retaining wall is the size and shape of your average concrete masonry block. For each stone we removed, we picked up and examined five or six. Every time with the dairy cockie's comment in mind, "Keep an eye out for tiger snakes, there are bloody hundreds of the bastards out there". Tiger snakes, among the world's more venomous snakes, nestled under our rocks, a full winter since their last meal so all of them out of sorts. I very quickly got into the habit of rolling rocks towards me, hoping a resident snake might be congenial enough to make its exit out into the paddock and not slither under my feet.

Wall near Stony Rises

Ross Forrester once told me of the routine to maintain water supplies on his Meekatharra station. Some 17,000 head of sheep scattered over roughly three quarters of a million acres were watered from 176 windmills. During summer in that part of WA animals without water might perish of dehydration within hours, so mills were checked from a light aircraft twice weekly and usually several needed attention each time. Most water was pumped from narrow bores but Ross also had windmills pumping out of some 35 old wells, most around 100 feet deep. Windmills work wonderfully most of the time, but every 12 months or so leather valves in their pumps wear out and must be replaced. To change valves in a pump in a well, the temptation is to climb down and do the job in situ. After all, to pull up and unscrew five or six 21-foot lengths of heavy steel pipe is hours of hard work, and several windmills might need urgent work after an inspection run. But there were disadvantages to taking this shortcut. Ross's wells were all deep and old, fairly dangerous in their own right. And they were always full of snakes – no well cover could keep them out. A nice flat shady well cover looked like an ideal home to any exploring snake. And water broke their fall nicely. It's amazing how long entire families of snakes can live down a well. The occasional morsel falls down and they certainly don't lack for a drink. But they are never happy, and become increasingly irritable over the months. Ross always shone a mirror down each well to see what might be lurking, then climbed down very slowly to allow his eyes to adjust to the gloom. And he always thought to take a stick with him as he climbed into the dark, not a long stick — there is precious little room to swing a stick in a well — but then again Ross did not care to take an unnecessarily short stick with him either. The record for a single well, I am told, was seven snakes and five big bungarras, racehorse goannas; all of them testy — enough to make Harrison Ford himself take pause.

The honeycomb stone we collected was a uniform dove-grey in colour, often enriched by the silver and green of colonising lichens and mosses. The rock's sharp edges easily locked into a wall and its colour was a good neutral backdrop to flowers. Building the walls was an epic job. Over that first winter Simon constructed some 250 square metres of wall. Many hundreds of tonnes of stones were wheelbarrowed onto the site and a fair percentage were useless; inferior rock we buried behind walls or used as footings. As winter's drenching rain settled in, our excavation became wondrously slushy, gumboots sometimes vanishing into mud, their owners dolefully paddling from the mire in just their socks. Using machinery soon became impossible and all construction materials were wheelbarrowed the 100 metres onto site: sand, cement, thousands of bricks and truck loads of crushed rock. In July, cloud descended and settled and stayed, day after day for five full days. It was very still, no actual rain, just constant mist, condensing and falling from trees in a continual patter, pooling in the beginnings of our car park, trickling down the access path into more pools and quaking mud under the wall we were building, and muddy water running off as a chuckling stream under tree ferns further down the slope; all this without a hint of conventional rain.

Our newly constructed cottage with brick archway entrance to the gardens on the left. Valerie on the end of the broom.

By spring we were making progress, despite bringing forward the construction of our reception cottage and nursery in order to have our business operating by late spring. Major walls were now complete and, with the occasional mild sunny day in September, we noticed a warm look to our weeping maples: leaf buds were expanding, crimson sprays of foliage unfurling and the old trees stretching themselves into chocolate soil around their roots. In October, the drot was back planting the many big rhododendrons that had been lifted from the ground in autumn and left in their root balls on the surface all winter. Terraces were deep ripped to counteract compaction inflicted during construction, then topsoil was shifted from storage piles and spread to form the borders. Later that same day we were all busily planting perennials from my collection of the previous 15 years.

Four weeks later, the gates to our car park opened just in time for the first weekend in November: the Melbourne Cup long weekend. Traditionally, the week of the famous racing carnival has been a favourite time for visitors to the hills enjoying later-flowering rhododendrons. In Cloudehill, Jim Woolrich's glorious specimens of *Rhododendron nuttallii* were heavy with white trumpet blossoms trailing honeysuckle-like perfume in the thick spring air, a superb *Rhododendron* 'Ightham Yellow' was vibrant with cool lemon bells, beech trees were in fresh leaf and hundreds of the late-flowering poet's daffodil, *Narcissus poeticus recurvus*, were tossing their heads across the meadow below Jim's cottage. Perennials in the borders had filled in a little, penstemons were showing an occasional precocious flower and *Delphinium* 'Völkerfrieden' had unfurled tatters of azure. With some nervousness, we suggested to nursery visitors that, if they didn't mind ramps of mud and gravel where there should be steps, they were welcome to wander into the beginnings of our garden.

28 September 2004

We suspect a peregrine falcon performed a 'stoop' through the garden this afternoon. Birds erupted into shrieking, flapping, windmilling hysteria, many more than I thought ever lived in our few acres. Within half a minute though, all was still again, not a sound and no birds. They'd tucked themselves into foliage, every one of them in hiding, except for the magpies, which were all clearly visible against the skyline in the topmost twigs of the tallest trees. The ornithologist of our party pointed out every magpie was searching the sky towards the southeast. Without our seeing it, a falcon, one of a pair that I knew patrolled further down the mountain, had flown into the garden and out again in that direction. Fifteen minutes later, silence still and no smaller birds yet emerged but not a magpie had wavered from its post, all still searching the same quadrant of sky with utmost diligence for the return of the falcon.

Poets daffodils near Jim's cottage

Views taken by Paul Cantlay and me from a travel tower hired in to clip beech trees (raised up 38.5 metres and its platform extended over the garden). I am very pleased with my photo – not so much camera shake evident as I thought was likely to be the case. The two right-hand shots are by Paul. That January morning was gloriously luminous.

THE GARDEN

At liquidi fontes et stagna
uirentia musco
adsint et tenuis fugiens per
gramina riuus

But let there be wet springs
and pools green with moss
and a slim stream slipping
through the grass

Virgil, *Georgics*, 4–18

Farmers in WA rarely took gardens all that seriously. A few trees to break the wind perhaps and a bit of lawn around the barbeque maybe, also serving as a spot to keep an eye out for snakes that might be thinking of moving in from the paddocks and settling under the house. Farmers weren't interested in gardens. The fence was there to keep sheep from the lemon tree. A farmer might stand at his back door and look straight past the strip of unpruned roses and the open paddocks and settle on the horizon. Did that wispy cloud mean anything? I remember an old cocky who lived on the difficult country out to our west. Fred tried to sell his farm many times. Each occasion he and the agent would agree on a price, a buyer would be found and persuaded to part with his money, the contract spread over the kitchen table, then old Fred's second thoughts would get the better of him and that would be the end of it. It was a hard farm, all useless sand, yet he never did sell.

BAMBOOS

The entrance steps to the garden are lined with a collection of bamboos. They are largely phyllostachys varieties, temperate bamboos, most not yet old enough to have produced culms to their full height. From establishment to maturity can take several years, so our bamboo clumps have yet to arch over the path in the way I intend. I hope to see them eventually several metres high, the canopies of individual clumps almost touching, foliage rustling with each breeze and the occasional crisp clack of culms knocking together as a hint of welcoming.

In the Dandenongs, phyllostachys are the best of the bamboos. Most gardeners are familiar with *Phyllostachys nigra*, the black-stemmed bamboo, its culms emerging deep green and turning ebony in their second and third season. Although planted as a vigorous root mass three years ago, our clump is still only 4 metres high. It should grow to 6 metres in our climate, I suspect. In subtropical gardens black bamboo can happily grow 15 metres and then set about colonising entire backyards, plus the neighbours' if popped in casually and ignored. This is true for all phyllostachys; they are running bamboos and we have planted our specimens with root barriers to control questing rhizomes. Substantial holes were dug and lined with very thick plastic to a depth of 50–60 centimetres. The bottom of each hole was left open for the true roots to explore for nutrients and moisture.

Phyllostachys nigra

Opposite *Phyllostachys nigra* I have planted perhaps my favourite of the group, *P. bambusoides* 'Holochrysa' (syn. 'Allgold'). This has the best yellow stems of any bamboo, a warm matte bronze. Our clump has around 50 culms rising a good 6 metres high. The leaves are a little larger than *P. nigra*, and are mid-green with an occasional fleck of cream variegation. The variegated effect is so subtle that most visitors don't notice it, yet it is sufficient to enliven the canopy and complement the upright to gently arching culms.

Next to *P.* 'Holochrysa' I have planted a very rare and desirable bamboo with a name that Bach might have composed a cantata to: *Sinobambusa tootsik* 'Albostriata'. Its culms are murky green but it makes up with dramatically variegated foliage; its mid-green leaves are longitudinally striped pale to rich cream and this will also grow to around 6 metres.

Phyllostachys 'Holochrysa'

We have several bamboos selected for their golden and green-striped stems. Perhaps the most notable is *Phyllostachys bambusoides* 'Castillonis'. According to textbooks, this is meant to have the same vigour as *P.* 'Holochrysa' and should only grow half the height of the species; however, ours is closer to 10 than 6 metres. It is glorious from the moment its early summer shoots appear; these are wrapped in pinkish-grey, parchment-like sheaths that fall away cleanly after some weeks to expose the pale bronze-green culms. Over several months this colour deepens to a golden yellow with a deep green stripe in the sulcus, the slightly recessed strip running between the nodes of each culm. These green stripes make for a rhythmic pattern running the length of the yellow stems and the foliage and the general demeanour of the clump is stately and handsome.

Sinobambusa tootsik 'Albostriata'

Beside our *Sinobambusa* we have *Phyllostachys aureosulcata* 'Spectabilis'. So far our spectabilis seems very similar to *P. bambusoides* 'Castillonis'; as the canopies of the two mature I suspect they will differ somewhat in character, however we need a year or

Phyllostachys bambusoides 'Castillonis'

Phyllostachys aureosulcata 'Spectabilis'

Phyllostachys aurea 'Koi'

two to find out. *Phyllostachys aurea* 'Koi', the smallest of our golden stem bamboos, grows beside our reception cottage. The mature height of *P. aurea* 'Koi' is about 4 metres and the lacy foliage is pale green, hence the 'aurea' as part of its name. Its stems are greenish-yellow with a broad green stripe filling the sulcus in the same way as *P.* 'Castillonis'. *Phyllostachys aurea* makes a superb container plant, partly because it seems to tolerate a confined root run, and partly because confining its roots seems to promote a strange growth characteristic. Rather than growing sensibly with uniform gaps between nodes, occasionally the internodal gap shrinks to nothing near the base of each culm – this happens with no reduction to the height of the culm. Thus, in any clump of *Phyllostachys aurea*, particularly those a little pot-bound, some culms grow with a congested series of nodes stacked one on top of another and this eccentricity adds handsomely to their character.

Each summer of the later 1970s and 1980s saw an increase in the grasshopper population in the Mogumber district to the degree that for a few weeks before Christmas every year they were in plague numbers. These were not the infamous Australian plague locust of eastern Australian agricultural areas, but a local species, the wingless grasshopper. Wingless grasshoppers favour sandy soils for egg laying; we first noticed them around 1975 on the western side of Merrie-Lea adjoining the sandplain and also over the belt of sand across the centre of Clover Downs. By the mid 1980s, they had moved onto the heavier soil paddocks, up rocky hillsides, right across both properties. Unlike plague locusts, wingless grasshoppers were not a problem encountered just occasionally; for Mogumber farmers they were a problem every summer. Being wingless, they could not travel any distance during their life cycle and they lived in the one district (almost in the one paddock), from season to season. In December, wherever I walked I would stir up a fizzing storm of the wretched things, leaping erratically, bouncing into my legs as often as not. They congregated wherever there was green to be eaten. Any pasture slow to dry off in November, in fact any lush, low foliage, attracted them. Through the 1980s we noticed no seedling trees, no seedlings of any sort, surviving their attention. The regeneration of the native bush along road verges and fenced off hilltops had effectively ceased. Wind-break trees, planted as part of our soil conservation work, did not survive through their first summer, the leaves chewed to pieces within days of the insects emerging from the ground. Grasshoppers also enjoyed my garden and I was forced to spray with an unpleasant pesticide every few days to prevent total devastation.

The problem was serious and solutions were in short supply, however chatting to neighbours we heard guinea fowl might help, at least in the garden. We were told guinea fowl were quick enough to hunt down the grasshoppers and big enough to eat quite a few each. So we invested in a couple of dozen guinea fowl and set them to work around the house.

Guinea fowl are handsome birds hailing from the African veldts. They are nifty runners, as any smallish ground-living bird would need to be coming from that part of the world and certainly speedy enough to catch grasshoppers; however, they soon decided a dozen grasshoppers each per day was really all they cared for, two dozen at best, then they wandered over to the garden to top up on salad greens. That left us with the remaining umpteen thousand grasshoppers within jumping distance of our flowers.

So we were stuck with our guinea fowl; still, they were not too greedy as they ate up the garden, and were handsome and strolled around cooing and peeping fetchingly. A drawback to guinea fowl, though, was their reveille call. This was in stark contrast with their melodious everyday calling. A guinea fowl's reveille can easily be duplicated by dragging a 6-metre length of heavy steel pipe over a bitumen road. Ideally, the road should have some embedded crushed rock to give vibrato to a full-throated metallic screeching. Guinea fowl are dim creatures. Certainly ours were hopeless mothers, laying huge piles of eggs of which they would only bother to incubate a few in the middle. Each evening the resulting chicks were left in a nervous huddle on the ground while their mums flew powerfully to high tree tops to roost. And every morning fewer chicks remained, until, until, there were none at all. This in mind, it puzzled Valerie and me that after swooping down from their roosts and stalking around our house, of the 12 available window ledges, the guinea fowl always jumped up to the best ledge to achieve maximum reveille impact. Thus, minutes before sunup every morning our bedroom rocked to their skull-cracking chorus. I would leap up and, throwing back the curtains, find a row of guinea fowl clinging to the window sill, earnestly eyeing me through the vibrating glass, screaming cacophonous good morning salutations. So happy they were to share their joy that unless I hurled open the window and yelled back expletives they would continue their glad tidings pretty well indefinitely.

We never did solve the puzzle of the grasshopper plagues. What controlling mechanism failed, allowing them to build to such numbers? Curiously, shortly after selling the farm the situation righted itself. Grasshoppers died away and disappeared. When I visited Ross and Shirley Forrester in 1997 I was delighted to see newly planted trees everywhere, growing nicely, not a grasshopper to be seen.

Planted half-way along the last of our golden and green bamboos is P. vivax 'Aureocaulis'. This has gleaming golden yellow stems with random narrow green stripes pencilled between the nodes. Aureocaulis is a seriously big bamboo, and though I suspect our specimen will reach 10 or 12 metres, in a warmer climate it could achieve 20 metres, perhaps more.

Phyllostachys vivax 'Aureocaulis'

Frittilaria meleagris (Snake's head frittilary) in terracotta pan on the entrance path

Contemplating taller bamboos, a scene comes to mind from the movie *Crouching Tiger Hidden Dragon*: a bamboo grove with arching stems rearing vertiginously into clouds of elegant foliage, shifting with the breeze against silk black shadows. But the scene was rather spoilt by the protagonists running impossibly through the leaves, waving swords and pulling faces. I was reminded of this when visiting a friend days after seeing the movie. A winter storm was heaving a grove of *Eucalyptus regnans* about on a steepish slope some 500 metres away. Regrowth mountain ash, all the same age, all approaching 60 metres high, were swaying vigorously, though slowly, some 10 metres back and forth, each arc taking five or six seconds. As we sipped our coffee it occurred to us that there was something odd about their movement: the trees were not responding to individual gusts of wind. As one tree swayed right to left, its neighbour swayed left to right; they were entirely out of time with each other. It dawned on us that the trees, all tall with immense weight high in their canopies, were behaving like gigantic pendulums, each with a slightly different rhythm. I remembered the bamboos in *Crouching Tiger Hidden Dragon* doing the same thing for similar reasons and made the comparison at the time. In both instances the plants seemed almost choreographed, performing a slow and stately ballet. I picture with impatience our small clump of *P. vivax* 'Aureocaulis' as it should be, in three or four years, with 20 or 30 stems arching high over the entrance path, swaying rhythmically and sedately and dominating our little bambouserie.

Sheep dogs were an essential part of the scene on any farm with merinos. We always had two or three, one lead dog, a younger dog learning the business and generally an older dog, semi-retired, who might chip in for an hour or two before wandering off to sleep in the shade. Moving sheep without a dog was well nigh impossible. I remember moving a small mob in an emergency, the details of which escape me. That there were no dogs I do remember, but there just happened to be three car loads of friends visiting, at least ten people, all in their teens and early twenties – surely sufficient to move a few hundred sheep through a couple of gate ways? However, watching the animals turning and trotting calmly through a cordon of arm-waving, yelling humans, it was clear one average dog outperformed the lot of them. That my friends were all from a rural youth club and all experienced sheep handlers made the moment doubly frustrating.

I can rattle off names of our various dogs going all the way back to my cheerful roly-poly kelpie, Meggy, who was really my pet from when I was learning to walk. We wandered off together and scared my mother half to death on several famous occasions at Moulyinning. Meggy was never much of a sheep dog; she would only help with the exciting bits, then left the boring work to Toodles. When Meggy was about eight she surprised us by producing a puppy; Mike and I called him Wagger. Wagger was much more interested in sheep work than Meggy and was on his way to becoming a top sheep dog when he took a poison bait. So did Meggy. They both died. I was told of this just as our car was pulling into the front gate, returning me for my first holiday back on the farm from boarding school. I was just 12 and the moment seemed an underlining of childhood's end. Years later, I asked Cam where he and Jan buried her but so many years later he could not remember.

Riley was an excellent border collie, given to Cam by a neighbour to fill the gap and he was our lead dog from 1964 for six years or so. Then Mr Chu, another border collie, who was second string to Riley but soon graduated to top dog, and Rick and Mintie, both kelpies, and Horace, a handsome, long-haired, brown and white border collie, obviously with a bit of kelpie in him and the best dog I ever had. Horace was backed up by Kimba 'the lion heart', who was given his name by my son Ben in 1985 or 86. Kimba was another kelpie. We thought it good to have both kelpies and collies. Kelpies kept going in hot weather when collies were inclined to linger in the shade or trot off for a cooling swim in a dam. Collies, on the other hand, were crucial for tricky jobs, moving mobs of ewes and young lambs for instance. Ewes tended to misplace their lambs as soon as a big mob was herded and any lamb instinctively wants to return to the last place it saw its mum (such a useful thing generally – if only children were so sensible). However, this made moving flocks hell for the dogs. The further the ewes were moved, the larger the congregation of lambs gathering to the rear, all pointing in the wrong direction, all awaiting their chance to pelt around the dogs, straight past us waving and yelling, back to where they were certain their mums were waiting for them, often miles away. It needed constant vigilance on the part of the dogs to prevent these breakaways. Kelpies, at least our kelpies, were inclined not to notice lambs gathering ominously in the rear. Border collies, Horace in particular, were on to them in a flash, eyeing them down, stepping into their path, just daring the lambs to put a foot wrong.

We brought Horace and Kimba with us to the Dandenongs and to our amazement they responded to this new part of the world by growing a much thicker winter coat than they'd ever bothered with in WA. They also chewed gaping holes in the under-floor heating ducts of our house. This was cunningly done over an extended period to camouflage the immediate impact; Valerie and I took most of the winter to figure out why our heating system was so hopeless, and becoming more useless by the week. It was spring by the time we spotted the cause for our discomfort, Kimba and Horace stretched under the floorboards, luxuriating happily next to their handiwork.

Horace was the one dog in my experience that seemed to show something of a sense of humour. As with every sheep dog, he was happiest on the back of the ute, his nose into the slipstream. I'm sure he missed working sheep in the Dandenongs though he quickly developed *new interests. As I drove through the hills, he kept a keen eye out for bicyclists up ahead, and as we passed he would lean over and bark right in their ear. The unfortunate athlete, half-way through a 600-metre training climb, would be seen in my rear-view mirror hauling his bicycle back from the gutter. I took both dogs walking every day those first months and one of our strolls was past a house patrolled by two of the nastiest rottweilers I have ever come across. A robust fence surrounded their yard but I found myself eyeing climbable trees as the rotweillers hurled themselves against the mesh and roared at us. This was repeated for weeks, Kimba and Horace dropping back to trot sedately behind my heels as we strolled past the rottweilers. Eventually, I noticed Horace pull ahead one day as we neared the house; he casually turned to the roaring dogs and gave one fierce decisive 'woof' right in their faces. The rottweilers flew from merely furious to positively berserk, shrieking and frothing, scrabbling hysterically at the fence to get at Horace. Horace glanced at me with the most nonchalant expression only a border collie is capable of and deviated not a whisker from the footpath running beside the diamond mesh.*

Hibanobambusa tranquillans 'Shiroshima'

Phyllostachys aurea 'Inversa'

Perhaps the most dramatic variegated bamboo we grow is *Hibanobambusa tranquillans* 'Shiroshima'. This is a hybrid between *Phyllostachys nigra* and *Sasa veitchii*. It features large green leaves with broad random buttery yellow stripes and is a low grower, perhaps to 3 metres, and its sideways lean makes it a good specimen to spill out from between taller varieties. We also have *Phyllostachys viridis* 'Robert Young', a bamboo big and strong enough to be useful for timber production. It is like a more vigorous and upright form of P. 'Holochrysa' with similar polished, sulphur-yellow stems enlivened with occasional thin green stripes. Given ample room it is highly desirable and we grow Robert Young in a spare far corner of the garden.

To further congest the yellow stems with the green stripes theme, we have two bamboos featuring the reverse. *Phyllostachys b.* 'Castillonis Inversa' is identical to the original but for green stems with its sulcus a broad stripe of yellow and the same is true for *Phyllostachys aurea* 'Inversa'. Both of these are very effective. If I had room, I would plant several specimens of P. b. 'Castillonis' with one or two clumps of P. 'Castillonis Inversa'. The identical canopies could be allowed to intermingle and the contrasting colour pattern made by the stems of the former planted close to its opposite could be an amusing detail.

When we arrived at Merrie-Lea in 1959 mother, to her horror, found the house full of mice. She bought all the mouse traps that the Mogumber post office/store held in stock, then heard that Les Tripp, the owner of the pub along the road, had one or two spare cats. And so it was that Penny arrived in our house.

Penny was a tabby with neat tabby stripes in two shades of grey and eyes the colour of dry grass. She arrived in a cardboard box and mother buttered her paws, then shut her in the kitchen – but it did not take Penny long to settle down. Calm, fastidious and nonchalant to a fault we soon found she brooked no nonsense from the sheep dogs and as a hunter she was unparalleled; in fact the finest mousing, ratting, parrot-collaring cat of all time. Mice melted away from the house and back to the grain shed within days of her arrival, never to return in the 12 years Penny was around. Late afternoons she could be seen strolling off to check on the rabbit warren in the shaly rocks halfway down the front paddock and half an hour later her 'come and see what I have' meowing could be heard from the back door; there she would be, with a blood-soaked rabbit, often bigger than herself, which she would gravely present to mother. Towards the end of every spring Mike and I would notice the soft mewling of another of Penny's litters in the dusty dark recesses under our house. We would crawl under the low floorboards to catch the handfuls of wriggling scratching kittens, moving them to a cardboard box in the laundry. Penny was the progenitor of generations of cats that moved off into the machinery sheds, the shearing shed, even the hayshed way behind the house hill, and ever further away into the hills. By the mid 1980s, all the wild bush cats for miles seemed to have a bit of tabby in them.

One last bamboo, one of the more intriguing: *Chimonobambusa Qiongzhuea tumidnoda* (syn. *Qiongzhuea tumidnoda*), the Chinese walking stick bamboo. Nodes are swollen in this species making extraordinary purplish discs threaded along narrow, whippy green stems topped with mid-green lacy foliage. In a pot it grows to around 1.8 metres; in the ground, it happily grows to 6 metres and sallies forth with rhizomes sprinting more than running and many metres in a season – the stuff of nightmares. This bamboo simply must be grown in a pot.

Chimonobambusa tuminoda

Chimonobambusa Q. tumidnoda comes from the high mountains of Sichuan Province in China. According to Ted Meredith, whose *Bamboos for Gardens*[1] is one of the more useful books on the subject, this bamboo has been used for the making of walking sticks since the Han Dynasty, more than 2000 years ago. Bamboo walking sticks were sold throughout China and some ended up in very distant lands but no one knew where the plant itself grew apart from a few canny monks and the local people of the Yi community. And certainly it was a prohibited export from China until recent years. In fact, I obtained my original piece from Jamie Stewart, a curator of the Museum of Western Australia. Courtesy of his position, Jamie was permitted to export a sample of the walking stick bamboo in the 1980s. He was fairly sure his was the first live specimen let out of China.

We grow our specimen of *Chimonobambusa Qiongzhuea tumidnoda* in a large handsome pot in three-quarter shade.

The theory of our entrance is that we have bamboos arching over the path, providing shade and a sense of enclosure before one walks into the first formal garden compartment. But in gardening, implementing ideas takes time. I suspect it will be a few more years before the effect we are driving at is obvious. By then several other plants along the entrance path will also be performing.

My grandfather, Mark Allan Francis, a big man, standing over 6 feet and broad shouldered, was renowned all his life as a sportsman. At Holt Rock, well into his 60s, he coached teenage neighbours in the niceties of tennis and was famous as the Dr WG Grace of the Lakes District whenever a cricket team went in to bat. Cam played both sports also, though mainly tennis, when he and Jan moved to Moulyinning; as a toddler I remember weekend tournaments all over the Great Southern. On clearing their first paddock, construction of sporting facilities, especially tennis courts, was pretty well the first item on the agenda for those little farming communities. Tennis courts were clay, made from crushed termite mounds and surrounded by rabbit netting slung between salmon gum posts. To one side there was generally a bower shed also made from salmon gums, with lengths of scrub woven into netting to form a shady roof and walls. Once rolled smooth, termite mounds made an excellent clay surface, superior to almost anything else, according to Cam.

Tournaments were highly organised, very fierce affairs. Teams from all those little towns thrashed each other to a standstill every weekend. Then a billy was boiled for cups of tea, with lamingtons, pikelets, sultana scones, sponge rolls, cupcakes, curried egg sandwiches, polony on crackers, cheese and gerkins pinned together on toothpicks, and perhaps a beer before heading off home. Or there might be a dance that evening, someone manning the rough old upright piano in the corner of the corrugated tin hall and everyone waltzing in the relaxed and easy way of those days. Every district, no matter how sparsely populated, fielded a cricket team along with its tennis players, generally the same people playing on alternate weekends, and in winter a women's hockey team and a men's footy team (playing that version of Australian Rules peculiar to WA, with slightly different rules and a bigger, heavier rounder ball to anywhere else in Australia). It was impossible to farm and not play sport in those days.

Towns of the Great Southern were generally built close to the railway servicing the region, often immediately beside the tracks opposite the co-operative bulk handling wheat bins. Most towns also had a Wesfarmers Co-op and many a grocery co-op; all these co-ops, I guess, arising from that intense sense of community generated by the shared sufferings of WW1, the depression and WW2, perhaps also the newness of the landscape. There was generally a meeting place for the local branch of the Farmer's Union, Parents and Citizens Associations attached to every school and a Country Women's Association. There were always working bees whenever anyone came down with a bad back during seeding or harvest. After a telephone ring around on the party line, cockies came for miles, clogging dirt roads with trucks and tractors and machinery to chip in and help out for the weekend; during harvest, the boys on the weighbridge worked through their Sunday off, holding the bin open for wheat deliveries. The only time the community feeling of those generations broke down was during stock sales or clearing sales. Ferociously bidding on a pen of prime wethers or two tooth ewes or a pile of broken machinery, it was definitely a case of every man for himself.

Cam helped to construct the tennis courts at Holt Rock over several working bees in 1933. They still exist and are, apart from several massive wheat bins, all that remains of Holt Rock. The tennis courts are not used however. At the end of a bumper season a few years back, after filling the bins to bursting, a momentous decision was taken by local cockies to store the last of the wheat on the old courts; this wrecked their surface and after more than 60 years the tennis club called it quits and moved, reluctantly, down the road to Lake Varley. My father was 13 when he helped with the collecting and crushing of termite nests and whip-arounds to raise funds for the rabbit netting. I have a crowbar, Cam says with a smile; he borrowed it from his neighbour, Jim Abernethy, to dig holes for the salmon gum posts and somehow never got around to returning it. It is the heaviest implement of its sort I have ever come across and generally sits in the garden shed and minds its own business.

Further down the steps on the opposite side to the *Phyllostachys* 'Holochrysa' we have a particularly choice shrub, *Magnolia sieboldii*. This will likely grow to just 4 metres and spreads out a twiggy canopy of the typical magnolia type, handsomely clothed with soft green deciduous leaves. Sieboldii flowers for many weeks from early to mid summer. Instead of hiding its flowers in the full foliage of early summer, it sensibly dangles small, crimson-centred, pristine white cups very conspicuously upside down, below its leaves. It is crucial when planting this species to place it over a path. One must walk underneath or the flowering may go unnoticed. Ours is planted right beside the entrance steps to have its canopy eventually overhanging, and will surely inspire people to tumble down in astonishment and admiration.

TREE RHODODENDRONS

Ross Forrester reckoned the manners of the West Australian bush, to a fair degree, came out of the committees that ran the Kalgoorlie goldfields in the 1880s and 90s. There were men on the many diggings, Bulong, Broad Arrow, Norseman, Southern Cross and the rest, who lived most of their lives under canvas. 'Forty Niners' from barren claims in the San Franciscan hills who had, in the 1850s and 60s, sailed to New South Wales and Victoria lucklessly chasing colour, then explored the icy ravines of New Zealand's Skipper's Canyon for a couple of hard winters, finally fetching up on the broiling, waterless red plains of Coolgardie and Kalgoorlie. By the 1880s, always in the backblocks, these men were long practised at living without the benefit of the rule of law; conventional authorities were regularly several rumours behind the frenetic rushes from one field to the next. There were, of course, clear reasons for dispute on the diggings – lode bearing seams ran from one claim to another and no one could ever be quite sure where the gold stashed in his neighbour's camp really came from. Yet security was, naturally, rudimentary. On diggings in other parts of the world this routinely led to violence and mayhem. Not so in WA. There was not much argument, certainly never bushrangers in Western Australia. After years of experience, older prospectors had it all worked out – fields of thousands of prospectors, their camps in wilderness hundreds of miles out in every direction from Kalgoorlie, were governed, with notably relaxed efficacy, by committees.

Prospectors took the voting of the committee members to their exalted position very seriously – the diggers were among the first anywhere to practise universal suffrage and secret ballot. And, perhaps as consequence, to any observer making comparisons with other parts of the world, the extraordinary thing was that weapons to maintain order were not to be seen. Committee members found no overt force necessary to uphold the right. In fact, the only sanction employed to deal with troublemakers was that most classical of punishments – ostracism. Miners causing strife or suspected of thieving were, in effect, ordered out of the community and off the field by the governing committee with absolutely no choice but to leave as their decision was enforced mercilessly by the local grocer, publican – and supplier of drinking water. Following pronouncement, these good people refused to deal with the offender. This modest level of enforcement easily instilled good manners. As gold ran out, miners and their families moved on and, wherever they went, that same understated, relaxed and democratic approach to disputes was in evidence. Most bush social occasions involved a committee or two. Every branch of agriculture had its grower marketing board. The several vermin fences running for thousands upon thousands of miles, erected against invasion by rabbits and wild dogs and worse from the east, were instigated by committees from throughout the southwest. And, Ross pondered, just a few years after that granddaddy of all rushes – the staking out of Kalgoorlie's glittering Golden Mile – the diggers took more than just the name with them to the beaches and cliff faces of Gallipoli.

Rhododendron 'Sir Charles Lemon'

The final plant of importance near these steps is a large specimen of *Rhododendron* 'Sir Charles Lemon'. We moved this elderly plant to this position 10 years ago, partly to screen off the next part of the garden and partly for its wonderful foliage. Its leaves are a particularly deep green and in late spring and early summer the undersides of new leaves are coated with a dense layer of deep brown, suede-like indumentum; its washing-powder-white flowers of October are a very handsome bonus. The plant is placed above the steps to best display its indumentum to visitors walking underneath.

Sir Charles Lemon must have been one of Jim's pride and joys. It is an arboreum hybrid, and as we cleared weeds we stumbled on a collection of arboreum rhododendrons growing throughout the upper half of the garden. Arboreums are the Himalayan tree rhododendrons. Think of trekking in Nepal, rhododendrons towering tens of metres overhead and studded with sometimes white, sometimes pink, more often red flowers. These, generally, are forms of arboreum. This highly variable species grows over much of Asia; from southwest China to the lower flanks

Pale, late-flowering form of *Rhododendron arboreum campbellii*

of the Nepalese Himalayas and into India; a population even in Sri Lanka. As one travels, forms of arboreum merge into each other from one region to the next.

The named forms we have include *Rhododendron arboreum campbellii*, from China, producing mid-pink flowers with white throats and its new foliage coated on both upper and lower surfaces with a particularly handsome rusty indumentum. We have more than 20 specimens of campbellii, I suspect grown from seed as they all seem to bloom at different times through August and September. I just about prefer them in new leaf, in November and December. Their dense canopies turn from a dramatic rusty suede to deep olive green and contrast wonderfully with the rugged grey bark of the trunk and branches.

Rough bark, though unusual in rhododendrons, is typical of the arboreums. It occurs again in the old specimen we have of *R. arboreum zeylanicum*. Our zeylanicum is 7–8 metres high and its massive trunk is very dramatic, partly because of its rugged grey bark and partly because it has a fair lean to it. The polished oval leaves are deep green and offset the small, garnet-red flower trusses with tremendous flair. This blooms for us in November, then carries on with a smattering of trusses through summer and autumn; even in early winter zeylanicum displays a bit of colour. Zeylanicum grows around tea plantations high in the mountains of Sri Lanka and I presume its eccentric flowering season is a consequence of its proximity to the equator.

Our old zeylanicum is hard to beat, but then we do have four specimens of *Rhododendron arboreum subsp. delavayi*. All these are magnificent but there is one specimen growing on the edge of our restaurant car park that is the most extraordinary and glorious rhododendron in the garden.

The delavayi form of arboreum also has the usual rugged bark of its kin, but in soft grey fawn and salmon pinks. Leaves are rich green and slightly rolled, effectively displaying their silvery dun felted undersides. Flowers are an intense blood red; some trusses open mid-August and the display builds right through spring with final blooms opening as late as November. Our big specimen stands 6 metres high, spreads more than 8 metres and it is full of character. To stand below, tracing its structure from massive trunk through heavy twisting branches and into an elaborately twiggy canopy, is a joy. The plant is glorious viewed from a distance and individual trusses are as handsome as anything in the garden. Finally, fresh leaves expand like felted, silvery green pennants and are a feature of late spring to early summer.

This plant was Jim Woolrich's favourite rhododendron. He called it 'the rocket', but I'm not sure that name is appropriate; its deep red trusses over the silvery, green-grey

Rhododendron arboreum subsp. delavayi

foliage makes for a faintly cool effect to my eye. But this, in the Dandenongs at least, is one of the great rhododendrons and one of the all-time best garden plants.

Sandplain to the west of Merrie-Lea was only thrown open to selection as late as the 1960s; I think it was the last Crown land to be turned over to farming in Western Australia. There was good reason for it to be at the end of the queue – none of it was inspiring, every block was entirely sand with occasional patches of gravelly sand forming the hilltops. The sand looked suspiciously like beach sand, finer grained perhaps and with a yellowish colour to it – just sufficient incentive for incoming farmers to hope to make a go of it. Vegetation was low banksia scrub, uniform in appearance all year but for several weeks when the scrub erupted to a kaleidoscopic wonder of intricate colour in September and October. Flowering of remnant areas of these highly infertile heathlands has become world famous in recent years but in the 1960s most was stripped of its vegetation by new landholders and the upper layer of sand exposed to the wind. Ploughing the soil in order to plant cereals

Ben and Alys, exploring a field of blue lupins growing on coarse sand near our rammed earth house on Clover Downs. They grow where nothing else will.

The sandplain, viewed from the 'razorback'. Our good silt soil cropping paddocks below, running towards the river. Beyond, the Dandaragan Plateau.

muddled the faint skin of nutrients into underlying coarse sand and the resulting harvest was more than disappointing. Only the foolish attempted a second crop and most blocks were turned over to West Australian blue lupin pasture; the powerful tap roots of this plant have the ability to draw up nutrients and moisture from deep in the subsoil.

I always looked to the sandplain with unease. One lunchtime in early April 1978, I glanced through a window to see part of the horizon to the northwest dissolved to a strange blur. The phenomenon made no sense at all. I called to Cam and Jan and we stood trying to figure out what might be happening. Whatever it was, it did not look like ordinary smoke or dust, just part of the sandplain that, spookily, seemed not to properly exist anymore. After a minute we could see – whatever it was – coming closer, and at a pace; but only when big white gums growing on Pat Kelly's hill bent suddenly almost to the ground could we be sure it was wind. No ordinary wind though, and seconds later the shockwave burst over us. That evening, news reports were filled with the damage caused by the precipitous arrival of Cyclone Alby to southwest WA.

That morning, Alby was reported as a tropical cyclone of moderate intensity, its centre north of Carnarvon. At the rate cyclones ordinarily travel, this meant it was several days away from us. However, in a rare piece of meteorological manoeuvring, Alby was 'captured' by a 'roaring forties' depression simultaneously approaching the lower west coast of WA from the southern Indian Ocean. The cyclone was reeled in, dragged south by the big depression, the cyclone's eye covering the best part of a thousand miles between breakfast time and lunch. Due to the strange geometry of the event, the layer of wind we first saw was extraordinarily shallow, hence there seemed to be no dust in the air. Within seconds though, debris ripped from the surface of the sandplain dropped visibility around the homestead to a few yards.

The following hours were a nightmare of dodging bits of tree, making windmills safe and weighing down loose sheets of corrugated iron to prevent shed roofs lifting off; all the while rubbish in the air stinging every inch of exposed skin. We were fortunate to have a burst of rain over Merrie-Lea around two o'clock, enough to dampen the soil and settle the dust, and making the soil relatively safe from further wind. There was still a lean, greyish look to the air though, and wind kept up strength for another 12 to 15 hours.

We were lucky that day. We lost many trees and one windmill but our soil stayed put. Most sandplain farmers received not a drop of rain and damage to their farms was catastrophic – in terms of human lifetimes, permanent. At the rate sandplain soils regenerate, the Dandaragan Plateau will need thousands of years to recover from Cyclone Alby. By the time I sold Merrie-Lea, a fair number of farmers were walking off their blocks out to our west.

THE WATER GARDEN

9 November 2004

A blackbird trilling and warbling from a twig high on the Chinese dogwood, its melody exquisitely intricate. It cocks its head listening to a neighbouring bird long enough to pick up the gist of the second bird's tune, then repeats its own little ditty with a cunning twist half way through, notes borrowed from the neighbour and spliced into its original song. The distant bird responds with an added trill while our bird contemplates its reply with indignation. Valerie and I relaxing at the end of a busy day, sitting in the sun on the theatre lawn enjoying this melodious quarrel.

Blackbirds began singing in the first weeks of August. Tiny songs at first, a few notes thrown to the winter wind, always in the dying minutes of the day; something about that last grey light inspiring birds settling onto their roosts with thoughts of the spring to come. Their singing increased with the sunshine and birds have marked their territories, selected mates and raised young almost to flying, singing all the while from first to last light. Months of practice and each bird now sounds as though it has acquired the tuitional services of a maestro to hone its performance. In a few weeks the young will be in the air and the adults will cease their singing and the garden the quieter until those tentative notes of next year's August.

*Candidus in sulcum miratur limen
Olympi sub pedibusque videl nubes
Et sidera Daphnis*

White Daphnis wonders at Olympus' unfamiliar threshold and sees stars and clouds below his feet.

Virgil, *Eclogues*, 5–56.

From the entrance steps, visitors walk down into the Water Garden. At its lowest, the floor of this compartment is more than 2 metres below original soil level. Earth banks to each side are retained with the best 'honeycomb' stone we could find; the beds are narrow – only 1.2 metres wide – and the stone walls are thus very prominent. As mentioned earlier, our engineer specified a maximum height of 1.5 metres for our dry stone walls so approaching this level we cut a shelf back 90 centimetres and retained the upper metre or so of bank with inferior rock.

Early spring – the hornbeam hedge still translucent

The ledge was meant to be just sufficiently wide to plant a hedge of hornbeam, *Carpinus betulus*, which would serve to hide the awkwardness of the upper wall.

Hornbeams were planted onto the ledges early in 1992 using seedlings rather than the fastigiate cutting-grown form. I puzzle over this now. The common hornbeam does have a tendency to retain dry foliage in winter, especially when clipped. Its leaves turn yellowish in autumn then shrivel to tatters hanging from the end of twigs. Alternatively, the fastigiate selection available in Australia seems to drop autumn leaves neatly and its winter outline is clean. Hornbeam bark is smooth, a wonderful silvery pewter and indeed very similar to beech. The effect of its winter outline is particularly lovely when hornbeams are planted as a hedge. Their silvery trunks, frequently fluted, and tightly curving branches and a tracery of fine twigs ending precisely in the clipped vertical plane of the hedge, recall a three-dimensional wood cut. However, this effect would be better without the common hornbeam's habit of hanging on firmly to its rat-brown dead leaves. Still, I am wary of using the fastigiate tree for hedging. Hedges look best when twigs intersect the face of the hedge close to 90 degrees. Shoots should grow out to meet the eye. Fastigiate hornbeams usually have twigs held at an acute angle to the plane of the hedge, making them difficult to clip and giving an awkward, untidy effect.

We planted our hornbeams, clipped and trained them, and within six years they were up to the 3.5 metres we required to give this area walls in proportion to the area of the rectangular floor of the water garden. Hedges are vital to the architecture of this part of the garden. Their generous green leafy panels over low grey stone walls are always a delight. I suspect our hornbeams are at their best in early spring, as the expanding leaf buds push off any remaining dead leaves. The silvery grey spine of the hedge is still exposed with just a shimmer of fresh mid-green. Simon Donald's stone walls immediately under each of the hedges give the effect of handsome footings. They are reminiscent of low stone retaining walls in Japanese gardens, which frequently have hedges planted onto them. This arrangement is something we have repeated in several parts of Cloudehill. For instance, English box, with its dense binding root system, is used to cap several higher retaining walls including the walls to each side of our water temple, the little pavilion constructed into the end of the water garden.

Each paddock on the two farms had its own character, its own mood, especially the hill paddocks on Merrie-Lea. The 'razorback paddock' for instance, with a thin strip of arable, gently sloping soil running the length of its ridge, was a difficult, even treacherous strip to cultivate because disc ploughs were inclined to slide out of the shaly soil and slip off the edge and with a bit of momentum the heavy plough would attempt to tug the tractor, along with its nervous driver, tumbling down the fierce slopes to either side. Near Merrie-Lea's northwest corner, sheoak woodlands grew along one ridge in our 'sherwood paddock'. Inspired by television stories of Robin Hood, Mike and I shot arrows at each other from vantage points among the megalithic-looking slabs of rock scattered through the trees. The rugged 'brecon paddock' received its name as a souvenir of Jan and Cam's tour of Wales in 1974. A gnamma hole, a tiny spring carefully lined with rocks with a big rectangular slab as lid, constructed eons ago by the Yuad people as a place, far from the river, where they could always be sure of a drink, provided the name for the surrounding steep, rock-strewn hill. We also had lazily named paddocks such as the northeast and the southeast and the south and the southwest. My wife Valerie found the paddocks named for compass bearings particularly exasperating, coming as she did from a background bereft of compasses.

The razorback

The gnamma hole (knocked apart by cattle)

Cropping paddocks tended to be the 60-acre or 180-acre or mill paddock or tank paddock or hay paddock. They each had their own character, which I remember as the sway of the tractor as I drove over them; each had its own texture and rhythm. Different soil types allowed differing levels of wheel slippage as the big rear tractor tyres bit into the loam. Shaly paddocks or pebbly paddocks or sandy paddocks all had a very different feel to them. Several of our front paddocks were littered with angular quartz pebbles and many larger 'boundies' (pronounced to rhyme with Burundi, I think one of the few Yuad words we white kids used). At night, quartz rocks flashed with sparks as the disc plough sliced through.

Each paddock also had its own routine when it came time to muster stock. Sheep dogs generally knew what they were about but there were often little tricks to keep in mind. Sheep approaching a gateway from a higher slope became apprehensive about what might be awaiting them around the corner down in the next paddock and could baulk and mill around for hours, ignoring the dog's barking, our whistling and clapping and cursing. A mob approaching from the opposite direction and sighting the hills arising before them would leap through the gateway serenely with us doing no more than to gently shoo the stragglers. On occasions, stock might respond to the character of the soil they were travelling over. I remember moving a flock across a sandy paddock on Clover Downs, the sand several metres deep over a layer of dense rock. One or two of the animals began jumping, out of nervousness or perhaps high spirits, and within seconds the entire mob was leaping, twisting, dodging chaotically in alarm at the echoing muffled boom of their own thudding leaps echoing through the sand off the rock below.

The broken nature of the Mogumber hills, the rapidly varying soils with their differing vegetation, made for immense variety in the landscape. Paddocks dominated by whitegums, wandoos, with their high open branch structure and pale dappled bark had a different mood to a neighbouring paddock of redgums, marries, with dense foliage, almost the colour of an English oak, cascading from the crown of each tree to the ground. I am thinking now of a particular slope covered in redgums, the angle of its slope paralleled precisely by the 'grazing line' of the trees, the slanting line formed by the lower limit of foliage left by the sheep as they grazed. This was clipped with smart precision by the merinos as they reared on their hind legs, reaching high for mouthfuls of leaves during hungry autumns. Every leaf within reach was stripped away. The resulting landscape was extraordinarily reminiscent of an 18th-century 'jardin anglais' made by Kent or Capability Brown.

The water temple was originally made as a simple alcove with brick side walls and a volcanic stone rear wall wrapping around a 1.8-metre square pond. My initial plan was to have water falling down the face of the 2-metre-high rear stone wall into the pool.

An exhibition of wood-fired ceramic pieces by Robert Barron

It was not a great idea. The alcove turned out to be a resonance chamber and the water fell with a plopping, teeth-chattering roar. I tried breaking the fall of the water halfway, which helped only marginally, and eventually I gave up. We have tried some dozen fountains of many and varied design in the alcove since. Fountains have been installed, temporarily, as part of garden art exhibitions displayed over past years, so there have been plenty of chances to experiment. I have found the less water splashing around the better. The best fountains create a mere tinkle of sound. Glazed ceramic fountains are often very effective, despite large volumes of water circulating through them, but only so long as the water clings to the smooth surface of the fountains and slides into the pond almost noiselessly, with just occasional drops thrown free.

The square pond in our little alcove is connected by a low stone platform to a rectangular, 1.8- by 6-metre pond, and having constructed and filled the pond, I sat back for inspiration to complete the project. Twelve months later, having reached the conclusion our alcove needed a roof, I sketched out a fairly classic design. The neo-Georgian design of the roof could readily be made to harmonise with its surrounds by making it from a contemporary material, such as mild steel, finished with a coat of paint.

Don Nixon, a friend living a few minutes away, fabricated the roof for what was now to be our water temple in his garage. He painted it a handsome blue, inspired by a deep blue hydrangea flower, and left me with the job of getting it home. The

A collection of aquatics. Bowle's golden sedge, *Carex elata* 'Aurea', in foreground. To the left, a water iris, *Iris pseudacorus* 'Variegata'; two clumps of *Schoenoplectus lacustris subsp. tabernaemontani* 'Albescens'; and in the far corner, *Spartina pectina* 'Aureomarginata'.

roof was a fair size but there was only a short distance to move it home. Loading the structure onto the ute I decided to take the back way, and drove onto the Mount Dandenong Tourist Road and quickly around a corner into a quiet road, except, blow me, there was a wedding party gathered at the little stone church on the corner. At least 200 guests spilled across the lane, all craning for a glimpse of the bride who, seemingly, was in the beribboned car immediately in front. Then there was me in this bright yellow utility with the brilliant blue Georgian roof roped on behind and draped over each side, taking up much of the lane's width. Everyone skipped hurriedly backwards except for the celebratory bagpipers, who were so preoccupied that I nearly scythed an end to their piping. I gave all a congratulatory wave and zoomed away down the road.

The temple roof now sits on the alcove as though it was always meant to be and we grow a juvenile form of Boston ivy, *Parthenocissus quinquefolia* 'Veitchii', through it and now we happily let the roof rust.

Planting in the beds on each side of the water garden is still at the experimental stage. Plants must be low so not to obscure our hornbeam hedges, and the dry stone walls under the hedges are likewise too handsome to be hidden. Thinking to add to the aquatic effect of this area, I planted ornamental grasses, sedges and New Zealand flaxes. This was mildly successful, at least while the hedges were growing, but as they reached full height the increased shade reduced the vigour of many grasses, causing them to collapse halfway through the season and the general effect became scrappy. As mentioned, the beds are narrow with room for not much more than one row of plants. Borders look best when planted four and five clumps deep, with opportunity to introduce minor themes, whether colour or texture. Simplicity and repetition are essential in the planting of narrow borders to avoid the 'dog's breakfast' look. This is something I am still working towards and am happy with only part of the original planting, mainly to each side of our little temple. As this faces due south, in full shade during hotter hours, we can grow a few hostas such as the statuesque glaucous green krossa regal, the blue-green halcyon and the lovely grey-blue hadspen blue. These are interspersed through yellow pools of Japanese temple grass, *Hakonechloa macra* 'Aureola'. Tucked in at the mid point of each bed we have *Sanguisorba obtusa* and *S. menziesii*, the former with elegant pinnate greyish-green leaves with soft rose pink bottlebrush flower in mid summer, the latter with glaucous blue foliage and flower tassels of dusky crimson.

To help achieve an air of restraint, the beds beneath the hornbeam hedges demand plenty of repetition. Eighteen months back I tried some 15 specimens of *Hydrangea quercifolia* 'Sike's Dwarf'. This is relatively new to Australia and I am not sure of its mature height but hope for around 1.2 metres. Its flowering is typical of the oakleaf hydrangeas: dusty conical heads of greenish cream to creamy white blooms in mid-summer developing dusky orange tints later. However, Sike's dwarf is meant to earn its keep with foliage. The leaves have the lobed leaf look of all the oak leafs but their smaller size and particularly neat shape creates a lovely textual effect. The foliage should form repetitive soft green mounds through the summer and die in winter in shades of yellow and pink and scarlet. Quercifolia is not totally deciduous in the Dandenongs – its autumn effects persist through most of winter.

Sike's dwarf is one of several new oak leaf hydrangeas. Others include *Hydrangea quercifolia* 'Snow Queen', producing upright heads of bloom covered in sterile flowers

Planting below hornbeam hedge dominated by *Hydrangea quercifolia* 'Sike's Dwarf', but also *Phlarlaris arundinacea* 'Feesey', upper left, the cream daisy flowers of *Anthemis* 'E.C. Buxton', centre, next to a small clump of *Calamagrostis x acutiflora* 'Overdam'

(or florets), and *Hydrangea q.* 'Snow Flake', displaying very persistent, double sterile florets in large pendulous cones. A couple of both of these are scattered amongst the Sike's dwarf for the sake of variation. *Hydrangea q.* 'Alice' is a vigorous form of this variable species and can grow to 5 metres and is making a superb feature on the edge of big rhododendrons elsewhere in the garden, producing flowers several times the size of its smaller kin.

Planting in front of the hydrangeas is still a puzzle but we persevere with some of the grasses. For instance, *Calamagrostis x acutiflora* 'Overdam' tolerates part shade well enough to grow happily and it complements the hydrangea blooms with excellent, stiffly upright variegated foliage in pink and white with the bonus of its early summer pinkish mauve flowers to around a metre. I am also trying several clumps of Mervyn Feesey's form of the old gardener's garters: *Phalaris arundinacea* 'Mervyn Feesey'. This lovely grass is almost entirely white, pencilled with the narrowest of mid-green stripes. Except for the first weeks of spring when it is suffused pink, this selection is perhaps the best grass for a silvery white effect. Feesey's form is also much less inclined to wander than true gardener's garters, and happier in sun, in the Dandenongs at least, than one might suspect.

On the southern side of the water garden we have a hedge of *Thuja occidentalis* 'Smaragd'. In 1993 I decided a conifer hedge was needed to contrast with abutting hornbeam

Early morning, late summer. The water temple now clothed with *Parthenocissus tricuspidata* 'Veitchii'.

hedges; both grown to full height now they work well together, the leafy soft green look of the carpinus against the dense mid-green of the conifer. The thuja does have a hint of yellow in its emerald during its summer growth period, which made me decide against using it as a backdrop to pastel colours in other parts of the garden, but lime as a backing to the predominantly flame colours of the warm borders is excellent. In winter, the thuja turns bronze, which I feel is appropriate for those downbeat months, making a nice change from its glittering lime livery of spring and summer.

A narrow gap at the foot of the thuja is open enough to try a little strip of the sun-loving *Cyclamen graecum*. This cyclamen revels in an exposed spot, growing in hot, low-lying parts of Greece and Turkey. Graecum has roots that hang on so tight that it is almost impossible to dig from its rocky crevices in the wild. It also has exquisitely patterned foliage that glitters handsomely beneath pink and white autumnal flowers. In the nursery I have first choice of its variable seedlings and the choosing of such delicious gems for their lovely leaf patterns arouses pure greed.

Hedges made of *Thuja occidentalis* 'Smaragd'

I guess I was on a tractor for a good two months in autumn and early winter in an average year, ploughing, scarifying back, harrowing and seeding the crop; spraying weedicide a few weeks later; ploughing fire breaks in spring in preparation for the coming fire season; or any number of minor jobs requiring a bit of horsepower. We even used a tractor-drawn harvester, so that was another five to six weeks in early summer sitting side-saddle on the tractor seat, twisted hard to the right watching the harvester, checking dozens of pulleys for signs of slippage (caused by blockages within the machine), monitoring wheat flowing into the comb, one hand always on the hydraulic lever controlling the height of the 16-foot comb, keeping it within an inch or two of correct level. The comb was often almost scraping the ground so there was always the danger of smashing it on a rock or stump – travelling at jogging speed and with the crop making obstacles difficult to see, one could never daydream. Occasionally I glanced ahead for trees and to gauge the approach to a corner. Twenty years on, my spine still has its twist to the right.

Memories settle around just a few places in all those tens of thousands of acres, and a few minutes in those months and years of tractor driving: seeding wheat over part of the northwest paddock, the ground broken into a long series of little dips and rises, the combine seeder pivoting behind the tractor, tynes rising and falling, adjusting to correct depth. The screech of case-hardened points scraping over a rock shelf forming the edge of the long breakaway, piercing the tractor's roar every few moments. It is always night in my memory, sowing the crop, always the pervasive growl of the diesel motor and the little space illuminated fore and aft by the tractor's lights; overhead, the mass of stars swivelling from horizon to horizon through the hours.

Harvesting is distilled now to a few acres of sloping ground in our 'barley paddock', a good heavy crop, speed down to a slow walk and the harvester shuddering with the sheer bulk of chaff and straw and grain moving through the drum, the constant shuffling roar of machinery, low whoomps as it comes close to clogging. Then the clean grain spilling from the rotating screen on top of the harvester, a deep river of that elemental stuff toppling through the sunlight into the harvester's bin.

I smell the wheat still, its dusty malt perfume; late afternoons when temperatures dropped with the sea breeze, plunging my outstretched fingers deep into grain piled high in a field storage bin, the sudden accumulated summer warmth of it, gritty kernels between the palms of my hands, lodged deliciously in the webs of my fingers, the firm bright knottiness of the wheat.

THE WARM BORDERS

A strip of sheoaks lined a rise in one of our cropping paddocks. The fine cascading, seemingly leafless twigs of the trees caught the winter breeze and turned it into the most lonesome sound, a vibrant keening that rose and fell in intensity with the changing strength of the wind. I was actually pretty cheerful at that moment, the wheat a few weeks out of the ground, thick and vigorous and a good deep green and no weeds that I could see. Apart from the occasional scudding cloud the sky was a glorious windswept blue. The unholy racket from the trees in front of me seemed thoroughly uncalled for but the wailing boomed across the open paddock nevertheless.

Or I am he who hunted out the source of fire and stole it, packed in the pith of a dry fennel stalk.

Aeschylus, *Prometheus Bound*

From the water garden visitors look down into our warm borders. These are the first of Cloudehill's double borders. At 22 metres long and 4 metres deep they give me 176 square metres of space to play with. The water garden is 1.2 metres higher than the warm borders, high enough to provide a nice feeling of walking down the short flight of connecting steps into waist-deep flowers. It was my intention when designing the garden to plant this enclosure to warm coloured flowers: reds, oranges, warm yellows, with Gertrude Jekyll in mind. Jekyll arranged her Munstead Wood border with rich colour foremost and central to lure visitors across a lawn to the heart of her garden. Misty mauves and blues and lemons suggest distant horizons and Jekyll grouped these to each end of her border. Reversing the arrangement would perversely have minimised the impression of space in Munstead Wood. Cloudehill's warm borders are meant to be a raucous welcome with just a hint of mauve and blue to be glimpsed through the central archways, to emphasise the length of the terrace and entice visitors onwards.

In 1994 I attempted a version of Hidcote's 'Red Border', using only red and orange flowers and plenty of purple foliage. Red flowering penstemons were planted, sweeping around clumps of the blood-red *Dahlia* 'Bishop of Llandaff' backed by orange cactus dahlias, crimson-mahogany heleniums and deep purple buddleias. Three and four weeks into the season I was having doubts. The effect was leaden. My orange-red perennials were banked around two medium-sized shrubs, good specimens of the purple leaf form of the Canadian redbud, *Cercis canadensis* 'Forest Pansy'. Forest pansy covers itself with superb purple foliage and is in every way a very amenable plant, but its bloomy purple is particularly deep and shadowy. Lapped with red and orange, the result was surprisingly lifeless and dispiriting and by mid summer I'd decided the Hidcote-style planting was too ambitious to easily emulate. That season certainly increased my respect for Graham Stuart Thomas who, I understand, did most to perfect the Hidcote Red Borders, as they are now in his advisory work with the English National Trust from the 1950s and 60s. However, his themes seemed not to translate to the Dandenongs and in 1995 I introduced yellows and 10 years later warm yellow is the dominant colour in this garden.

Summer, 1994

Cloudehill's borders rely on a number of shrubs for muscle, especially, of course, the forest pansies. Herbaceous perennials dominate the frontal planting and weave back through the shrubs. All woody plants, trees and shrubs are heavily pruned and frequently pollarded to keep them to scale and a little topiary is included for winter interest. We have eight domes of clipped English box spaced out four to a row on each side of the central path. They are almost the 1- by 1-metre I think they need to be to give a solid look during the bare weeks of winter.

The forest pansy form of the Canadian redbud is an outstanding plant. Clipping makes their growth dense and lush, and with a hard winter prune, we keep ours at 3 by 3 metres. Their heart-shaped leaves are deep aubergine purple, overlaid with a silvery iridescence, similar to some varieties of black table grapes. In fact, I struggle to think of anything other than black grapes fresh from the vine, their bloom mottled with dew, to give an idea of this colour. No other purple-leafed plant comes close. But how did it come by its name 'forest pansy'? I had a customer come to our nursery saying, "My wife visited last week and she asked me to stop in and buy a forest pansy". "Fine" I replied, "we have some good stock – what do you think of this one?" I pulled out a cercis in a 33-centimetre pot and presented it to him. He looked at it suspiciously and replied, "Listen mate, you are trying to have a lend of me. I know about plants, I know what a pansy is. A pansy is a little thing with flowers and it shouldn't cost anything like this much", and away he stormed to his car,

Opposite: October, with tulips in pots. *Phormium* 'Dark Delight' to the right, *Cotinus coggygria* 'Golden Spirit' behind; our weeping maples in fresh leaf and to the rear on the left, our historic *Fagus sylvatica* 'Roseomarginata'

me trailing in his wake, attempts to explain quite ignored. Our cersis are deep velvety purple all through summer and in mid-April fade to autumn colours: yellow, flame-orange and crimson. Leaves fall to reveal purple-black willowy twigs emerging from the pollarded stems. These are sufficiently interesting to leave pruning to the last weeks of winter. We generally place pruned twigs in a vase, perhaps mixed with stems of silvery honesty. Occasionally cercis twigs react to warmer indoor temperatures by popping out crimson-pink, pea-shaped flowers. These make an arrangement even more handsome and also remind me of its common name, the Canadian redbud. Redbuds flower in spring with wands of cerise pink, the small spreading trees dominating landscapes from southeast Canada and New England to Texas and the mountains of Mexico. Flowers emerge not only from young wood but also from old stems and even trunks in a display of profligate eccentricity that is only matched by its Mediterranean cousin, *Cercis siliquastrum*, or the Judas tree.

21 December 2004

A warmish evening, cicadas calling from the dry bank above our work area. Melbourne cicadas are harsh and shrill compared with the cicadas of our Clover Downs garden. I always enjoyed walking that sandy garden in the evening, often in bare feet, loose earth giving a little with each footfall and the dry air so often filled with the soft, high-pitched roar of the local cicada. The sound rolled in banks between the red gums, each pool of sound quietening as I approached, cicadas responding to my presence. I particularly enjoyed late evening, watching colours changing minute by minute, softer colours becoming more prominent while reds and oranges sank to shadow.

Several big West Australian 'Christmas trees' to the west of the house also blossomed around the summer solstice, during walks each tree darkened against an oyster-shell evening sky. Above their dense canopies, orange flowers became flaring chunks of colour that caught the prolonged pale light skipping across the ocean from Africa. The Christmas tree, Nuytsia floribunda, *was one of the few plants to leave its flowering to the onset of summer heat; as a consequence, and because of the sheer abundance of nectar produced, each mass of bloom attracted insects for miles. Ants trekked across the paddock at furious speed and entire hives of bees gathered to enjoy every tree's prodigious feast.*

Western Australian Christmas trees are really giant, free-standing mistletoes. Their roots run out from grey, elephant-hide trunks some distance and attack anything in their path – other trees, shrubs, even grass – and parasitise the victim. I asked the contractor laying the below-ground telephone line to our newly built house why on earth his trench was swinging all over the paddock. He replied that, "The bloody Christmas trees will latch on and rip the guts out of the cable if I go anywhere near the buggers".

Opposite: General views, in October with hybrid rhododendrons flowering above the water temple (top); four weeks later (bottom)

All shrubs planted in the warm borders are used more for foliage than flowers except for three specimens of *Buddleia davidii* 'Black Knight'. The grey-green leaves of

this buddleia are sparse but it makes up with long spikes of perfumed inky purple flowers from every growing point. We do have to work on this plant as Black Knight is gawky and wants to grow metres every season. Ours are cut back to 60 to 90 centimetres in winter and they grow easily to 2.4 metres and flower in January with a colour that fits wonderfully with the predominant themes of this garden. They are one of the few borrowings from Hidcote we persevere with. In fact, Black Knight was one of the plants packed into my 1988 collection with the thought it was indispensable in the planting of a warm coloured garden. It must be dead-headed immediately after the first flush of bloom. Subsequent growth is a lovely silvery grey rather than the dull green of earlier months and it has a sprinkle of flowers from early March for a further 10 weeks.

Other shrubs in the warm borders include the ruby honeylocust, *Gleditsia triacanthos* 'Rubylace', the smoke bush, *Cotinus coggygria foliis purpureis* and two specimens of the splendid *Rosa moyesii* 'Geranium'. Our altitude of 600 metres puts us above Melbourne's smog into a layer of pleasingly clean air, also humidified by our proximity to Bass Strait. In other words, wonderful conditions for black spot disease and I am reduced to growing only roses most resistant to this nuisance. Forms of *Rosa moyesii* are among the few to thrive. Our specimens of geranium produce lacy

Plants arranged around *Rosa moyesii* 'Geranium'
Left to right: *Phormium* 'Dazzler' and *Spiraea* 'Goldflame'; *Physocarpus* 'Dart's Gold' and *Crocosmia* 'Lucifer' in late-spring foliage; *Phormium* 'Anna Red' and *Cotinus coggygria* 'Golden Spirit'

canopies of grey-green leaves, 2.5 metres high by 2 metres across on unusually upright stems for a rose. The narrow space taken by the stems means we can easily tuck shade-loving plants under their skirts. The small, garnet-red flowers produced by this selection are exquisite for three weeks in December and bristly bottle-shaped hips glow warm orange for many weeks in March and April, or at least until the crimson rosellas notice them.

Unlike forest pansy, the rubylace honeylocust is well named, especially so in the first half of the season. Its tiny bipinnate leaves are mahogany ruby through mid summer and slowly turn a very curious ochre in late summer, and in autumn an even more curious rich milky copper, which is actually good, for by now the entire border is softening to similar colours. Rubylace is a smaller grower than its several golden-leafed counterparts and we prune gently each winter.

Cotinus coggyria foliis purpureis is an older selection of the common smoke bush with smoky purple rounded leaves. As we prune, or rather pollard this plant back to a metre-high stump in August, we eliminate the fuzz of purple-pink flowers it otherwise displays. A shame, as a smoky pink haze would be wonderful with the surrounding yellow of heleniums, rudbeckias and *Achillea* 'Coronation Gold'. However, without a serious prune there would be no sunshine for its neighbours, so we grow it for leaves and plant cotinus varieties elsewhere for flowers. Because the soil is moderately rich, its autumn tints are a strange wash of coffee orange and not the fierce colour smoke bushes exhibit in ordinary, unimproved soil. I might add this is true for a fair number of plants grown for autumn colour, but especially so for smoke bushes. The winter outline of our foliis purpureis is fun. Strong seasonal growths splay from the pollarded trunk in splendidly eccentric loops and twirls and these are revealed with the falling of leaves. In the corner adjacent to our purple smoke bush we have planted *Cotinus c.* 'Golden Spirit'. This more upright form is over 2 metres now and its lime-gold foliage contrasts splendidly with the neighbouring New Zealand flax, *Phormium* 'Anna Red'.

To provide contrast with the fuzzy, often nondescript growth of herbaceous perennials, certain plants are included for decisive foliage patterns: several varieties of New Zealand flax, cannas and clumps of *Miscanthus sinensis* 'Gracillimus' all provide strong texture. Gracillimus is the oldest of the narrow leaf forms of this indispensable grass, producing mounds of fountain-like foliage 1.5 metres high by 2 metres across. It can be wider if the clumps are left undisturbed for too long and we divide every two or three years. The rumpled, crimson mahogany flowers emerge very late in the Dandenongs, perhaps April or even May; the same plant in Western

Australia flowers around February. Flowers can reach 2.4 metres in warmer climes; we expect 1.8 metres at best in Cloudehill. Half a dozen clumps are scattered along the rear half of each border.

This season I am experimenting with the recently introduced *Miscanthus nepalensis*. This Himalayan species flowers to 120 centimetres high with pendulous, silky yellowish feathery tassels displayed high above the foliage in February, March, April and onwards deep into winter. Half a dozen clumps are growing close to the path on both sides to give a hazy foreground to calm the otherwise raucous blare. At least, this is the theory. Other plants flowering with dusky tints, used to the same end, include a warm mauve blooming bergamont, *Monarda* 'Donnerwolke', and a mauve-pink eupatorium called Gateway. The thought behind mixing these colours through the yellows and reds comes from seeing an exhibition of oils by Criss Canning in the early 1990s. One of Criss's paintings featured the Bishop of Llandaff dahlia, its blood-red flowers and purple-black foliage arranged in a burnt-orange vase. The vase was placed on a brown tray with three ripe passionfruit to one side and a hefty swatch of dusky burgundy and pink striped cloth as backdrop; the latter complemented the dahlia brilliantly. On first seeing Criss's extraordinary still life I was standing in the crowded gallery for long minutes wondering how might plants in a garden be arranged to similar effect. Criss, naturally, did not have to include green in her painting. Garden borders, even with plenty of plum and purple and grey, will always be dominated by green, so my little tribute to her painting had to be modest. What I took away from the gallery was the thought that vibrant colours are enlivened wonderfully by intermingling them with soft, dusky, complementary colours. A border devoted entirely to hot colours risks becoming overbearing in the way my 1994 scheme failed. Criss's lesson took a while to sink in; I began seriously including dusky colours in the late 1990s. However, we now have lots of mauve-pinks and pale crimsons among our oranges and reds and yellows. I hope the clumps of *Miscanthus nepalensis* underline this theme as they produce sprays of coppery yellow all late summer.

Completing five years of boarding school and returning to the farm I threw away my wristwatch and stopped wearing shoes. Not having a clock strapped to my person was no great matter as, apart from the front boundary following the curves of the river, all Merrie-Lea fences ran exactly north and south or east and west – shadows from posts told me the time to within minutes. However, to discard any form of footwear in paddocks thick with rocks and prickles may seem perverse, and especially tricky working the merinos in sheepyards. Walking between them, sharp hooves inches from bare feet, was decidedly risky and catching

Miscanthus nepalensis

the animals by their muzzle, to check their teeth for wear perhaps, was begging for strife. Sheep usually responded to this indignity by stepping sideways with a stiletto hoof onto my foot, then rearing onto hind legs while pirouetting. Still, looking back, to feel the earth under my feet seemed important at the time and after a while they calloused to the degree I could jog a distance through an occasional double gee (three cornered jack) patch, accumulating prickles impaled a centimetre and more into my flesh. Eventually I stopped to peel them away, but it was a matter of pride to ignore them for a few hundred yards.

After a couple of years I began wearing boots. At first, only in the coldest part of winter or in the sheep yards during spring, the ground covered in sloppy manure but, season by season, in the way of the world, comfort won out.

Spiraea 'Goldflame' in the foreground; at left, *Phormium* 'Platt's Black', *Hemerocallis* foliage, *Physocarpus* 'Dart's Gold', *Arctotis* and *Euphorbia dulcis* 'Chameleon' at the rear

Phormium 'Dazzler' is a dramatic strap-leafed plant for frontal planting. It thrusts its scimitar-shaped purple-brown leaves to 80 and 90 centimetres high, each having a central broad stripe of crimson red. The colour is much closer to true red than more recent selections: evening glow and crimson devil, but sadly, Dazzler is a pusillanimous grower. It is an old selection I saw first in Christchurch, New Zealand, in 1975 and I remember my lust, even more so because I could not simply buy it and take it home. In Australia, I eventually tracked this variety down to David Thompson in Adelaide, who sent me a piece in 1989. In the 16 years since, this has become two and a half clumps, but only just, and they are quite small and low. Two big clumps of the exuberantly growing *Phormium* 'Anna Red' are placed a metre or two back from the path. Despite its name, Anna Red has leaves closer to plum mahogany than red, but there is a silvery infusion to this colour on the underside of its leaves. This two-tone effect is particularly good because its habit is stiffly upright to 1.8 metres.

As I worked yellows into the borders in the mid 1990s, it occurred to me that one large advantage of this scheme was the abundance of plants with yellow foliage. Don Teese, of Yamina Rare Plants, gave me some specimens of *Physocarpus opulifolius* 'Dart's Gold' to experiment with around this time. Dart's Gold is a nondescript plant for its flowers and general demeanour but by early summer the raised surface of each lobed leaf appears brushed with gold, due to recessed veins turning green. From a distance, the effect is strongly lime-green and this persists the entire summer. I scattered Don's Dart's Gold through the planting to give an immediately dramatic effect. Each physocarpus is cut to within a couple of centimetres of the ground in winter. Buttery yellow buds swell early in spring and quickly assume lime-green tints. I imagine without pruning, our plants might grow metres high.

Even with a drastic winter cut back, Dart's Gold grows a metre every summer; our plants are within easy reach for someone in December to shape back to the 60–80 centimetres we want.

Another shrub I use in a similar way is *Spiraea* 'Goldflame'. This is smaller, easier to use as a frontal plant and several are scattered beside the central path. Again, every plant is cut almost to the ground in early winter and with the first days of spring, tiny leaves expand in a blaze of orange and bronze. As leaves reach full size they turn warm yellow. Unfortunately, early summer also brings its puce-pink flowers, which we try to clip off, but not in too much of a panic as by this time there is plenty of nearby colour falling within the theme of the garden.

Among the first of the herbaceous perennials to flower is *Achillea* 'Coronation Gold'. Its ferny, silvery green leaves alone make this plant so good to grow that flowers are almost a bonus. Above its foliage, flower stems rise 60 centimetres topped with superb 12-centimetre-wide corymbs of tight-packed, tiny ochre-yellow flowers for weeks through December and January. One drift of this plant sits very nicely against a backdrop of *Ligularia* 'The Rocket', the horizontal saucer-like flowers of the achillea contrast almost too logically with the vertical yellow spires of the ligularia. The ligularia also possesses elegant deep-green jagged leaves on stems polished bronze-black. It forms mounds of foliage to 80 centimetres and narrow spires of its yellow flowers rise with stately aplomb 1.5 metres in front of the yellowish green of our thuja hedge. *Achillea* 'Coronation Gold' and *Ligularia* 'The Rocket' is perhaps an obvious combination, except the first requires sun and dry soil and the second shade and moisture. It so happens the thuja hedge beside the entrance steps throws sufficient shade across the ligularia to keep it cool during the hotter hours of the day. As the hedge is on top of a metre-high brick retaining wall, conifer roots do not compete with the ligularia, so the rocket enjoys more shade and lots more moisture than any other plant in these borders. I thus have one precisely defined corner to grow what is essentially a cool climate woodlander. The ligularia was planted with heart in mouth though, but after performing well for eight years now I feel rather smug with this glorious shade lover, while fractionally to the left *Achillea* 'Coronation Gold' revels in its sunny spot.

To the other side of the entrance steps, tucked against the brick retaining wall to reduce this plant's propensity to run, I have planted the marvellous *Euphorbia griffithii* 'Great Dixter'. This herbaceous spurge has narrow oblong, glaucous green leaves stained plum-red, and flowers in late spring with orange blooms faintly infused with crimson. Again, Great Dixter enjoys the extra moisture below the wall at this end of the border. It prefers more light than the ligularia so is planted on the sunnier side of the path. At the other end of the borders I have used *Euphorbia schillingii*. This summer-flowering euphorbia produces chartreuse-yellow blooms over handsome sea-green leaves; these often appear variegated due to pale mid-ribs. *Euphorbia schillingii* grows 60 centimetres high and seeds itself gently. I also use *Euphorbia dulcis* 'Chameleon' with a great deal of nervousness, as it seeds wantonly. Chameleon is a fabulous plant however. It produces lush, low mounds of metallic purple foliage and the nodding flowers of spring and early summer are bright crimson-purple. The effort required removing numerous stray seedlings from among other plants is easily worthwhile.

One unsettling thing about living in the Dandenongs is Cloudehill's easterly orientation. Our views are of sunrises, softened perhaps by mist. We rarely notice sunsets. Generally a clear evening sky pales to oyster lavender tints and at best an occasional pale blush reflects from over the ridge. Before now, I have always lived in houses facing west – most West Australian houses do. Sunsets viewed from the old homestead on Merrie-Lea out over the sandplain were often torrid with apricot crimsons and vermilions, especially in summer. In the early 1960s a volcanic eruption in Indonesia flooded the upper atmosphere with dust and for months sunsets were suffused oily emerald and purple. The colour filled the sky and the bare hills in summer were turned lurid.

Summer holidays on the beach at Cottesloe in Perth or tiny beach shack settlements along the coast meant we were always watching the sun over the Indian Ocean. Reflected afternoon and evening light was shattered into kaleidoscopic fragments by fierce sea breezes chopping across the water.

Four years after first planting the warm borders, I decided to reintroduce *Penstemon* 'Schoenholzeri', or 'Firebird'. I did this with trepidation remembering how its brick-red flowers so dominated in 1994 – our Hidcote summer. However, 15 plants were ordered from a local grower and planted along the front edges of the borders and grew away happily as penstemons are wont to do, and flowered in the early summer in glorious shades of wine-scarlet. This colour settled so easily into the garden that it was a while before I noticed the plants were not the warm brick red flowering Firebirds I had actually ordered. They were actually P. 'Andeken an Friedrich Hahn', or 'Garnet'. Garnet is one of the finest of all the penstemons. Its coolishly tinted panicles thrown up so profusely made me appreciate how effectively this colour, a red with just a touch of blue, served to enrich the surrounding yellow, orange, warm red theme. Occasionally one needs to be jolted by serendipidous mix-ups to find the

Penstemon 'Andenken an Friedrich Hahn', pulling the colour theme sideways

Opposite top: *Ligularia* 'The Rocket' at the rear with *Achillea* 'Coronation Gold', the latter infiltrated somewhat by *Euphorbia griffithii* 'Great Dixter'
Opposite bottom: A few years later, the corner intensified with the purple *Salvia nemorosa* 'Ostfriesland' and the bronze foliage of *Crocosmia* 'Solfatere'

best plant for a position and accidentally planting garnet certainly provided impetus towards exploring Criss Canning's use of colour.

Another plant with flowers of a colour that slide into cooler tints is *Potentilla* 'Hamlet'. This has silvery green, pleated leaves in the style of a sophisticated strawberry plant and neat, five-petalled blooms of sumptuous burgundy red, deepening towards the heart of the flower. The similarity to the strawberry is not coincidental. They are both members of the rosaceae family and potentillas are closely enough related to fragrarias to occasionally hybridise.

The warm borders begin to show some colour in spring but don't fill in and flower with any great drama until early December; by Christmas and New Year we have the finest of our crocosmias providing a trumpet blast of bloom. The glorious *Crocosmia* 'Lucifer' has pleated, sword-like leaves, handsome in their own right, and topped by elegantly poised flowers of the warmest possible red. I have used four or five clumps of Lucifer planted a metre or more back from the central path. They rise to 140 centimetres and the clumps are positioned so that the flowers and foliage show above the surrounding planting. Lucifer dominates the garden through to late January.

This photograph, taken at the same time as the photo opposite, demonstrates nicely the importance of repetition planting a smaller length of border. Every week of the season I attempt to have at least one plant at its best, underlining this point. For most of January, *Crocosmia* 'Lucifer' serves the cause.

Longer borders provide the luxury of a progression of themes; for this reason, when making the garden, I was determined to allow much more space along this terrace for the cool colours.

Crocosmia 'Lucifer' was one of several crocosmias brought back in our luggage in 1988. Others were C. 'Emily McKenzie', C. 'Solfatare' and Beth Chatto's form of montbretia. The latter does raise one problem with this family: their propensity to hybridise and seed themselves around. Certainly, montbretia itself is a weed of the Dandenongs, though very handsome brightening up road verges in mid summer with spikes of small yellow and orange flowers. I dead-head most of our crocosmias, especially early flowering varieties, to eliminate seeding, which also serves to reduce the tendency of foliage to flop after flowering. Beth Chatto's form of montbretia blooms a little after Lucifer with starry, brilliant orange blooms to 90 centimetres. Unlike common montbretia, Beth Chatto's montbretia has upward-facing flowers which, along with the intensity of their orange tint, make this plant very much more effective. Hard on its heels we have *Crocosmia* 'Spitfire', again around 90 centimetres, displaying the deepest red flowers of all, very dainty and elegant. Late-flowering crocosmias include C. 'Emily McKenzie', C. 'Solfatare', and the longest in bloom of the group, C. 'Star of the East'. The last produces spidery, soft tangerine flowers, all of 5 centimetres wide and is good for five to six weeks. Emily McKenzie has blooms only a little less substantial, in burnt orange with a chestnut eye zone. *Crocosmia* 'Solfatare' is outstanding for its splendid ochre-yellow blooms and its superb bronze-green leaves. In fact, Solfatere has foliage with presence enough to deserve space for this feature alone. Finally, in one or two other parts of the garden we are using a new import to Australia, C. 'Golden Fleece'. This has soft butter-yellow flowers over pale green leaves to around

Mahogany-orange phygelius, sharp chartreuse euphorbia and warm kniphofia

Physocarpus 'Dart's Gold' with *Crocosmia* 'Solfatare' behind

Our seedling dahlia with *Alstroemeria* 'Red Fury'

60 centimetres. Unlike our other crocosmias, Golden Fleece has blooms of such a gentle yellow it serves nicely as a highlight in a planting of pastel colours.

If the inestimable *Crocosmia* 'Lucifer' sets the mood for Christmas and January, then *Dahlia* 'Bishop of Llandaff' is its counterpart for February and March. This famous plant is perhaps still the best dahlia for deep purple-black, handsomely dissected leaves. I remember seeing it at both Sissinghurst and Hidcote in 1981 and it took years to track it down in Australia. A number of nursery people knew it and several were sure that so-and-so grew it just after the war but no one could lay their hands on it. Eventually, in 1989, the last year we were farming, David Glenn sent me one precious tuber. After just one summer it was retrieved from my Clover Downs garden and packed into our luggage for the trip across the Nullarbor to Melbourne. This was handy because David had lost his only other tuber in the meantime. Every specimen of the bishop we now have, in Australia at least, derives from my one scrappy plant. Yet, I have met scores of people who remember it from their childhoods. The rise and fall and rise of the Bishop is the best example I know of fashion in horticulture. It was introduced to this country in the 1920s and was popular between the wars but the poor old Bishop survived all those years of pastel and white gardens in the 1970s and 80s by the skin of its teeth.

Edibles – ruby chard with bronze fennel

We have several clumps of *Dahlia* 'Bishop of Llandaff' scattered along the front and middle sections of the borders. Most clumps have not been touched in 12 years. The tubers seem curiously slow to multiply. This is also true for some of the newer dark leaved dahlias. In soils sufficiently free draining to leave tubers underground, the bishop requires less maintenance than nearly any plant I know. Certainly, I have never staked my plants; only a modicum of deadheading is required to provide a continual display of bloodiest red blossoms from Christmas to mid-autumn, the flower stems eventually rising to 120 centimetres high. Mind you, any gardener with poorly draining clay soil should be lifting and storing dahlia tubers in late autumn to avoid their rotting in winter.

Several other dark-leafed dahlias are used in these borders, the best of which, I think, is a selection by Keith Hammett in New Zealand, which he named 'Clarion'. *Dahlia* 'Clarion', like the Bishop, has single yellow flowers sharpened by a hint of green. The foliage has broader lobes than the fine, lacy cut of the Bishop, but the leaves are at least as dark: a velvety purplish black, even with an iridescent sheen which adds intensity to the colour. I also grow one clump of *Dahlia* 'David Howard', with coarsely lobed purplish bronze foliage and fully double-orange flowers. Finally, we have a number of other black-leafed dahlias, all seedlings and, I suspect,

Opposite bottom: Warm borders, high summer; *Crocosmia* 'Lucifer' dominating, with kniphofias and *Euphorbia schillingii* in foreground and *Arctotis* 'Blaze' with rich orange daisy flowers and silver-grey foliage scattered along the brick edging

Helenium 'Moerheim Beauty'

Dahlia 'Clarion' and *Phormium* 'Dark Delight'

all hybrids between clarion and the bishop. Seedlings pop up here and there throughout the borders, generally out of a clump of crocosmia or around the back of a buddleia and are often an unsettling yellowish pink. There is one nice plant with butterscotch blooms and we watch and wait. One never knows. We might make our fortune yet with the ultimate black-leafed dahlia.

4 January 2005

A midsummer rainy day. Showers both gentle and heavy all afternoon. The garden filled with water and every plant catching the light as clouds thin between showers. A bamboo on our entrance path has arched over to brush the steps, crocosmias along the border lie collapsed onto the gravel path. From the peony pavilion I watch the beech trees, their outstretched leaves receiving the rain, wind rising towards the end of the shower, shaking the trees and freed water raining out over the mollis azaleas. What are those lines of Basho? "Long rain in May/the sky is a single/sheet of paper/under the clouds."

Remembering this haiku from many years ago and thinking of Merrie-Lea in January – a cloudless sky acid blue, the air white, the entire landscape from mid-distance to horizon shuddering with summer.

＊　　　＊　　　＊

The sky is so close in the Dandenongs, clouds often whipping past just above the hill, very active, ever-changing, propelled at breakneck speed as though by time-lapse photography. Am thinking of an afternoon lying on the lawn watching small clouds breasting the ridge in a southwest wind, moving out over the valley, shrinking minute by minute; reduced to half by the time they were over Silvan and just smears and shreds left over Wandin, the rest of the valley clear. The Merrie-Lea skies seemed infinitely high, clouds, when they appeared, seemed fixtures, unvarying in shape, not obviously moving faster than the sun or the moon; weather systems inched their way across that immensity of space.

One final plant vital to these borders is the canna. We use several, including two variegated selections: *Canna* 'Tropicana' and *Canna* 'Pretoria'. They both produce very similar rich orange flowers but Tropicana has broad purplish leaves striated pink and cream while Pretoria's leaves are mid-green striated with yellow. They are dramatic plants. I prefer the clean effect of *Canna* 'Pretoria', or 'Bengal tiger' as it seems to be becoming known in the Australian nursery trade. I also have a clump of the fabulous old *Canna* 'Wyoming' with broad orange flowers over rich purple and burgundy foliage, and finally an unnamed variety throwing up beefsteak tomato red flowers atop its broad green leaves. We do need green. It is easy to overfill the garden with aubergine and bronze accompanying warmer colours – green is hard to beat, so convenient too. I noticed some seasons back this canna with its lushly handsome mid-green foliage was crucial to moderate the purples and reds and yellows.

Photos from different angles of *Canna* 'Tropicana' with *Physocarpus* 'Dart's Gold', *Dahlia* 'Bishop of Llandaff' and, in the larger photo, *Crocosmia* 'Emily McKenzie'

Green is especially important in the instance of the left-hand border. This border is backed by a hedge made from copper beech, *Fagus sylvatica* 'Purpurea', which gives the deepest aubergine purple of any plant in the garden. Opposite is the dry stone wall retaining the original earthen bank. This is capped with a box hedge, the two totalling a little over 2 metres high. Our beech hedge is clipped to about the same height to balance and it just may be the first formally clipped beech hedge to be planted in Australia. No nurseryman I could find was aware of any beech hedge planted locally. Or could recommend the best spacing between trees. After deciding copper beech should be used for this crucial position I planted them with a degree of nervousness. Would they do what we wanted of them? We used trees Simon Donald had grown 'in ground' with loving care and annual root pruning and were around 120 centimetres high. They went in towards the end of our first winter at 90-centimetre spacings and within two years easily reached 180 centimetres high. Four years on, the hedge was dense and giving the impression it may have been there for decades; 15 years later, it is by far the best hedge in the garden. We clip around Christmas each year. Removing the yellowish-pink growing tips takes the plants back to purplish-black under foliage. This is naturally very soft and prone to burn so we time the clipping for a cool showery period to allow a day or two for leaves to acclimatise to the extra sunshine. (Clipping during a spell of cool weather should be the rule for all hedges in summer, especially in warmer climates.) Over the next month the beech puts out new growth; this is brilliant crimson, all the more startling

Dahlia 'The Bishop of Llandaff' with a wisp of *Miscanthus sinensis* 'Kleine Fontaine'

for the dense black mass of the underlying foliage. In any other part of the garden this late summer effect could be a little over the top, even vulgar some may say. Here however, with a tide of red and orange and yellow lapping against the crimson and black hedge, the combination of colours seems quite relaxed and almost understated.

Our hedge turns bronze as the border softens late March and April. The subdued and tawny effects of these months are in keeping with flashes of autumn colour in other parts of the garden. Beech trees warm to old gold and brown in May, and by June the hedge is in its brown and copper winter dress. Clipped beech holds previous-season leaves through winter giving a nicely sere look. Near the end of May we cut back untidy perennials, leaving only those plants with interesting seed capsules or dry foliage. Fountains of pale-yellow grass remain along with stiff helenium stems; English box domes glitter greenly with the rustling dry leaves in the beech hedge in the first winds of the winter.

After years working with these plants I think perennials flowering in warmer colours are easy in Australian gardens. Heleniums and rudbeckias are robust growers, and dahlias, cannas and miscanthus are much longer flowering and more suited to our climate than the dubious summers of Gloucestershire and Kent. If an Australian gardener wishes to try a serious planting of perennials, perhaps these are the best to begin with.

Lower warm border rolling away from the (still untrimmed) copper beech hedge

Late season effects; glass sculptures by Daniel Jenkins

Imagine a tree on a hillside, a still, cloudless day but the tree twisting and lashing as though in a storm of wind and rain. The image comes from a science fiction story read so long ago I no longer remember the title or author – just the image. The story concerned scientists experimenting with a time machine capable of dislocating a small circle of hillside out of time and wrenching it forwards by 48 hours. A storm forecast for two days ahead is detached from its time and place and is focused around the tree, producing a vertical column of wind and rain around the gyrating tree on an otherwise still day.

The story goes off in other directions but the introductory image is the important thing. The image can be reversed – the tree glowing and still on a dark stormy day and is just as intriguing.

The tree on its hillside shaking in a storm on an otherwise quiet sunny day is something that has haunted me for 30 years. As a concept for an impossible piece of sculpture it is perfect; still, just one of innumerable ideas that may or may not be incorporated into a garden.

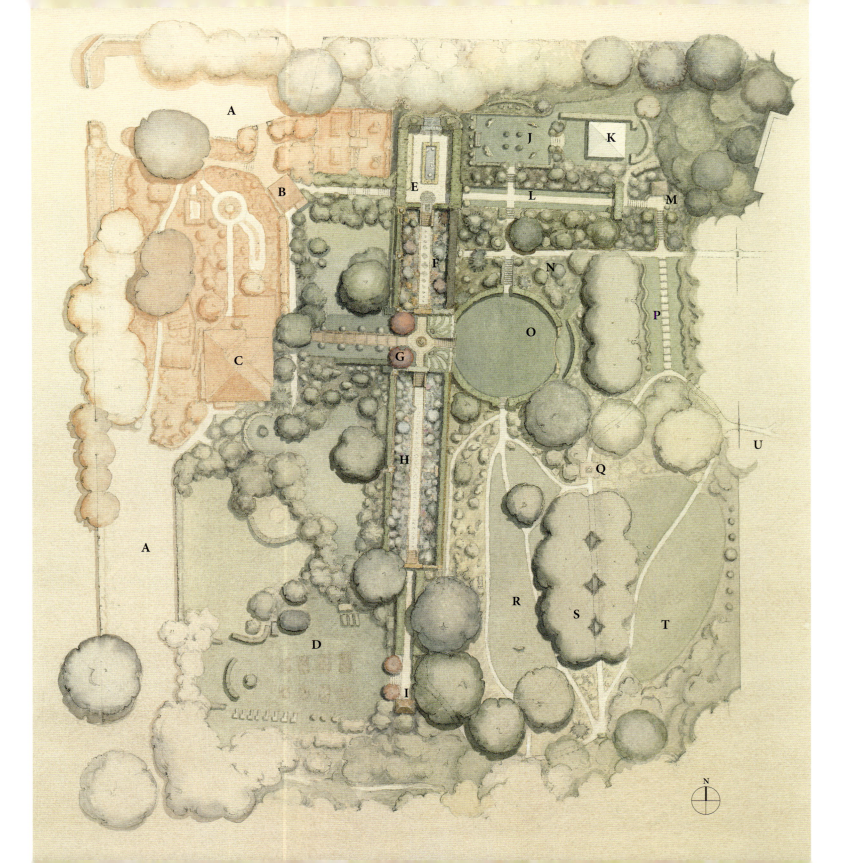

Ross McLeod's watercolour plan of Cloudehill (opposite) gives a good idea of the joys and puzzles in making a garden out of Jim Woolrich's flower farm. Larger trees were already growing of course, the proximity of several of these to the main terrace underlines the care required as we excavated that first autumn. This terrace, including the formal brick steps linking the Maple Court with our restaurant, was all planned on paper weeks beforehand. Other garden compartments were constructed with a good deal more spontaneity. The extent of the eastern end of the Shrub Walk was determined largely by how much surplus soil was available from excavating the Quadrangle and Marquee lawns. The precise line of the bank between the Shrub Walk and the Green Theatre was decided by the importance of maintaining original soil levels around existing trees on the slope. (Burying the roots of an old tree is an excellent way of slowly suffocating it.) Of our excavations though, that for the Green Theatre was the trickiest. The plan illustrates nicely how closely we approached a number of mature trees, drastically changing soil levels; each time thinking very hard. It also illustrates that almost none of the axes in the entire garden intersect at a decent, regulation 90 degrees.

We allowed plenty of time to plan each step. From memory there were five separate projects involving serious excavations, scattered over 11 years. And since this plan (which Ross made in 2007) we again have had earth-moving machinery visiting. The slope above the Summer House has become a Commedia dell'arte *lawn, with cut out figures of Pierrot, Il Capitano, Scapino, Pulcinella and Harlequin floating above curving strips of rough grass that happen to be filled with Jim's bulb plantings of 70 years back. Yet another beech hedge has been planted around this lawn and the ensemble will be worth admiring as this fills in – in another four or five years. Patience is everything in gardening. A new path links the* Commedia dell'arte *lawn with the path immediately below the restaurant. And we have made a generous terrace on the lower side for edibles: our vegetable plot. Lining the new path on the higher side is a Belgian fence made of 'Gorgeous' crabapples. That leaves just the pocket next to our restaurant car park and one or two last ideas to put into place.*

THE MAPLE COURT

*Tantus amor florum et
generandi gloria mellis*

Such is their love of flowers
and the glory which they
find in building honey

Virgil, *Georgics*, 4–205

Nearly every weekend, Jan and Cam would go for their Sunday afternoon drive around the farm. For 25 years this was one of their rituals; Valerie and I kept it up for another 10. Dams were inspected for water levels, windmills checked to be sure they were pumping properly and wheat crops looked over to see how they were performing. Still, those two or three hours were always pretty relaxed. Sunday afternoon drives were meant to be time to enjoy the scenery. To see spring pasture thickening into seed, to enjoy the faint haze of a sea breeze moving over the hills in summer, to watch an autumn sunset burn dust-dry ridges vermilion and purple. This was a time to allow the landscape to steal upon us unawares, to surprise us.

Stock inspections were part of the routine. Lambing ewes were viewed from a distance in June so not to lure mothers away from newly dropped lambs. As lambs grew older, we could approach more closely, then the task was to guess the lambing percentage, the number of ewes that had successfully reared young – always a guide to the quality of pasture and the season in general. Calving cattle were inspected regularly in case cows fell into difficulty. I remember dramatic episodes pulling calves from their mothers and, after appalling battles, the astonishment of the calf hitting the ground, kicking and blathering itself into life and the mother turning to lick it clean and suckle it, the previous few agonising hours already forgotten it seemed. During the 1970s, Cam and Jan built up a handsome herd of Murray Greys, very popular cattle at the time. They came in two colours: mostly rich toffee brown, but my parents particularly favoured the silver version of the breed – silver suffused with creamy dun. It was a grand thing to hear Jan and Cam arriving home from their Sunday drive, bubbling with joy over the new crop of calves, exclaiming over the beauty of them, talking of an entire crèche, perhaps a dozen calves, gambolling away in a corner; another, just born, lying low, instinctively still, concealed to the best of her ability by its mother in stems of long grass. After 12 years the herd was entirely silver and it was noticeable at the district bull sales that silver Murray Grey bulls sold for twice the price of their dowdy brown cousins. Hereford growers were worse, though. Our next-door neighbour culled and culled his herd until only those creatures with the loveliest possible cream and mahogany dappled hides remained. The poor animals became so inbred they suffered appalling rates of eye cancer, something unheard of in other breeds.

It was easy to become attached to farm animals. I found pigs the easiest – they were way too intelligent to treat as ordinary farm stock; they oozed character. When I was a kid Jan and Cam ran a few sows, traditionally, in large pens with sties, small huts, to shade them in hot weather. They were fascinating animals, usually friendly and only ever tricky when with very young piglets. The mothers became extremely protective. One squeak from a newborn and, whatever the cause, even a sibling biting its tail, mum would lurch to her feet, roaring and wild and ready to attack anyone within handy distance. Even now I can feel my feet flying over the earth nosed loose by the animals everywhere in their pens, hurling my feed bucket behind me, a huge old sow, easily four, five times my weight, galloping and chomping and frothing at my heels; my final leap over the high outer mesh fence always seemed effortless, the barbed wire on top cleared with feet to spare. Still, despite the occasional bit of excitement, it was easy to find oneself chatting away to one of the sows, especially the older ones who in quieter moments listened so attentively. Even my fastidious mother became intrigued with the pigs. It occurs as I write she was the one to name them. They all had names, of course. Jan named them for friends, and wives of neighbours: Mrs Pat, Mrs Fred, Mrs David and so on. It was a whimsical thing on her part, I'm sure. She was never deliberately unkind; tact and forbearance infused her very soul. I cannot recall her once saying anything ever to upset any of those fine people, all those friends of hers, at least not to their face. Jan would have been mortified to have been thought rude or unkind.

Over the years I became ever more sensitive to the joys and grumbles of the old sows; every load of porkers going to market was a wrench and on taking over management of Merrie-Lea my first decision was to give up farming pigs.

While designing the garden much thought went into how best to use the big weeping maples. These magnificent trees cried out for appropriate surrounds. Looking for inspiration I came across a woodcut in Jane Brown's *The English Garden in our Time*[2] showing a pavilion enclosed on each side by reflecting curved flights of steps, these leading away from a low paved foreground. This paving was in a black and white

Weeping maple in fresh foliage

The Teinturier grape, *Vitis vinifera* 'Purpurea'

diamond pattern laid to distort perspective. In fact, the garden was imaginary, a conceit. The black and white diamond paving was meant as an eyecatcher. With this surreal and impossible garden in mind, all through that first winter I scribbled designs for a garden around our maples that I hoped could be the focus of Cloudehill.

The quality of the two Yokohama maples made it imperative they play a leading role in our plans. I came to speculate whether the maples might be used to highlight the intersection of important axes. As mentioned previously, the starting point for the design of Cloudehill was to allow room for a substantial terrace across the property. The terrace needed to be long and broad enough to accommodate two sets of double borders and beyond the borders, an entrance garden and a transitional garden. These four would need a generous length each of the terrace, so, as we were taking possession I crawled under banks of blackberry-infested rhododendrons with a tape measure trailing behind, checking how much space might be available. After hours on all fours and not a few scratches I felt confident that, along with these gardens, there should be room for another small garden dedicated to the maples, perhaps near the centre of the terrace. I also scrambled around, exploring towards Jim's house to be sure various shrubs were either weeds or could be shifted. We were already considering converting the cottage into a restaurant and it seemed logical to connect the building with the heart of the garden via formal steps – there seemed just space for a flight of steps beside a row of big *Magnolia soulangianas*. Meanwhile, below the terrace, I was hoping to find space for a 'green theatre'. It was essential that all these parts of the property be free of historic trees, anything of importance too big to move. To my relief this seemed to be the case.

No one could ever say no to my mother. She was generally a champion fundraiser for the Anglican Women's Guild and the op shop, and in the 1970s raised as much money during the Red Cross annual appeal as every one else in the Moora Red Cross put together. Always a few thousand dollars, usually sums well into five figures, pretty impressive for 30 years back. For weeks in autumn she toured Mogumber and Gillingarra visiting every farmer along every lonely track, convincing them to donate a bale of wool oddments or a truckload of seconds wheat to the cause of alleviating world suffering. She came to take little pleasure in her success though, and was particularly rueful over the crusty old farmers out to our west as they handed her a cheque for what was probably a sizable share of their annual income at the end of a cup of tea and a plate of Mills and Wares biscuits. With time, as their plight became dire, she felt everyone should be contributing to their cause and came to loathe the annual appeal.

*   *   *

My mother was the only person to have had a lost dog notice read out on the ABC Radio 'Country Hour' program in all the years I listened to it. As a puppy, Horace went missing one day and Jan duly arranged for the notice to be read by the hapless program manager. I have no idea how long he held out against Jan but suspect it wasn't very long. She never raised her voice, was always sweetness and light, but no one was going to win an argument against her. Horace turned up a few days later dragging a dislocated hind leg. He was a lovely dog and brilliant sheep worker but never any good at jumping after that.

Thirty metres below and almost parallel to the proposed terrace grew a lovely row of European beech, which could conveniently serve as a screen behind the intended theatre. There were eight trees in total, three copper beech intermingled with five greens, making a tapestry effect on the grand scale. Uniformly young, vigorous, approaching two-thirds of their mature height, they were likely planted the winter after the 1962 bushfires. To the right was a magnificent multiple-stemmed copper beech. Huge, and appearing to be of the same vintage as the big tricolours and fernleaf, it would have been part of the collection imported from Fred Street in 1928. The tree seemed to correspond to *Fagus sylvatica* 'Riversii'. The riversii beech was distributed by the famous William Rivers Nursery operating in the suburbs of London in the early years of Queen Victoria's reign. Of the many plants William Rivers grew, I suspect this one magnificent form of the copper beech is what he is mainly remembered for. To the left of the theatre site, the natural left-to-right slope contributed a nice hint of enclosure. All seemed very propitious.

12 January 2005

A memory from a spring day in the early 1980s, of moving a flock of sheep out from the yards into the powder bark paddock; a magpie was chasing a crow, the slow-moving crow cawing in distress attracting two more crows to its rescue. They buffeted the lone magpie, which in turn cried in alarm attracting, seconds later, two more magpies swooping to its rescue. It was one on one now and the crows were at a severe disadvantage and clearly fearful; could they outlast their ferocious attackers? The fast-moving magpies' attack demanded expenditure of huge levels of energy; they could maintain this for less than a minute, then the advantage was back to the crows and their more leisurely, energy-saving flight. But could the crows survive that time without injury, loss of an eye or broken wing, before the pendulum swung their way? It is the only time I have ever seen crows and magpies in a no-holds-barred battle.

A wedgetail eagle was circling this morning, reminding me of an afternoon back when we were making the garden. We were relaxing at the end of an exhausting day building dry stone walls. Several of us were lying back, talking, beers in hand with the sun slipping below the ridge to our west. A dot circled high above us, came closer and resolved itself into an eagle. Minutes later and much closer, we could all see it was a wedgetail and as it wheeled closer and closer we began to wonder why it was zeroing

The parterres, taken shortly after their early December clip

in on us. The penny dropped. I sprinted to our chook house, no bantams to be seen and, opening the door, there were the hens all huddling nervously and two hours earlier than usual onto their nighttime roosts. The pint-sized cockerel, however, stood guard at the hatch, just a sliver of his cocked head protruding through into the open and one beady eye scanning the heavens; now the eagle was brushing through the mountain ash, wings spanning the garden, darking the sky.

After allowing room for four compartments along the main terrace there remained some 12 or 15 metres spare for the maple court; with the terrace around 13 metres wide, the maple court could be made square. Central paths bisecting the square, north–south and east–west, would require nearly 2 metres each, leaving 5.5- by 5.5- metre beds in each corner. In 1992 our maples were around 3.5 to 4 metres in diameter. In my sketches they seemed to sit happily in the two upper beds and, after moving, our trees looked demure in their new positions, with plenty of space around them. However, out in the sunlight and away from root competition the maples have doubled in volume and at least quadrupled the surface area of their canopies. Not bad for 80-year-old trees. And 15 years later the old maples are enthusiastically overflowing their carefully constructed raised beds.

The weeping maples are notable not only for their size but also their branch structure. Both are grafted onto 60-centimetre standards and their lower branches writhe and

Above, left to right: Andrew MacGregor playing shakuhachi, his Japanese bamboo flute. Andrew helped instigate twilight concerts staged in the theatre every summer in the late 1990s and early 2000s. The last year or two has been devoted to *en plein air* Shakespeare; Japanese lantern by Ted Secombe; winter view

Opposite: The parterres; 'firebox pot' by Robert Barron

loop back over themselves, in fact have formed a series of horse collars. Beeches ingraft, develop horse collars occasionally and several on Cloudehill have done so. Figs do this frequently, but with maples this phenomenon is rare. Japanese weeping maples are also famous for arguably the finest foliage to be found on any garden shrub. The exquisitely feathery leaves of the atropurpureum form are bright purple-red as they expand, emerging early in September and filling out over some two weeks. The trees require a bit of warmth and sunshine to unfurl their leaves fully. A burst of cold weather can bring things to a halt and if low temperatures persist for more than a few days, maples become prone to aphid attack. Aphids can do serious damage, as we discovered in 1994, a year our trees looked very thin all summer. We watch for aphids now and spray at the first opportunity. The flower of the Japanese maple is relatively insignificant, certainly in the dissected forms. One of the upright forms, *Acer palmatum* 'Bloodgood', has crimson seed capsules that are almost ornamental, but the flowering of weeping maples generally only serves to disrupt the luxuriant sleekness of their canopies. Through spring and early summer the leaves of our atropurpureums sink into ever-deeper tints of mahogany-purple and late summer soften to bronze-green. During April the trees flush to a shadowy purplish-green and around the third week of April they change almost overnight to gleaming coppery orange, flushed on the sunnier side with crimson. Autumn colour is good for six to 10 days and is pretty reliable. However, I sometimes wonder if our maples are not best in winter – their bare branches writhe with such eccentric aplomb, especially good when dusted with snow.

Ploughing the windmill paddock one late autumn in the mid 1980s; the paddock grown to sweet lupins the previous year, lupin stubble raked into a windrow in late summer, stretching in a spiral kilometres long. Banks of crumpled dry foliage lay heaped every 10 metres as one walked from the side of the paddock to the centre, the windrow perhaps half a metre high by a metre wide. For the plough to do its job properly the earth needed to be bare – it did not take much straw to clog machinery so a clean stubble burn was essential and also helped to reduce insect pest populations. Outer stretches of the windrow had been burnt days before but rain during the burn meant that most of the lupin stubble towards the centre remained.

I commenced ploughing in the late afternoon, expecting to get a few hours in before running up against unburnt windrow and by eight in the evening, having been forced to stop and unclog the plough several times, was thinking to return the next day to complete the burning. However, with a box of matches from the tool box and rake from the back of the ute, it seemed worthwhile experimenting. I was pleasantly surprised to find, despite the evening's dew, the day's sunshine had dried the remaining windrows sufficiently to enable the stubble to burn. Once alight, it was easy to catch some of the ignited stubble on the rake, walk to the next windrow, shake burning fragments to ignite it and carry on. By zigzagging over the paddock I eventually had the spiral of lupin stubble burning in hundreds of places. Each section of stubble burnt slowly around the paddock, like a wick, flames rising to a metre high.

At first the light was only sufficient to illuminate occasional gum trees standing between the windrows but with more fire even seams of rock high up on the hill sides were caught in the glow. Soon 60 acres of softly crackling bonfires crept along the windrows and the entire night scene was glinting coppery persimmon. Trees close to the flames were made seemingly transparent, soft light caught within their canopies and they turned to giant lanterns. For a time the entire amphitheatre of circling hillside was picked out in coppery light, ridgelines etched, colourless but clear, against the black night sky.

I stood awhile, watching: a curious mood, very still, flames rising bolt upright. Paddocks were frequently burnt in preparation for a new crop; cool grass fires and wheat stubble fires were part of the autumn routine. Those burns were always daytime affairs; this was different. These were like campfires of a bivouac, evenly spaced, almost ceremonial; propitiatory perhaps, with the embracing hills sloping suddenly towards the stars. The line came to mind, 'Erxias, where is this useless army gathering to go?'

I climbed into the tractor cab, hit the ignition and drove, following the edge of broken earth. The plough threw up dusty ash every time its discs passed over a burnt windrow and smouldering ash heaps fountained with rusty sparks high into the night as the machinery crashed through. The shattered fiery necklace retreated towards the paddock's centre, flames faded into night, individual fires shrinking to glowing spaghetti tangles of

Conifers on the slope above the weeping maples.
Left: *Cupressus cashmeriana* on the left,
Chamaecyparis nootkatensis 'Pendula' in the centre
and *Abies lasiocarpa* 'Compacta' on the right

Right: *Abies concolor* 'Compacta' to the right of the
Abies lasiocarpa 'Compacta' with the cool borders
below

disintegrating lupin straw. And the fires died away, leaving the familiar swinging beams of tractor head lights, the diesel motor's hypnotic thrumming roar and the metallic scream of plough discs tearing the pebbly soil through the remainder of the night.

While still constructing this part of the garden I began to feel the maple court was much too bland, certainly lacking the intrigue of that original woodcut. Some architecture seemed called for and it occurred to me that one way to emphasise the axis along our terrace might be to build archways over the entrance and exit of the maple court along the central path. I was thinking along these lines while leafing through a book on a particularly famous English garden and spotted the design for my archway. Having gone to some trouble to not copy structural elements from other gardens, I'm not keen to own up to which famous English garden this might happen to be. It is a particularly well-known garden with many high walls and a few low walls, one of which happens to have an archway built into it. I simply counted bricks and sketched it out and over several days Simon and Richard built two such structures. We took great care to line the archways up along the main path, as they serve to focus the eye to the centre of the axis and also help frame a series of receding views. It is amazing how much nonsense one can get away with when garden making. It is difficult to carve a straight bank with an unwieldy drot to provide backing for a dry stone wall. And string lines somehow are moved and mistakes are made and, truth be told, there are precious few right angles anywhere in Cloudehill. It is good to have everything line up along central paths though.

The design of the parterres in the two beds below the weeping maples was originally governed by their unusual shape. The centre of the maple court was paved to make a small square with its centre coinciding with the intersection point of the main axis and the cross axis from Jim's house to the theatre, but the square revolved 45 degrees. The four surrounding beds thus each had their corner closest to the centre snipped off. As mentioned, the upper beds were reserved for the two big weeping maples; the lower beds I initially planted to geometric box parterres, each with three domes rising out of an arrangement of triangles. As it grew, the effect seemed a bit pedestrian. More so some five years on when we installed ornamental railings by Kim Kennedy to each side of the brick arches. Kim's handsome railings made the somewhat traditional parterres look irredeemably twee, so we dug up the nicely grown box and sold it. One thing about a nursery beside the garden is that disposing of mistakes is so easy, and sometimes profitable.

Digging out our parterres did give me time to think how best to redesign the area. The loose, asymmetrical growth of the maples suggested a simple organic treatment. Again, a photograph from a book provided inspiration[3]. Russell Page, a landscape architect of the years after World War Two, designed a garden in northern Italy featuring twin parterres with triangles of santolina emerging from platforms of neatly clipped English box. The fine, silvery grey santolina foliage displayed a little

Parterres, with a glimpse of the green theatre

proud of the deep green box was a brilliant juxtaposition on his part, but my experience with santolina suggested this combination could only be good in the Dandenongs for a brief time around mid-summer. For us, santolina needs a radical chop each winter to avoid soft spring growth eventually flopping apart. After clipping close to the ground, cotton lavender grows into tight mounds and flowers mid-summer, generally with strong yellow blooms contrasting raucously with its leaves. To have a clean 'table top' of silvery, unflowering foliage sitting 2 centimetres above surrounding box for as much of the season as possible seemed like a good deal of work. However, ferreting around a few of the many growing nurseries in Monbulk and Silvan I discovered a dwarf pittosporum: *Pittosporum tenuifolium* 'Argenteum Nana'. This is very compact and produces rounded canopies of tiny, silvery green leaves that flush rust-pink in winter, an effect more handsome than santolina and much more persistent. I had never seen it grown as a hedge, let alone a component of a parterre, but pittosporums are such forgiving creatures I thought it worth the risk. Then there was the matter of a design. Over several weeks a sketch pad or two were used up until I settled on a relatively simple flowing pattern to complement the old maples. The box and pittosporum were ordered in and the new design planted late in the spring of 1997.

Railings covered with the giant Japanese grapevine, *Vitis coignetiae*, intermingled with the Teinturier grape, *Vitis vinifera* 'Purpurea'

Over the seasons I have experimented with various plants under the two maples; for instance, the slowly spreading ground cover *Viola cornuta*, both the elegant mauve flowering species and its albino form. And woolly thyme, *Thymus lanuginosus*, tumbling over the low stone walls retaining the maple beds. This softens the walls somewhat, the tiny grey green twigs trailing airily over the sharp volcanic stone. Unfortunately, the walls happen to be sitting height and the woolly thyme appears so soft and springy and so inviting it is forever being crushed to nothingness by bulky posteriors.

I have a collection of hostas under the maples and these, on the whole, seem to enjoy the heavy shade. Glaucous blue-leaved varieties such as *Hosta* 'Big Daddy' and *H.* 'Blue Wedgewood' are well-suited to their surrounds, the bronze reds of the overhanging maple foliage, as are hostas with leaves variegated sea-green and chartreuse such as *H.* 'June'. I am persevering with *Hosta* 'Zounds' despite its brilliant chartreuse-yellow leaves clashing blatantly – it is just too mouth watering. One or two rich green hostas look splendid, likewise a couple of creamy white variegated varieties tucked into very shady spots. The winter before last I thought, so far so good, let's pop in some variegated Solomon's Seal. A mistake, I'm afraid, as

Erythronium californicum 'White Beauty'

it has surprised me with its vigour, shooting off into surrounding hostas. It is taller than I imagined and is turning the entire planting into a muddle. So, a job for next spring – retrieve *Polygonatum falcatum* 'Variegatum' from under the maples and try under the *Enkianthus campanulatus* shading the summer house at the end of the terrace.

Left to right: *Astrantia major, Hosta* 'Hadspen Blue', *Hosta* 'Striptease', *Hosta* 'June' and *Viola cornuta*

SOUTH PERTH

His breathing raw with morphine, and
My father's hand, restless, searching,
Unresponsive to my touch.

Outside, above the river, there are so many birds.
The air is filled with bird call, the sound of city
Traffic smothered under a
Tremendous wave of birdsong.
Mewling seagulls float
Into the wind, swallows
Flick past our window and shrill
Rosellas barrel belly sideways between the
Apartment towers. It's odd how
Many of these are the birds of my father's childhood,
South Australia – eighty years ago, and
Still the same carolling of magpies through the mallee scrub
On the banks of the slow brown Murray.
Beyond our balcony,
A great flight of
Tremulously shrieking
Cockatoos are
Wheeling lazily
Around
The gum trees.
And in the distance, the
Dark, aching,
Call of
A single crow.

Beside the river I can see a
Young woman walking two border collies,
Children playing and the sea breeze ruffling the water.
A glorious and gloriously mild afternoon after
Days of mid-summer heat.
Beyond the water, the
Inconstant city skyline, and
To the right, those weathered hills stretching north, past
The horizon, to bleached and stubbled wheat fields.

My father's hand resting now in my hand

And still the birds call, and
Still they are calling.
5PM

*   *   *

After an illness of some four months Cam died at this time in his home in South Perth. I was fortunate enough to have been with him for the previous few days and to have enjoyed a relaxed chat with him as late as that Wednesday evening. He collapsed the following morning and died much more quickly than we were told he might. My sister Jenny, my daughter Alys and I were with him that final afternoon.

Around three o'clock that Saturday afternoon we were visited by a home-care nurse, a quietly spoken young man. Because he was on a high dose of morphine, in those last hours, my father needed to be moved regularly to prevent bedsores. The nurse explained that as Cam was showing signs of terminal restlessness there was a chance of his passing away as we helped change his position. However, all went well and at the end of it the nurse asked Cam if he felt any pain. My father shook his head vigorously to indicate no; he had been beyond speaking to us all day.

Those moments following were extraordinary in many ways. Cam's third-floor apartment overlooked 'Perth Water' on the Swan River estuary. Perth Water is more like a substantial lake than a stretch of river at this part of its journey and served to reflect the office towers of the city's business district on the far side of the water. Away to the east, the Darling Escarpment formed the horizon, running due south, and north to where it eventually becomes the western face of the Mogumber hills; the district's grain harvest would have been completed some weeks earlier.

The view over the river was tantalisingly peaceful, yet for some 20 minutes the space down to the water was cacophonous with birds. For all of the following week, around five o'clock, many hundreds of white cockatoos flocked past the apartment's balcony and settled in nearby sugar gums. Every time, the cockatoos' raucous arrival caused the many other birds living beside the river to respond with their own territorial calling. Back in Melbourne, when I showed Valerie the lines above, she said that the intensity of birdsong made it difficult to hear me as I spoke to her on the phone both a little before and a few minutes after Cam died.

The lines were mostly composed that evening, partly during following days, and I read them to those attending Cam's funeral on Thursday the tenth. The following poem, which was originally included in my mother's funeral in 1997, was then read to complete the service.

*   *   *

So What is Love

So what is love? If thou would'st know.
The heart alone can tell.
Two minds with but a single thought,
Two hearts that beat as one.

And whence comes love? Like morning bright.
Love comes without day's call
And how dies love? A spirit bright,
Love never dies at all.

(Anonymous)

THE COOL BORDERS

Climbed down from the tractor cab having finished ploughing our 180-acre central east paddock. Two am and this the last night of nearly three weeks of night-shift ploughing, 14 to 15 hour shifts, seven nights a week. Very still, silent and cool after the warmth of the tractor cab. A moonless night, the entire Milky Way brilliant against an anthracite sky. A loud clicking was emanating from the tractor's diesel motor as it cooled and the air filled with the not unpleasant smells of hot diesel and ploughed earth. As I stood, I noticed a layer of cooler air gliding down the slope towards me, so shallow it reached only to my knees. The air around my bare thighs and arms and face felt absolutely still.

There was no vehicle, so that meant a 4-kilometre walk back to the house and some rest. It was too dark to cut across paddocks and thus my route around the farm tracks formed three quarters of a large circle. Walking carefully in the starlight, feet following vehicle ruts, I could hear a mopoke from somewhere near the circle's centre, calling steadily all the way home.

Gardeners discovering herbaceous perennials almost invariably seize on those flowering in pastel colours. I remember first reading Anne Scott-James' *Sissinghurst*[4] while visiting Christchurch, New Zealand, in 1975. The book was in the window display of a little bookshop a street or so back from the cathedral square and seeing it reminded me of the pleasure reading Harold Nicholson's diaries years earlier.

Clockwise from top left: Cool borders, early October; 'Fern Goddess' by Graham Foote; *Parthenocissus tricuspidata* 'Veitchii' over the archway

Horse chestnut in flower beside the Avon River, Christchurch, New Zealand

I bought a copy of Scott-James' book and leafed through it while sitting beside the Avon River, the stream forming the perimeter to the city's botanic gardens. Late spring and the gardens were vivid with colour that day, beyond anything ever to be seen in WA and sunlight on the stream might have inspired an idyll by Elgar, long emerald waterweeds swaying with the water's flow. Scott-James wrote of Vita Sackville-West using cool colours to accentuate the mood between Sissinghurst's mulberry brick Tudor buildings – a planting in every tint of cerise and purple described planted below one ancient wall, an astonishing thought. Then I was poring over poor-quality yet intriguing photos of the rose garden with smoky iris beside crimson gallica roses and amethyst ornamental onions lining a path. And then a garden, entirely white, inspired by owls in moonlight with snow on the ground, seemed positively otherworldly. The following days I was exploring footpaths over the Cashmere Hills, the sudden range of hills that divide Christchurch from its harbour at Lyttleton. From their slopes, one overlooks the city and the Canterbury Plains. Beyond the level plains, the vertical wall of the Southern Alps formed the entire western horizon, their ragged peaks still white with October snow. At my feet, little gardens dug into the slopes of the Cashmere Hills brimmed with spring perennials and in my imagination I arranged them into the colour designs Anne Scott-James wrote of. My mind's eye was full of creamy pinks and lavenders and lemons threaded with trickles of silver. A taste for the sunset colours of Vita Sackville-West's cottage garden was to come later.

As with the warm borders, our cool borders, though predominantly herbaceous, are really mixed borders. Shrubs and heavily pruned trees provide out of season substance to herbaceous plantings. Among shrubs used are several buddleias. B. 'Pink Delight', for instance, with dense, silvery grey foliage and rich lilac-pink flowers, and B. 'Lochinch', its leaves pewter silver and powdery blue flowers. These are the best of our buddleias and for foliage, Lochinch is perhaps the finer of the two.

Silver is vital in these borders. There is a much wider range of colour used here than among the warm perennials; also the cool borders are close to twice the length of the warm borders. As there is not so much repetition in the planting, silver foliage is crucial to unifying the diverse colours and textures of the 300 square metres' worth of beds. An effective plant deployed to this end is the weeping silver pear, *Pyrus salicifolia* 'Pendula'. A small tree with very narrow leaves for a pear, its foliage is coated in short white hairs that catch sunlight and give an intensely silvery appearance from late spring to late summer. Although called weeping, the growth is wayward to the point of eccentricity, with twigs shooting off in every odd direction. In fact, a specimen of this pear allowed to grow naturally can look thoroughly awkward in winter. For this reason, and also to keep our two trees within bounds, we prune hard in June, to within a bud or two of the previous cut and this way keep them to a little over 3 by 2 metres.

Another large shrub we use here is the purple-leaf hazel, *Corylus maxima* 'Purpurea'. This seems to grow more slowly than other hazels, yet can achieve 5 by 5 metres. It grows with the typically stooling habit of the hazel family, the hamamelidaceae. These are all superb plants for the garden, generally small and medium-sized shrubs. They include witch hazels, or hamamelis, the true hazels, or corylus, and the corylopsis and fothergillas, all handy shrubs for coolish gardens. Just when we think we have this family figured out we come to parrotias and liquidambers, trees definitely, able to grow 30 and 50 metres high. Both the latter, the sweetgum in particular, tolerate lots of heat and a degree of drought. Our purple-leafed hazel is only 5 by 4 metres after about eight years, its many suckering stems clothed in large round corrugated leaves tinted rich coppery purple. Its purple is nicely flushed deep green when in fresh growth and the result is excellent in a nicely understated kind of way. I have it towards the end of the lower border, about half way back. The purple hazel helps to conceal a last flurry of planting, leaving visitors, wandering past, puzzling what may be around the corner.

Buddleia 'Lochinch'

Weeping pear and Alstroemeria

Lake Camm

18 February 2005

My older sister Jenny was saying a few days back that, as a child, she was occasionally sent by our mother to stay at our grandparents' Lake Camm farm. She remembers the wind in the sheoaks growing around the big rock up beyond the garden wall. Although she was little, perhaps seven or eight, sometimes she walked over to our Uncle Hector's house a mile and more away to the west to play with our cousin Wendy. Jenny remembers two or three times she and Wendy walked on further, through a sheoak forest and down to the shores of the big salt lake that formed the western edge of the farm. In summer, the lake bed dry, they walked way out over the salt. On turning back, the shoreline and the farm beyond seemed a faint rippling smudge floating high above the crisp salt floor of the lake.

Valerie and I brought several artemisias back from England in 1988. I knew these Mediterranean plants would probably grow well on the farm and most also possess attractive silvery perfumed foliage. *Artemisia* 'Lambrook Silver', a selection, or perhaps

Left: A bank of *Viburnum plicatum* 'Newzam' and *Buddleia* 'Pink Delight' in fresh spring growth
Above: *Rosa moyesii* 'Highdownensis'; *Berberis thunbergii* 'Rose Glow'; *Calamagrostis x acutiflora* 'Overdam'

a hybrid, of *A. absinthium*, has the most extraordinary silvery blue aromatic leaves. Unfortunately, it has a tendency to run up to an untidy flower in mid-summer. If lambrook silver is cut back before Christmas the foliage comes again and is effective for the remainder of summer, then dies away. With leaves good for 12 months, the most useful of the wormwoods released from quarantine in 1988 is *Artemisia* 'Powis Castle'. This gives a low mound of excellent silvery grey, filigree foliage, perhaps 50 by 100 centimetres. Powis Castle is a non-flowering selection of *Artemisia arborescens*. I remember arborescens itself growing by the road to Moora, WA. That specimen cheerfully dealt with seven months of summer drought and fierce root competition from surrounding salmon gums. It was also growing 2 metres high, flowering very untidily for most of summer and flopping open with easterly winds. The dense, windproof foliage of Powis Castle is much superior. Both Powis Castle and Lambrook Silver are very reliable and fast-growing plants, useful especially when first planting a border. I used many specimens of both as we established the cool borders and even now half a dozen of each remains.

Other wormwoods include *Artemisia alba* 'Canescens', with silvery tangled, thread-like foliage reaching around 30 centimetres and *Artemisia ludoviciana* 'Valerie Finnis', forming a suckering thicket of 30-centimetre-high stems with handsomely jagged

silvery leaves. Finally, we try to keep one or two mounds of *Artemisia pedemontana*. This must be placed at the front of a planting as it grows only 2 or 3 centimetres high by 30 centimetres across. Obviously, it needs care in positioning to avoid being overwhelmed by neighbours. Pedamontana deserves this for the ethereal beauty of silken, thread-like foliage. The word 'pedemontana' has something of a ring to it. The Latin means 'foot of the mountain' and refers to those parts of central Europe where this artemisia originates, in other words, places with cool sunshine, always difficult to find in Australia, even in the Dandenongs. *A. pedemontana* is tricky; it is herbaceous, its low framework of stems die in the autumn and stiffen, I suppose, to hold a blanket of insulating snow over its tightly curled leaf buds, waiting tucked against the earth for the coming spring.

Shasta daisy, *Echinops* 'Veitch's Blue'

A number of ground-hugging silvery plants are planted to spill over the brick edging and onto our central path. These include *Dianthus* 'Hidcote', with a soft cushion of glaucous foliage and deep crimson flowers in late spring, and *Tanacetum ptarmiciflorum* (syn. *Pyrethrum ptarmiciflorum*) with exquisitely intricate and softly tactile leaves described dutifully in the *Royal Horticultural Society A–Z Encyclopedia of Garden Plants*: 'elliptic to oblong-ovate, 2- or 3-pinnatisect, silver-hairy basal and stem leaves, to 10cm (4in) long, have 8–22 linear-elliptic, scalloped segments'.

Another excellent spilling plant is the newish *Geranium* 'Silver Cloak'. This has very pretty, deeply cut greenish-silver geranium-style leaves and by early summer it throws a glittering sheet of ground-hugging foliage half way across our path, profusely studded with small, lilac-pink flowers. I am also using an arctotis with passable, pale greyish foliage and daisy flowers of an indeterminate pink, which flush alarmingly to yellow in cooler weather. There must be something better. Another job: find a good arctotis for edging of the cool borders.

A further family of plants dependable for edging are the stachys, or lamb's ears. They have prostrate stems rooting from nodes as they go with a blanket of pale grey-green lamb's ears leaves covered in short white hairs. This latter characteristic is nearly always a sign of drought tolerance and, in the instance of the stachys, the tougher the going the happier they seem. We use the common *Stachys byzantina* (syn. *S. lanata* and *S. olympica*) but have gradually replaced it with a non-flowering form, *S.* 'Big Ears', with more handsome, felty greyish leaves. The flowers of byzantina are generally a nuisance – scrappy purplish-pink affairs protruding from the 30- to 40-centimetre-high woolly spikes. Perhaps this is unfair. On first appearance I guess they are presentable, but the flowers quickly discolour. *Stachys* 'Big Ears' has larger leaves than *S. byzantina*, more green-grey in colour and producing few, if any, flower

Opposite top: *Berberis thunbergii* 'Helmond Pillar' and *Phlomis russeliana*
Opposite bottom: Collection of pots from Crete and Southern France, arranged around a bench; in the foreground, *Salvia* 'Caradonna' with a dwarf red gladioli to the right

Stipa gigantea in early summer. To its left, *Calamagrostis acutiflora* 'Overdam'; in the foreground *Salvia* 'Caradonna' with deep purple-red narrow spires and *Salvia microphylla* 'Heatwave Blast' tucked behind to the right.

spikes. Another stachys handily sends up flower spikes but no flowers. This is the very curious and reasonably handsome *Stachys b.* 'Cotton Boll' with flowers modified into congested cotton bud affairs. The flower spikes are good for an extended period, I suppose because the actual flowers are never fertilised. We also grow a close relative, *Stachys thirkei*, which is like a very neat dwarf version of *Stachys byzantina*, in fact, both its flowers and foliage are less than half size. Finally, planted under a pollarded golden catalpa in another part of the garden altogether, we have the yellow-leafed form of common lamb's ear: *Stachys byzantina* 'Primrose Heron', which is rather fun and very good for its matte-lime effect, and best in shade.

Several taller silvery plants are planted into the second rank of these borders. For instance, a few specimens of *Santolina* 'E.A. Bowles', with excellent sea-green silvery foliage and cool lemon-tinted flowers. Generally, santolinas form mounds of harsh greyish white foliage and smother themselves with jarring, yolk-yellow flowers so we were very pleased to find and squeeze Mr Bowles' santolina into our boxes in 1988. Valerie and I also collected *Achillea* 'Moonshine', a glorious hybrid from Bressingham nursery made by Alan Bloom between *A. clypeolata* and another lovely species: *A.* 'Taygetea'. Taygetea produces an abundance of small, horizontal plates, corymbs, of lemon flowers over pale sea-green filigree leaves which, curiously, is exactly the same combination of colour, both flower and foliage, as *Santolina* 'E.A. Bowles'. *Achillea* 'Moonshine' throws up slightly larger plates of flowers than taygetea, which, again, are a creamy lemon. However, Moonshine also produces fabulous masses of heavily filigreed, intensely silver foliage. *Achillea* 'Terracotta' has good green-grey foliage and flowers of terracotta orange and yellow. Terracotta is a plant we use in both the warm and cool borders. Finally, we grow *Achillea* 'Credo', with silvery green leaves and creamy lemon flowers produced on stems 80 and 90 centimetres tall, a useful plant for a mid-border position. All of this group enjoy an Australian summer.

About half way along on the lower side of these borders, I have one specimen of *Melianthus major*, planted with trepidation as the thought that comes to mind is straggly specimens commandeering entire vacant building blocks through suburban Perth. Each plant could reach quite a few metres by quite a few metres in those dry sandy soils with their underlying high water table. But its boldly toothed pinnate leaves are always good; their colour ranging from silvery sea-green to pale grey-blue, depending on the soil and the season. In summer, it produces spikes of dusky crimson flowers, which we happily sacrifice in the cause of restraining this plant. By chopping it hard in winter, we keep our specimen to 1.5 by 1 metre and I would class it as close to the best plant to carry the silvery blue theme through the garden.

Artemisia lactiflora 'Guizhou' and *Veronica spicata* 'Icicle'

Phlomis tuberosa and *Achillea* 'Moonshine'

23 February 2005

My Uncle Hec and Aunty Eid's house was stacked with books, often first editions, frequently autographed, many with plays of the 1930s, 40s and 50s, and English magazines full of theatre reviews such as John O' London's Weekly*. Uncle Hec also collected bird books; Vincent Serventy, the famous naturalist of those years would come to stay and he and uncle would go bird watching down on the lake. A white piano stood pride of place in the lounge; apart from regular practice, Uncle Hec used this for composing keyboard pieces. The surrounding garden was extraordinary – trees and shrubs and roses and green grassy walks, with a sundial perhaps, maybe a birdbath; I really cannot remember at all for sure now. I have the faintest of memories of a grand garden in the midst of those big dry paddocks and the huge salt lake just down the slope. I wonder now how on earth he watered it, in that country, with the irrigation gear of the 1950s. Jenny tells me the water was all carted by truck from a communal catchment tank installed by farmers next to one of the big rocks common to the district. Concrete walls constructed around the perimeter of the rock funnelled water into huge storage tanks. This supply was used by farmers for watering stock and household purposes, not really for gardens. Uncle Hec had nothing else for his plants, and according to Jenny, he irritated his brothers beyond telling by taking time off every day or two, even during harvest, to carry water for the garden.*

In the early 1960s a crop duster spraying nearby wheat accidentally poisoned Uncle Hec's garden and within days everything was dead. My uncle immediately left his garden, walked away from his house, sold his farm, and left Lake Camm and everything else in his life behind.

My Aunty Margaret tells me Uncle Hec, as a young child walking along a street, stopped by a house to listen to piano playing. The owner noticed him sitting on a stump in her front garden and invited him in, suggesting he might like to try for himself. Apparently,

My uncle's lounge room, in spring 2007, a day of strong wind with faint drizzle occasionally resting on the grass, not nearly enough to actually moisten the soil; exasperating weather in a dry season. The house was never lived in again.

within minutes of sitting at the piano, he seemed to be playing with the skill of many months if not years of practice. I remember he was never without gloves to protect his hands while doing farm chores – much to the amusement of neighbours.

A water collection wall in the Lakes District

We use a fair number of ornamental grasses in the cool borders. Most are at their peak in late summer but two or three flower earlier; perhaps the earliest and best of these is *Stipa gigantea*. Three specimens of this grass are scattered strategically through the borders. Its insignificant clumps of 40-centimetre-high foliage produce tall, wiry stems radiating out 150 to 200 centimetres in November, topped with huge coppery bronze, wild oat-type flowers. The effect is gauzy, ethereal and dramatic, especially with arching stems swaying in the wind. The plants are showy for a long time. Seed heads slowly turn from coppery yellow to pale straw in late summer. They remain interesting throughout, especially as the borders build with late-season perennials. In winter, stems break and need to be snipped off. There are a couple of points to keep in mind when growing this plant. Unlike most ornamental grasses, it is evergreen. If leaves are cut back in winter the flowers will be lost. When foliage becomes untidy the solution is to don a leather glove and rake through the leaves with one's fingers to remove dead material. Also, keep in mind that the stems splay out nearly 2 metres sideways. *Stipa gigantea* should be planted back from a path by this distance so passersby do not snap flowers.

The giant oat is an extraordinarily handsome plant and deserves thought in placing. The great thing about its gauzy 'see-through' effect is that other plants can be grown through it. We have ours with pale straw stems floating above crimson sedums, rich pink asters and mauve verbenas, all plants with solid chunks of colour in autumn and foliage low enough they can be planted immediately around the base of the grass without casting shade. Finally, this oat is curiously difficult to propagate. Startlingly difficult, keeping in mind it looks a bit like every wheat farmer's nightmare. Having too much experience for my own good spraying unpleasant chemicals to eliminate annual wild oats from cereal crops, I was highly suspicious on first seeing *Stipa gigantea*. However seed is difficult to germinate and accidental seedlings rare, and the giant oat usually responds to division by falling on its face and dying.

We grow several mid-season, smaller grasses along the central path. *Achnatherum calamagrostis* produces silky beige flowers arching out from under our *Corylus maxima* 'Purpurea' to some 50 centimetres. The flower heads of this outstanding plant are persistent for the bulk of the summer. We also have two species of pennisetum. The first of these, *Pennisetum orientale*, produces lovely wands of dusky opalescent pink flowers to 45 centimetres from Christmas to early autumn. And by mid-summer,

Clockwise from top left: *Pennisetum orientale*, *Phlox paniculata* hybrid to the centre and *Dahlia* 'Sophia' behind; *Pennisetum orientale* in the foreground, Lepechinia sp. behind with purple-pink salvia-like flowers and see-through spikes of the purple *Verbena bonarensis*; *Stipa gigantea* with *Buddleia* 'Royal Red' looming behind

our *Pennisetum villosum* is uncurling and fluffing out fat racemes of greenish cream flowers. Both of these spill across the path and are reliable and well behaved in Cloudehill. Unfortunately, *Pennisetum villosum* in a slightly warmer and dryer climate than the Dandenongs is more likely to ripen its abundant seed successfully, and is potentially invasive. Conversely, *Pennisetum orientale* seems to seed rarely, in the southern half of Australia at least.

27 February 2005

Two days before Cam collapsed I read several pages of this manuscript to him, mainly on his childhood, checking for mistakes and his comments. He told me the make of the family's first truck: a little 'Thirteen Hundred Weight' Bedford (good for eight bags full of wheat each trip), and that they managed to clear 50 acres and sow their first wheat in the autumn of 1930. It "went very well, five bags per acre", due to the ash from the previous autumn's burn off which they carefully ploughed into the soil. I quickly figured at the one shilling and eight pence per bushel he remembered they were paid, and at three bushels per bag, the family's gross income for all but a few weeks of their first three years farming was 62 pounds and 10 shillings. "We had to pay for the bags the wheat was packed in", Cam replied when I pointed this out, but he could not remember how much the jute bags cost.

He was intensely tired those last days and we were only talking for perhaps half an hour. I finished my reading with the paragraph about his experiences in the RAAF. He laughed and laughed, a little embarrassed, but laughing so hard he could not reply.

*   *   *

Cool borders in full colour. Top: towards the summer house; bottom: towards the maple court.

Atriplex hortensis Rubra with *Sedum* 'Autumn Joy' – still 'in the green'

By odd coincidence, couple of weeks after my father died I was reading Albert Facey's A Fortunate Life *and found that Facey specifically mentions 1930 as an* annas mirabilis *for the WA wheat belt; an unparalleled bumper year. On his farm near Wickepin, Facey harvested a phenomenally good crop of 15 bags per acre. However, due to the depression, there were no export markets for wheat that season and Facey's entire harvest was put into storage. In his instance he received an advance payment of three shillings and sixpence per bushel with the expectation of a considerable final payment to come. However, long after the original money was spent, his grain sold for the ludicrous price of one shilling and sevenpence a bushel. Having to repay the difference forced Albert Facey to sell his farm and move to the city.*

For early summer colour the penstemons are hard to beat. We imported a reference collection from Graham Trevor in Sandwich in 1993 to confirm names of the varieties then available in the Australian nursery trade. As it turned out, the finest of our collection turned out to be new to Australia: the lovely *Penstemon* 'Alice Hindley' with jacaranda-blue flowers paling to a white throat. Penstemon hybrids range in colour from white to soft pinks to rich cerise and scarlet, to mauves and purples. Several have white throats, occasionally with pencilled markings. Most grow to 30 centimetres, a few to 60 and 90 centimetres. They all bloom heartily in early summer, rest a little, then with deadheading carry on through the season; in fact they usually spot flower from late summer deep into winter. Penstemons are mostly highly drought tolerant.

There is a bit of an argument as to how far penstemons should be cut back in the winter. I find if they are clipped close to the ground they become prone to fungal diseases lurking in the soil. Spring rains seem to splash spores into open wounds and plants die back and occasionally succumb. Stems pruned 10 or 15 centimetres above the soil seem safe from infection, however, new season shoots emerge from the very base of each stem, older stems die and shrivel and dry ends become exactly sharp enough to neatly spear between fingers and fingernails as one attempts to weed near the clumps in spring. Or, in our genial and almost frost-free garden, penstemons can be left unpruned, in which case they rampage to 50 centimetres high by metres across and fall open half way through each season. The choice is yours.

Lysimachia ephemerum is an excellent mid-season perennial. Most of its loosestrife relatives prefer moist soils and sometimes shade, but ephemerum is best for us in full sun. I did try it in shade for a while through my experience with *L. ciliata* and *L. clethroides*, both dislike too much heat. One of our unhappy clumps of ephemerum managed to seed out into the sunshine and instantly its progeny grew away with upright stems and narrow glaucous foliage and spikes of coolly elegant, pale grey flowers with such alacrity that I could but stand and admire. *Lysimachia ephemerum*

Best of mates: Brock the border collie and Tillie, the border terrier

flowers to 90 centimetres and is good for all of February and a little of January and March. I use *Lysimachia clethroides* in a moist, partly shaded spot elsewhere in the garden where it grows to over a metre with paddle-shaped mid-green leaves, colouring orange and red and yellow in the autumn and throwing out spikes of tiny crisp white flowers which, as they begin to open, hang poised in such a way as to exactly represent a shepherd's crook, or the flowering spikes of any in the clethra family: the splendid shrubs *Clethra arborea* and *C. delavayi* and others.

True herbaceous geraniums are excellent for early to mid-season colour. Spilling over the brick edging to be noticed as one enters the cool borders, I have the albino form of *Geranium sanguineum*, with simple white flowers over a low mound of rich green filigree leaves. Two or three specimens of *Geranium* 'Sea Spray' are scattered further along the path. Sea spray is also an ideal frontal plant, producing rapidly expanding mats of dull mahogany bronze foliage studded with blush white button flowers. This, I think, is the best of the Alan Bremner hybrids, of those I have had experience with at least. It is curious to think that this plant, hybridised and selected in the Orkneys off the coast of Scotland, seems very at home in the Dandenongs, and warmer parts of Australia when given afternoon shade. *Geranium* 'Pink Spice', with darker foliage and soft pink flowers and the same growth habit is also good, perhaps more resentful of sun. The recently released *Geranium* 'Orkney Pink' is an excellent variation of this group, with cerise-pink flowers over similar foliage. I also like *Geranium* 'Mavis

Geranium 'Rozanne' with the globular shaped flower heads of Russian garlic, *Allium ampeloprasum* and *Filipendula rubra*

Eryngium tripartitum and *Stachys byzantina*

Simpson', one of the riversleanum hybrids, which forms neat low mounds of dull grey-green leaves and has pale pink blooms all through summer.

Through the years I have tried many of the blue flowering geraniums, although they need cosseting and are never robust enough to use in the borders. Not so, however, *Geranium* 'Rozanne'. This recently introduced hybrid of the species himalayense and *Geranium wallichianum* 'Buxton's Variety' is outstanding, in fact one of the all-time great herbaceous perennials. Its glorious flowers are mauve-blue, suffused with scarlet and fully 4 centimetres across. The plant is sufficiently robust to throw up 50- by 90-centimetre mounds of matte, mid-green foliage with a generous display of blooms from late spring to late autumn. I understand Melbourne's mild beachside gardens have rozanne flowering most of the winter, but for us, the leaves eventually turn scarlet and die back to a mallee root affair. Our specimens in full sun flag a little on a hot day. Those I have planted under tree peonies and in half sun sail through the hotter months. A customer from inner Adelaide reports that she has Rozanne in a pot on her verandah in a few hours' morning sun, then shade, and the plant flowers its heart out all summer and, apart from enticing hundreds of passersby to push open her gate and bang on her door asking, "What is that thing with the amazing flowers?", she is quite happy.

Sea Hollies are also good for adding blue to the January and February scene. I have accumulated several that I no longer have names for. They seem to lurk for a few years before they have strength to flower with enough of their steely blue, thistly flowers to put on a reasonable show. *Eryngium x tripartitum* though, has more vigour than most and is pretty good. Its flowers are small, excellent grey-blue and tripartitum has blooms by the score to around 40 centimetres. Its stems can be floppy; a friend suggested growing tripartitum through *Sedum* 'Matrona' and the combination works beautifully, silvery blue thistles interwoven through the pruinose flowering spikes of the sedum. We also grow a few of the central American species: *E. agavifolium*, *E. horridum*, *E. proteiflorum* and *E. yuccifolium*; despite their unsettling names they all have handsome rosettes of silvery green foliage topped by stems with greenish-silver thistle flowers. This group is very distinct from European species, generally taller and more heat- and drought-tolerant and excellent mixed into Mediterranean-style plantings.

February is the best month to see bergamots and phlox in bloom. Again, I seem to have been given several phlox, which have been popped in without due attention to labels. Each has multiplied into a colony sufficient to flower with a showy display of perfumed pink or white or mauve, or in one case, molten purple flowers. I can only

scratch my head when asked for names. Or perhaps the old plastic labels are still there, buried underneath the crowns? One of these springs, as we divide, we may find out. These are all paniculata types, all prone to mildew. We also use two of the maculatas with narrow, glossy, disease-free leaves: *Phlox maculata* 'Alpha' has lilac pink flowers and *P.* 'Omega' white blooms with a pale pink centre.

Sadly, disease is also a problem with most of the bergamots, or more correctly, monardas. We have grown eight or ten of these with mixed success; they are happiest in a wet summer, not so good in heat and drought when mildew can be devastating. *Monarda* 'Beauty of Cobham' is perhaps the prettiest, with whorls of

Top: *Monarda* 'Sahin's Lavender' with the very pink, slightly lavender flowers, with *Verbena bonariensis*, *Stipa gigantea* and *Buddleia* 'Royal Red';
Bottom: The globe thistle, *Echinops* 'Veitch's Blue' with creamy achillea

One of our unnamed *Phlox paniculate* hybrids

narrow, pale pink flowers protruding over apricot calyxs. The most mildew-proof of the bergamots is a plant I obtained from Kurt Bluemal in the USA, *Monarda* 'Donnerwolke'. Donnerwolke translates as thunder cloud, and the flowers are a nice stormy reddish lavender. The colour is notable because it sits so well over its lavender-tinted, aromatic foliage. The spicy perfume of the crushed leaves is predictable as one watches the plant in the spring, its runners oozing their way across the soil, forming a dense prostrate mat in the way of all the mint family. Stems rear up through the summer, in the instance of Donnerwolke to a metre high and each stem is topped with a flower. *Monarda* 'Donnerwolke' also branches vigorously as it blooms and the successively rising fresh flowers keep the clump handsome and tidy and full of colour for six to eight weeks. As mentioned earlier, the dried flowering stems of the monardas are austerely handsome through winter and can be left until August.

6 March 2005

Cam first mentioned the little seepage tucked beside the Holt rock many years ago and I always took it he was entirely responsible for collecting water every day and carrying it home. Anyway, in those last days I asked him about my grandfather, wondering what sort of man Mark Allan might have been. Cam replied he was "gentle, quiet, reserved". And Emily May, who, though uncomplaining, all the settlers of Holt Rock could readily see was a lady perhaps more at ease welcoming friends to an Adelaide hills drawing room than to a makeshift tent in the West Australian bush several hard days' travel from any sort of town. Then we were speaking of the tiny spring on which the family depended those first summers; Cam corrected my telling of the story. He certainly collected water to fill the two kerosene tins every day but apparently, after a time, Mark joined Cam in order to carry them back to camp. A ten-year-old could not easily lift the brimming five-gallon buckets and the water was too precious to risk spilling. Actually filling the kerosene tins took ages; this was my father's task. As my grandfather waited for Campbell to scoop the very last drops of water from the slowly oozing sand, father and son took the opportunity to ponder the doings of the day.

At the end of two years my grandfather installed a corrugated iron tank to collect rainwater from the roof of their newly constructed shanty. This was neat timing, Cam told me, as the little spring dried up that third summer and in nearly 20 years following there was never a sign of it.

Agapanthus are the most foolproof of perennials and given the hundreds of varieties producing flowers from spring to autumn, in shades of white to pearly grey, jacaranda blue to azure, from navy blue to purple, one can hardly garden in Australia without them. However, a couple of the species and a few of the named forms are seeding themselves seriously, especially in dryish coastal areas. In my experience the majority of garden hybrids are safe. I imported several back in the 1980s: *Agapanthus* 'Bressingham White', *A.* 'Bressingham Blue', *A.* 'Isis' and *A.* 'Loch Hope'. I am fairly certain these are all from the Headbourne hybrid group. They are herbaceous, they die down in early winter, leaves fading in yellowish browns, and for me they begin flowering in February, much later than the evergreens. Loch Hope produces large spherical heads of brilliant true blue flowers to a metre high, with the advantage of a prodigious number of buds to each head and so an extended season in colour. Isis and Bressingham Blue both have scintillatingly deep blue blooms, Isis blooming first and Bressingham Blue taking over the baton for late summer and early autumn. The latter two produce smaller flower heads. I particularly like A. 'Isis' for its sheer neatness: its low strappy leaves, its bolt upright stems to 60 centimetres and its perfectly globular flower heads of intense deep blue. I have yet to see a seedling from these.

The last of the mid-season plants I will mention is *Cimicifuga racemosa* (or *Actae racemosa*), a lovely dark-leafed form of the species that came from a little Mt Macedon nursery some years back. The 'bugbanes' are really woodlanders, preferring rich moist soils and cool dappled light. They have divided lacy leaves and elegant narrow spires of white bottlebrush flowers. Mine is a seedling and was a small, bronze-green-purple nondescript seedling when purchased. As it gained strength, the colour improved to the degree that I feel it is now the best dark-leaf form I have seen. Its foliage is soft charcoal and its recessed veins deep purplish black. Blush white flowers are produced in elegant wands to 90 centimetres and naturally these provide breathtaking contrast with the foliage. I first placed this cimicifuga in

Tulbaghia violacea in front of *Cimicifuga racemosa* dark-leaf form, a few pale blue flowers of *Geranium* 'Nimbus' and sprays of *Pyrus salicifolia* 'Pendula' cascading from above. Ceramic pot by Ted Secombe.

The silver pears catching the early morning light

Clockwise from top: Misty morning: *Lysimachia ephemerum* in foreground, *Clematis viticella* 'Huldine' on the silver pear; *Berberis* 'Rose Glow', *Calamagrostis acutiflora* 'Overdam', santolina and yellow phygelius; *Verbena bonarensis*, seedling aster, lepechinia, *Melianthus major*

nearly full shade to find the plant grew slowly and the leaf colour wishy-washy. After two years it was divided, half left in situ and the remainder moved to more sun. The sunnier clump was much stronger and its colour richer. Three years later I decided to press the issue; one precious specimen was moved into the borders and tucked below a silver pear in full morning sun. This grows magnificently, the extra light intensifying the purple-black of the cimicifuga wonderfully. With the tangled silver of the pear above, our *Cimicifuga racemosa* looks positively awe inspiring and a little boast definitely warranted.

11 March 2005

The South Perth apartment was full of letters. In nearly 45 years, Jan and Cam were only apart for a few weeks altogether. Every parting seems to have been memorialised by a cache of daily letters held with an elastic band and stuffed into a shoe box or desk drawer. They make impossible reading. Bundles of letters are mixed with photographs; one of my mother watching Cam unload bags of wheat from a small truck into a co-operative bulk storage bin, the back of the photo marked: Lake Varley, 1947. Another tiny snap, faded and blurred, is of Cam, perhaps 14, larking about, waving from billowing sheaves of hay piled high on a wagon pulled by a big draught horse. Turning the image over, one reads 'Star'. There is even a batch of disintegrating congratulatory telegrams tied with a ribbon sent by their friends when I was born.

The writing is all neat longhand with odd flourishes I suppose, in my father's instance, dating to correspondence lessons in 1929 and '30 when copperplate was still the ideal. Neither Jan nor Cam attended a secondary school, neither had their handwriting styles coarsened by taking dictation from a teacher, having to write speedily; both preserve something of a child's neatness and are a pleasure to read.

Together with the letters is a 21st-birthday card, a silver key embossed on the front and signed by what was likely the entire Holt Rock community on 26 November 1940. Weeks later, with the harvest complete, Cam signed up with the RAAF; a difficult decision as he was leaving the farm to be run by his two sisters and his father who, by this time, was 71. Cam was in a reserved occupation and was not required to fight but off he went and shortly after met my mother. The curious thing is, despite the proximity of their families, my parents only came to meet and fall in love at this time; my mother nursing in Perth and my father serving with the RAAF at the Pearce base, just north of the Swan Valley.

Haycasting and seeding in the 1930s

On top of a great pile of Cam's letters I found a copy of my mother's funeral service in 1997, which included the poem So What is Love? I asked Cam the whereabouts of the poem during a visit a couple of years back. The lines were selected from an anthology for my mother's funeral but later we couldn't find the book and, years after the event, I couldn't remember the poem with any accuracy. The anthology was probably left with the undertakers, it has certainly remained lost; I spent an hour or two looking for it that day without luck. Anyway, when the time came, there it was, the poem, printed within my mother's funeral service, rescued from the mass of his other papers and left by my father on top of his correspondence; top drawer of the desk, left hand side.

HIGH SUMMER

*Quali fioretti dal notturno gelo
chinati e chiusi, poi che 'l sol li 'mbianca
si drizzan tutti aperti in loro stelo,*

As the little flowers which the night
    frost has bent and closed
become erect upon their stalks
when the sun whitens them,

Dante, *Inferno*, II–127–129

Cam's foolscap pages, penned in 1994, noted his increasing difficulty in understanding Jan, and to actually hear her. Her Parkinson's, or rather her Louie's Whole Body Dementia as it was eventually diagnosed, had worsened by then and her vocal cords so weakened that her voice had softened to the quietest of whispers and Cam no longer understood anything much of what she was saying. His slight deafness did not help. This was happening along with a general weakening of my mother's entire muscular system, a sort of paralysis I suppose. She had earlier been physically strong. I think of her keeping up with a herd of cattle on foot for miles over rough country around the age of 70; keep in mind cattle move at a pace that a very fast walk must be interspersed with serious jogging. Cam wrote in 1994 that the worst thing was that he "no longer could enjoy her beautiful voice". A little piece of jigsaw fell into place as I read. They met, of course, in those desperate months around the time of Rommel's Western Desert campaign, Dietrich's singing of 'Lili Marlene'. It occurred to me that Jan's speaking voice, always low and throaty, and their memories of those times, were a kind of talisman for them. He also wrote they married with the thought ten years together would be enough, would justify everything, and that anything further would be a bonus. And by 1994 they had "been blessed with 43 years".

Late-season perennials I find are some of the best, especially in Australia. The asters, the sedums, the salvias and dahlias all look promising through the season and pick up and carry colour themes into autumn. Around 50 percent of our perennials are later flowerers, some 30 percent mid-season and we try to plant not more than 20 percent early summer bloomers. This ratio keeps the borders fresh throughout and keeps mid-season dead-heading to a minimum. With the experience of a few years now we count on reasonable colour from late November to mid March. Some flowering will persist through to early winter and softening colours of the foliage and developing seed heads provide interest to justify an occasional wander up and down the path throughout April and May.

Dahlias become a mainstay in February and March. *Dahlia* 'April Portwine' is an old collarette variety with a single row of deep burgundy petals and a creamy white petaloid centre; although this combination of colour is a bit jarring, its relative simplicity of form makes a good effect among other flowers. I try to avoid dahlias with large, heavy blooms because they so often bend and crimp. There is not much worse than a dahlia displaying good numbers of perfect flowers and others half snapped and dangling. *Dahlia* 'April Portwine' has relatively lightweight flowers with sturdy stems to around 1.2 metres. A creamy lemon collarette, given to me without a name, has been planted among late-flowering deep-blue agapanthus and this variety is also robust enough to withstand autumn wind and rain without becoming an eyesore. *Dahlia* 'Cruden Farm' is close to a nymphae type with silky white double blooms. It is quite low, less than a metre, and so out of the wind somewhat and reasonably tidy. *Dahlia* 'Sophia' is a decorative type with very full flowers and taller, 1.2 metres and more. It is well worth risking wind damage for the drama of its splendid crimson-purple blooms. Sophia was given me by David Glenn after my noticing it in his border at Lambley a few years back. It is a very good plant. David did require me to go down on bended knee for a tuber or two.

We use quite a few asters; while I don't keep track of all the names, several are worth taking note of. The classic *Aster x frikartii* 'Mönch', famously used beside the moat walk at Sissinghurst, is a thoroughly reliable performer, flowering with elegant jacaranda-blue blooms through February and March. The crown builds up for a season or two from first planting and is at its best after three years and carries on from there with little attention. Snails helping themselves to the new spring shoots is the only problem I can think of. Several clumps of frikartii are scattered along the front of the borders; we divide them every five years or so. Most asters need constant lifting and dividing but forms of lateriflorus also require little maintainance. *Aster lateriflorus* 'Horizontalis' is another of my 1988 imports. It forms an upright mound of tiny, deep purplish-black leaves good from October to the end of February. In early autumn the foliage pales to dull bronze-green and masses of tiny crimson-centred white flowers smother the plant for two or three weeks. *Aster lateriflorus* 'The Prince' is similar, its leaves darker again, almost coal black, and I'm

Aster laterifloris 'The Prince', *Allium sphaerocephalon* and alstroemeria

Berberis 'Helmond Pillar' and *Cortaderia selloana* 'Silver Comet'

Sedum 'Autumn Joy' and *Geranium* 'Rozanne'

Above: Globe thistles – *Echinops sphaerocephalus (top)*
Pennisetum villosum detail (centre)
Pennisetum orientale detail (bottom)

not sure an improvement. Very dark foliage can look like rather shadowy among surrounding colour, and is especially noticeable in photographs. *Aster lateriflorus* 'Lady in Black' is a willowy, tall growing form, to 90 centimetres and more, at least twice the height of The Prince. Its leaves are a little paler but still very dark and it seems faintly thirstier than its smaller brethren but generally I find them pretty tough.

Aster divaricartus is another I squashed into those cardboard boxes I brought back with me from England in 1988. This is a very unasterish aster. Divaricartus has deep green, paddle-shaped leaves with intriguing glossy black stems. Small daisy flowers are faintly off-white but pale enough to be effective over its little tangle of black stems in early autumn. The plant is low, 30 centimetres with support, but is inclined to flop. Gertrude Jekyll is often quoted as recommending *A. divaricartus* be grown over the glossy round leaves of bergenias, which is not a bad idea. The aster is certainly better with support, they both enjoy half sun, half shade, and the rich green of the bergenias make a handsome backdrop to the leaves of the aster as they turn yellow and orange and red in the late autumn. This is one of only three herbaceous perennials worthwhile growing for autumn colour. The others are *Lysimachia clethroides* and *Gillenia trifoliata*, and now I think of it, fragrarias and *Persicaria campanulata*, and perhaps one or two of the grasses. Still, autumn colour in asters is unusual.

Aster cordifolius 'Little Carlow' is one of the best of the traditional asters. Over several seasons it will build to a 1.2- by 1.2-metre clump with 2.5-centimetre-wide, cool lavender-blue flowers with tiny yellow centres. Little Carlow is robust, almost mildew-free and thoroughly reliable. The novae-angliae varieties are also good in gardens where plants have to manage without spraying for mildew – such as Cloudehill – and we have the famous old *Aster* 'Harrington's Pink' tucked behind a clump of *Stipa gigantea* as an excellent example of this group. This has a double row of clear rosy pink petals, the flowers about the same size as little carlow. Harrington's Pink makes a sturdy mound of colour as the stipa winds down to its late-season wispy effect. I noticed a seedling of Harrington's Pink sneaking up on the other side of our stipa last season. Its flowers were a richer pink, very distinct, and worthwhile remembering for next year. Any number of asters of the novi-belgii group have been popped into various shrub borders. They rely on other plants to conceal their scruffy, mildewing foliage and surprise us with little bursts of colour through late summer and autumn.

The McPhee family first settled on their selection at Lake Camm in the late 1920s. For a year or two they lived in tents and in their spare time from clearing set about building a small house with timber my grandfather brought with him from the jarrah forests. During those

Lake Camm, drying up quickly after the meagre rains of 2007

first summers, pioneers of the district noticed a number of bushfires, seemingly caused by lightning strikes. With no one living in outlying parts to fight them, fires burnt great swathes of the scrub, stretching away in every direction from the tiny Lake Camm community. One fire burnt for weeks along the horizon, for so long in fact that everyone came to ignore it. One morning the wind changed direction and gathered speed and the fire front, which had taken so long to sneak past them, swung sideways and within a startlingly brief time an immense wall of flame was exploding over the nearest rise and racing to engulf them.

They had no water to fight the fire and could only run; there was time to save just one item from the half-built house: an upright piano. The family leapt onto the farm cart to hold the thing steady and with my grandfather laying leather around the horse's ears, they headed for the salt lake, down through the sheoaks and out onto the salt. Several neighbours soon joined them in what everyone could see was the only safe place in the district. Once all were accounted for, my Uncle Hec climbed back onto the wagon and began playing music hall tunes. Everyone sang along to 'Roll Out the Barrel', and 'It's A Long Way to Tipperary' and all the songs they could think of.

The fire burnt the entire district black, burnt the McPhee's house with all the belongings they had not rescued, clothes, photos, books (including a big old family bible with generation upon generation of the Clan McPhee listed in the fly leaf); the fire burnt the lot as they stood around on the bare salt lake and sang and sang.

Claire Takacs

Claire was a student when she introduced herself to me. She was hunting for a subject for her portfolio, hiking through the mountain ash forest looking for inspiration. After exploring Cloudehill, Claire asked if she might pop back to photograph the following day. I agreed, but was taken aback a little when she asked if it was possible to gain access before 5 am. "Well, there is a gap in the hedge and a bit of netting you can climb over". Arriving at a more respectable hour myself I saw she was just climbing out, on her way home, couldn't stay for a cup of coffee. Only recently did a member of her family point out she was travelling two hours each way to get here. And in the several years since, her finest work always seems to involve missing breakfast.

That was the first of many shoots and, admiring her work after a few visits, the penny dropped – Claire was by no means your common garden-variety photographer. A few years on, with major awards and numerous articles illustrated by Claire in magazines around the world, I thank my lucky stars for that first serendipitous conversation.

According to our computer file the photo on the front cover of this book was taken at 5.32 am on 23 October, 2007. Thus we see the sun rising and flaring through a copper beech, spring foliage still translucent. That was a glorious morning. Over the next 60 minutes Claire shot what became some of the finest Cloudehill photographs, including the image on this page.

Many herbaceous sedums are now available in Australia. After trialling quite a few, I think only *Sedum* 'Autumn Joy' and *S.* 'Matrona' are robust and long-flowering enough to grow in the thick of other herbaceous plants, certainly in the Dandenongs. I have grown one or two of the smaller sedums, *S.* 'Ruby Glow' and *S.* 'Vera Jameson', tucked against the bricks edging the central path. These both perform nicely so long as we take care they are not overgrown, in which case they shrivel to nothing in a flash. I do rather like *Sedum hidakanum* (syn. *Hidakanense*), but this is a very dwarf species, to 5 centimetres high only and not at all suitable for mixing into the borders. It is an exquisite plant nonetheless, with tiny circular, pewter-blue leaves and soft rosy pink flowers. For years I grew hidakanense in a shallow pan carved from red

Below left: Autumnal wisps of *Stipa gigantea* trailing in front of the deep ruby 'cauliflower' heads of *Sedum* 'Autumn Joy', *Aster x frikartii* 'Mönch', *Salvia leucantha* and *Dahlia* 'April Portwine'

Below right: The filigree silver of *Senecio vivavira*, *Sedum* 'Autumn Joy' to its left, a pink monarda, with *Salvia involucrata* 'Bethellii' heaving up under the skirts of the silver pear

Indian sandstone and there it was happy, very pretty and safe from competition. A deal larger, S. 'Ruby Glow' and S. 'Vera Jameson' both grow to 12 to 15 centimetres, Ruby Glow with bluish glaucous leaves and Vera Jameson in glaucous purple; they each have sparkling pink, late summer flowers. *Sedum* 'Autumn Joy' and S. 'Matrona' will grow to 30 to 50 centimetres and I use a few clumps of both back into the borders a little and they are happy to fight it out with smaller asters and santolinas. *Sedum* 'Autumn Joy' is a famous stalwart and grown by the acre by James van Sweden in the USA. Deservedly so; I am sure that every serious gardener has it in their top ten of absolutely dependable plants. I remember the first time I saw it flowering, at Sissinghurst no less, in 1981. The Sissinghurst gardeners had Autumn Joy next to *Santolina* 'E.A. Bowles', the latter with creamy primrose, pincushion flowers over sea-green foliage. Nearby was *Senecio viravira*, an upright mound of lacy, narrowly lobed, silvery grey leaves topped with little button flowers, which cunningly, were exactly the same powdery primrose as the santolina's. The clump of Autumn Joy was simultaneously flowering with a great cauliflower mass of dusky pink. Even now I think this is one of the cleverest planting combinations I've ever seen and in its honour I imported all three plants. We try to have a version of this grouping somewhere in the border each season. Unfortunately, the sedum flowers weeks later than the santolina for me in the Dandenongs, even after hard pruning the santolina in spring to delay its blooming. Returning to our visit to

Below left: Apple-blossom pink flowers on ruby stems of *Sedum* 'Matrona', *Aster lateriflorus* 'The Prince' behind and a few blooms of a pink alstroemeria at the rear right

Below right: The fresh, hazy-pink flowers of *Calamagrostis acutiflora* 'Overdam' to the rear on the left, *Salvia nemorosa* 'Ostfriesland' below, lavender-blue flowers of *Nepeta* 'Dropmore' to its right and crimson-red *Knautia macedonica* behind

Achillea 'Coronation Gold' and *Salvia* 'Lye End'

Salvia 'Caradonna'

Salvia greggii 'Bicolor'

England in 1981, I remember S. 'Autumn Joy' flowering in garden after garden, for weeks, in every shade of silvery green, of pale pink, of rich dusky pink and flaring coppery red. Autumn Joy, which I had read about but never seen before, was the motif for me of that glorious summer.

Sedum 'Matrona' is a relatively new plant and I think the best of a long series of recently introduced sedums. It seems even more robust than autumn joy, producing mounds of bruised purplish green foliage, 40 centimetres high by 60 centimetres. In late summer pale greenish-purple buds open to display the typical cauliflower formation of apple blossom pink flowers. The flowering has not the persistence of Autumn Joy but S. 'Matrona' makes amends with its flower heads and stems, which dry off to a glowing chestnut during autumn. The foliage yellows and falls away and the dry seed heads are superb all winter. We collect these during the final tidy up of the borders in August to make an arrangement of them.

I know of enthusiasts who have entire gardens of salvias and little else. Most prefer dry sunny gardens. We have salvias in Cloudehill flowering every part of the year except late winter and the first week or two of spring. *Salvia nemorosa* 'Ostfriesland', with 50-centimetre-high wands of deep blue-violet flowers, was one of my 1988 imports along with *S. nemorosa* 'Mainacht', its shorter flowers an even deeper blue-violet and very evocative of the night sky in May. The nemorosa group dominates the early summer borders. *Salvia* 'Lye End' has 75-centimetre stems of lavender-blue flowers and *S. nemorosa* 'Amethyst' has stems a little lower and its blooms are almost amethyst. All these bloom in November and December but will repeat flower in late summer if the surrounding competition is not too fierce and with timely dead heading.

I have experimented with a few mid-summer blooming salvias, the microphyllas for example, and greggii varieties, in pinks and raspberries and creamy yellows, but late-summer and autumn flowerers have been vital in Cloudehill from our first summer onwards. *Salvia guaranitica* grows to 1.2 to 1.5 metres and produces a cloud of true azure flowers for many weeks, almost into winter. It is a wonderful plant and I might be entirely over the moon with it if only it did not go on to produce wheelbarrow loads of tubers that simply must be dug every year if the plant is not to entirely colonise the surrounding garden. *Salvia* 'Black and Blue' is similar in appearance, its azure flowers on slightly lower stems, which are almost black and accentuate the flowers. This, happily, has no tubers. The Mexican sage, *Salvia leucantha*, is a robust and reliable sub-shrub, flowering as long as guaranitica. It also has attractive narrow, grey-green leaves and rich violet woolly calyces from which the small white woolly flowers protrude in a lively way.

We have tried any number of late-flowering salvias in the borders and other parts of the garden. *Salvia* 'Black Knight' for instance, with large, deep purple flowers protruding from purple-black calyces, and S. 'Waverly', with smallish mauve-white flowers and rosy purple calyces and stems, and S. 'Indigo Spires' with indigo flowers; but I think my favourite of the autumn sages is *Salvia mexicana* 'Lime Bracts'. This has slate-blue flowers that emerge from substantial lime-green bracts, which are quietly showy and very persistent. The plant is generously branching and flowers to 1.2 metres and the hazy lime effect is good for months. One final sage, which is excellent from late autumn to the depths of winter, is *Salvia involucrata* 'Bethellii'. This has good lolly-pink flowers on rosy purple stems to a metre, and the foliage has just the right hint of lime green to contrast nicely with its flowers.

In March 1954, in what should have been the driest part of the year, an intense low moved up from the Southern Ocean and hovered off the south coast and dropped a year's worth of rain in just two or three days all over the Great Southern. By the end of it, the Bletchley homestead was on a low island surrounded by an endless lake of water. Fortunately, harvesting was complete and most of Cam and Jan's stock were safe on a few acres of high ground to the south of the house. But the breeding ewes were stranded almost 15 miles away on a small block of land they owned at Dongalocking. Of course breeding ewes were the core of the flock and Cam decided he simply had to check them, and this would mean wading and swimming all the way.

Thinking a dog essential at the other end, he called Toodles and the two set off into the flood. It was all pretty level country and the water deepened so very gradually that it was some time before Toodles found himself swimming. Now Toodles was a mite past his prime and after a bit he swam over to Cam and made it plain he was already tired and not happy with swimming all the way to Dongalocking, so Cam lifted him around the waist to give him a rest and carried on walking. A while later, water almost up to his chin by now and old Toodles draped over one shoulder, it dawned on Cam that he was on a hiding to nothing. He had not reached the lowest point of the first valley and Dongolocking was still more than 12 miles away, so after a bit of cogitation he turned back. This was a very wise decision. He was to discover later the flood had transformed the little gully he was approaching into a river broad and strong enough to have floated the pair of them downstream all the way to the middle of Lake Dumbleyung. And besides, they were eventually to find the Dongolocking ewes had all been so sensible as to stroll to the highest place in their paddock and wait patiently for the water to go away. So they were happy and all was well.

Salvia nemorosa 'Amethyst'

Salvia mexicana 'Lime Bracts'

Salvia gregii 'Raspberry Royal'

Grasses, left to right: *Briza major*, an interesting weed of road verges and bushland areas; Veld grass, a pasture species of the Dandaragan Plateau, adding warm rust to a predominantly yellow-grey summer landscape; Kangaroo grass, or *Themeda australis*, on the Chittering road verge

I was just a little over two years old and have no real memories of the big flood except, in younger years, my sleep was disturbed by a series of nightmares involving black clouds and endless rain and water in general.

Browsing through a bookshop around 1976 or 77, I came across Roger Grounds' monograph on ornamental grasses[5]. I was not then aware of any big grass other than pampas grass regarded as ornamental enough for gardens and so was puzzled and intrigued. It was immediately obvious almost none of the plants Grounds described were actually available in Australia, certainly not in Perth nurseries. My curiosity aroused, I began to take notice of grasses growing naturally along the Mogumber road verges. I say naturally, but soon came to appreciate that the southwest of Western Australia has few indigenous perennial grasses and these are not hugely ornamental. Perennial grasses growing along roadsides sufficiently notable to catch my eye were mostly introduced accidentally with shipments of fodder from South Africa or Europe; this fodder supplying the livestock also on board. A number of grasses and plants such as capeweed arrived this way on sailing ships in the first years of white settlement. One such grass was *Briza major*, which as kids we called 'blowfly grass'; this appeared almost within months of European arrival and by the 1980s was naturalised everywhere, including deep into national parks. In fact, only after reading Grounds' book did I appreciate it was not a native and actually came from the Mediterranean. Other grasses I spotted along roads around this time included *Paspalum dilatatum*, with not unattractive fine grey-green seed heads to half a metre, and red natal grass, *Rhynchelytrum repens*, with low mounds of blue-green leaves and almost crimson flowers quickly fading to sandy pink. I remember my small triumph identifying a little colony of red Natal grass growing beside a gateway from the Moora road into our mill paddock. I was carting a load of wheat down to the Mogumber bin and stopped to pick a few stems to take home, so it must have been a week or two before Christmas. Heaven knows how it got there. There seemed to be no other red natal grass in the district and I was lucky to notice that small colony; its flowering was only good for the first weeks of summer. I also suspected it had weed potential and decided to keep an eye on it and not spread it around. As it turned out, the natal grass stayed put, did not seem to move at all, at least over the following 10 years.

Themeda australis, or kangaroo grass, was another plant featured in books and articles. At long last, a native species making it on to the ornamental list, I thought, surely this should not be too hard to get hold of? However, though common in the eastern states of Australia, kangaroo grass is rare in WA, apart from in the Kimberleys; and the Kimberleys are somewhat more than a Sunday afternoon drive from the southwest of WA. However, taking the scenic route through the onomatopoeically named Chittering Valley on my way to Perth one day I spotted the handsomely scruffy inflorescences of kangaroo grass growing on yet another road verge and managed to detach a small piece (very much against the rules, I'm afraid: please don't do likewise) and planted it in pride of place between two massive rocks and a little to the fore of a variegated pampas grass.

Another grass, which I'm sure actually first appeared at exactly this time, was *Pennisetum setaceum*. I remember digging a few clumps from a railway embankment near the Gillingarra siding around 1983 or 84, without qualms as it was obviously an interloper. The clumps grew vigorously despite months without rain, with grey-green foliage to 60 centimetres and magnificent burgundy-purple foxtail plumes to more than a metre in early summer. Under garden irrigation *P. setaceum* grew more vigorously still, flowered for eight months and became a highlight of my collection. For a time, this species was thought to be an Australian native and sold as such by nurseries. However, it was being confused with *Pennisetum alopecuroides*. The latter has been found growing, mysteriously, as one small colony in a heavily forested, northern part of the Blue Mountains in New South Wales, so is counted indigenous despite the fact it is otherwise found only in Japan and east Asia. *Pennisetum setaceum*, on the other hand, is now thought of as an African species. I'm positive it appeared

Pennisteum setaceum flowering on the road verge a few minutes' south of Moora beside *Alyogyne huegelii*, October 2007. I remember the latter, this actual plant, putting on a showy display every spring in the 1980s. Clearly long lived as well as immensely tough.

in WA in the late 1970s, the early 80s at the latest. A truck driver friend of mine told me that by the late 1980s he had seen 'foxtail grass' beside roads from Meekatharra, with its highly erratic desert rainfall, through to Margaret River, 1000 kilometres south and the recipient of 1.2 metres of rain every winter. Foxtail grass is undoubtedly a magnificent thing, but its astonishing adaptability and the speed with which it can move illustrates how much care is needed as we experiment with plants in the garden. I think this grass is quite safe on farms with stock – it will not tolerate grazing pressure and sheep eating the crown kill it. In suburban areas, where notice can be taken of seedlings, foxtail grass can also be grown, with care. In pristine areas, however, near undisturbed vegetation, watercourses or national parks, *Pennisetum setaceum* is without doubt a serious weed. The spread of foxtail grass along roads in rural districts is something of a disaster. Road verges are often the last stronghold of indigenous plants and should be free of gratuitous competition.

Over the years I found further reference to ornamental grasses in Graham Stuart Thomas' superb book, *Perennial Garden Plants*[6], and an entire chapter in E.A. Bowles' equally remarkable trilogy, *My Garden in Spring, Summer, Autumn and Winter*[7]. Allowing that Bowles was writing in 1912 and 1913, he must be regarded as a pioneer of the field. Gertrude Jekyll grew a couple of forms of miscanthus and also lyme grass, *Elymus arenarias*, in the 1890s. And who was it first grew pampas grass as an ornamental?

One evening in the weeks before they retired, Jan and Cam went to visit Ross and Shirley Forrester for a farewell glass or two. Driving up Syke's Road and approaching the final bend, Cam, out of high spirits and skylarking, accelerated around the corner, skidded on loose gravel, off the road, down the road verge, somehow avoided immediately turning the car over on an awkward gutter, missed several big trees by centimetres, down a long slope dodging between boulders, where he eventually slowed and crossed the bed of a dry gully without bellying too badly, then drove sedately up the other side and back onto the road half a kilometre on. All this in total silence and, according to Jan the next day, absolutely nothing was said between them for the rest of the short distance to the end of the road and saying hello to Shirley and Ross. It happened very close to the entrance gate to Clover Downs; spotting the tracks the next morning, I followed them to find the errant vehicle had exquisitely negotiated the only possible path through many rocks and stumps and trees, and unerringly found the one narrow place along the gully a car might cross without wrecking its suspension and smashing its sump. The whole thing happened in darkness and the vehicle out of control. To exactly repeat the adventure successfully involved odds of a thousand to one against, I imagined;

Sedum 'Autumn Joy' and *Achnatherum calamagrostis*

Opposite: A patch of wine crimsons and purples; a phygelius in the foreground overtopped by a few stems of an intense crimson alstromeria, *Gaura lindheimeri* 'Whirling Butterflies' mid-ground to the left, the true *Salvia leucantha* to its right and a purplish seedling of *Aster novae-angliae* 'Harrington's Pink' behind

more, really, to get out of it without even a scratch on the paintwork. Jan intimated Cam was a bit mortified. With a lifetime's familiarity with bush roads, never before had he done such a thing.

A couple of days later, while chatting to Ross, he asked, "Was that your folk's car taking the long way around the bend?" It was unnecessary of him to ask, really. All the Forresters read tracks with ease enough to recognise their neighbours' vehicles; they could usually pick how long back the tracks dated, for a while, until rain or wind smudged them. To their beady eyes, vehicle tracks might well have been an embossed and gilt-edged calling card left in the dusty gravel. "They did seem quiet for a bit when they arrived" Ross pondered, shaking his head when I confirmed Cam's misdemeanour. "Not at all their usual selves."

Even at the time it seemed the incident almost epitomised their life together. Cam and Jan both could tempt fate in a pretty bloody-minded way at times yet, for whatever reason, she generally withheld her hand. After selling Merrie-Lea in 1989 Cam was told by several old-timer neighbours that everyone around Gillingarra was sure he would bankrupt himself as he struggled to pasture and fertilise our rocky hills in the 1960s. No one had dreamt of using an aircraft to do this until Cam called on Bob Conn to help out.

*   *   **

At a time when I was very unhappy, Cam, driving me home from boarding school, parked beside the road to discuss the social practicalities of the type of roughhouse teasing found

The hornbeam walk

The silver pear in autumn with *Miscanthus sinensis* 'Silberfeder' to its left. The hedge behind is *Thuja occidentalis* 'Fastigiata' which provides an excellent greyish-green backdrop to pastel flowers.

in any big, unfamiliar institution. We had stopped within view of the Pearce RAAF base and my father spoke of his memories of the barracks: a recruit returning from leave via an hour or two at a local hotel. His dormitory neighbours took advantage of his condition to haul his bed level with the rafters with ropes at lights out and the following morning all woke early to enjoy his plight. Then, perhaps the proximity of the same buildings setting him musing, he spoke of love; plumbing its depth, understanding its meaning. He talked of sitting with the beloved in silence, without speaking, for all of an evening as a way of knowing these things. I remember I could think of nothing to say. I was not 13 years old.

With much reading and not a few exploratory drives through neighbouring shires, by the late 1980s I had accumulated a respectable collection of grasses to intersperse through my perennials. They eventually came across the Nullarbor and during the mid-1990s were augmented by the grasses brought back from England in 1988. Quarantine authorities released the latter in exasperating dribs and drabs; there was ample time for deliberation over the placement of each variety into our newly made borders.

Miscanthus sinensis 'Silberfeder', or silver feather, is a very old selection with coarse green foliage to 1.6 metres topped by silvery beige flowers to over 2 metres. Its flowers have a silky quality, especially when caught in angled light; a clump is placed to one side of a silver pear to be backlit by morning sun over the hedge and glows and

Collection of succulents, corner of summer house

shimmers for weeks in February and March. Unfortunately, silver feather does tend to fall open. *Miscanthus sinensis* 'Gracillimus' is more upright through the season and flowers very late, April to May, with rich, bronze-crimson flowers to 2 metres and more. Gracillimus was the first narrow-leaved miscanthus selection. It has been almost superseded by *M*. 'Sarabande', with foliage as fine as gracillimus and more upright again. Sarabande has soft mushroom-coloured flowers in late summer to around the same height as gracillimus and is a superb plant. *Miscanthus sinensis* 'Flamingo' has rich coppery pink flowers and its habit is somewhat cascading, which is excellent in an open position but requires more precious room in the borders. Flamingo also has coarser leaves. *Miscanthus giganteus* is flowering in Cloudehill for the first time this season and it is mightily impressive. The narrow clump of foliage rises to well over 2 metres and is topped with dazzling, almost iridescent silvery pink flowers reaching over 3 metres. We have placed one clump two-thirds of the way along the border and against the retaining wall at the rear. The last of our Erst Pagel miscanthus selections is *Miscanthus s.* 'Graziella'. Graziella is compact, with smoky mushroom-tinted flowers to barely a metre and some autumn tints in its dying foliage. I am experimenting with it among Japanese pines in another part of the garden.

The grass theme is carried to the end of the border with a clump of creamy white variegated pampas grass in front of our hand-made brick wall. Although rare, this pampas grass has been in Australia for years and seems to correspond to *Cortaderia* 'Silver Comet'. I first obtained it in the mid-1980s and planted it in my Clover Downs garden, where it produced a symmetrical fountain of lush silvery foliage to 1.2 metres, and dense plumes of creamy flowers at least 2 metres high, glorious from before Christmas to late summer. The same plant grown at Cloudehill is not quite so lush and flowers in autumn. I understand it rarely seeds but cannot vouch for it.

The big grasses dominate the cool borders during the last weeks of summer. Their pale flowers catch low autumn light and parchment leaves add to the mood as decay sets in. We cut untidy stems of perennials back to earth late May or early June, when bleached grasses and a few seed heads of monardas and eupatoriums are all that remain. Winter storms gradually strip the miscanthus leaves away from rattling flower stems and the upright stems topped with skeletonised inflorescences we leave to spring.

A month or so before I was born my father was woken early one morning, partly by bright moonlight, partly by a strange racket from the garden. Rising and going to the window he could see a hobgoblin-like creature sitting in a crook of a peach tree. Snarling, screeching,

Sedum 'Autumn Joy', lower right corner; *Echinacea purpurea*, behind. The last wisps of *stipa gigantea* and *Miscanthus sinensis* 'Flamingo' rising to the left of a trio of conifers: *Juniperus* 'Blue Arrow'.

Opposite: *Miscanthus sinensis* 'Silberfeder', February

Right: Mid May, *Melianthus major* at the rear to the right, *Salvia leucantha* in the midst of its flowering, rich violet calyxs and tiny white flowers and the dry stems of *Sedum* 'Autumn Joy' in the foreground

Hornbeam hedge walk, autumn

chattering with baboonish malignity the goblin was making threats to kill my mother and her unborn child as she slept; boasting there was nothing my father could do to prevent this. The creature then burst through the open window and Cam wrestled with the thing for some time. Not a physical battle, you understand, it was more a battle of willpower, but still, with the certainty of my mother's death if he weakened or in any way failed in the struggle. Despite the agony of the moment, my father eventually noticed moonlight was streaming into the room in a way impossible for a south-facing window, and instantly the goblin was gone. Cam reawoke and in that quiet morning he could see the garden was, indeed, full of moonlight, every twig, every petal on the little flowering peach was like polished silver. Standing at the window he easily could see an empty (goblin shaped) crook in the tree, its configuration he was sure had never noticed before. But all was still and my mother slept on quietly. She had been close to miscarrying and ordered to rest and had been in bed for some days at this time.

Something of the verisimilitude and intensity of the dream made a profound impact on Cam and Jan. Years later it was mentioned to me, in passing, with some embarrassment. They were farming people, after all, not given to mulling over such things. As it happened the nightmare seemed not to prefigure anything untoward, except perhaps, weeks later, on the afternoon of the day I was born, torrential thunderstorms lashed that part of the Great Southern. Unharvested crops were ruined and stock killed and vehicles caught in the worst of the weather appeared to suffer sledgehammer blows from falling hail.

Autumn decay

THE MEADOWS

Pro molli viola, propurpureo
narcisso carduus et spinis surgit
paliuris acutis.

In place of the soft violet, in place
of the purple narcissus, comes the
Christ's thorn with its sharp spikes.

Virgil, *Eclogues*, 5–39.

14 April 2005

Drizzle as we woke up and by late morning rain is falling steadily, shreds of mist through the trees. With the dust of the last weeks washed away and today's soft light, the early autumn colour is incandescent. Our Acer japonicum aconitifolium *is a medley of scarlet and soft burgundy and the two big weeping maples are glinting with orange and red over the faded bronze of their late summer foliage. Pink and yellow autumn leaves of Boston ivy lie floating in the brown-black pond of the Water Temple.*

Mid-April: I imagine the cockies out in the Victorian wheat belt are thinking that they deserve some rain by now and after today perhaps the tractors will be moving into the paddocks.

I remember trading our little 60-horsepower John Deere on a J.D. 4040 with its 105-horsepower engine. I remember driving this new tractor, with its big sound-proofed and air-conditioned cab, its fancy radio and its hydraulically cushioned operator's seat, around the paddock for a while, just for fun, no machinery attached. It swayed across the hillsides with an exhilarating sense of relentless power. Chatting to Jan later: "Feels as though nothing could ever slow it down"; nice autumn day in 1979, waiting for the 'break'.

Mid-October, the fern leaf beech

The great privilege of working in Cloudehill is that much of what we have has been here for a generation or two; the mature rows of beech for instance, likewise the spring meadows. Bulbs in the meadows have been a talking point for nearly 50 years and these have needed little work on our part to incorporate into the garden. Walking to the end of the main terrace and reaching the terracotta-shingled summer house, one finds bluestone steps on the lower side of the terrace to explore down below Fred Streeter's big fern leaf beech. Further, winding steps lead on under a tall arching holly hedge

Mid-October, sunup

'Wings of Desire' by Rudi Jass

The meadows, clockwise from top left: Spanish bluebells, *Scilla hispanica*, with occasional clumps of an older daffodil; *Sparaxis tricolour* variety; the rather weedy buttercup, *Ranunculus repens*, with a creamy rose *Ixia speciosa* hybrid; Spanish bluebells hiding a path with a drift of *Sparaxis tricolour* on the far side.

(*Ilex aquifolium* 'Camelliifolia') down the south boundary to our meadows. All we have done here is cut paths across the slope towards a choice of destinations.

I understand the lower corner of the property was planted to bulbs in the early 1930s, ample time in intervening years for the plants to naturalise. Spanish bluebells and grape hyacinths have spread from their original rows throughout the meadows. As the bluebells commence their flowering, the hyacinths fade, the two providing a magnificent ground of blue for the many daffodils, from palest cream to yolkiest yellow from late July to almost November. As the daffodils finish and the bluebells run to seed, South African bulbs, ixias and sparaxis, along with various meadow grasses, begin to flower. The most attractive of the grasses is Yorkshire fog, *Holcus mollis*, with loose, mauve-lavender inflorescence over dusty grey foliage. With luck, the flowering of Yorkshire fog coincides with colonies of *Ixia maculata* throwing up papery, rose-blushed

Yorkshire fog, *Holcus Mollis*

creamy blooms through the grass's lavender haze. Even better, one bank of ixia grows below some copper beech that have now deepened to sombre aubergine – a ravishing combination. Ixia and Yorkshire fog are so perfect together it is a shame they are weeds elsewhere in the garden. This ixia seeds itself around, however, and Yorkshire fog runs. We enjoy both without concern as they are slashed before any seed ripens. And paths surrounding the meadows make ideal barriers to rhizomatous plants. The Yorkshire fog flowers are just the right height to nicely conceal the masses of unsightly dying daffodil foliage. And brassy little buttercups, *Ranunculus repens*, pop through and are a feature for two or three weeks in late October. In November and December, ox-eye daisies turn the lower meadow into a pointillist's dream, with flecks of dead white scattered through the green. And then, generally in mid-summer, a thunderstorm rolls over the ridge and bowls the entire assembly flat. To avoid a tangled eyesore for the remainder of the season we allow things to dry, then slash close to the ground. This can be in January, but more usually February; though the best time to slash varies, the more wind and rain the sooner it needs be. If the job can be left to February then colonies of tangerine alstroemeria and burnt orange montbretia flower through the yellowing grass to glorious effect.

Curiously, annual slashing and mowing is how a traditional hay meadow is maintained. Hay meadows were part of every farm and rural community in northern

Alstroemeria flowering through fading Yorkshire fog

By January montbretia is flowering

Europe from the first days of agriculture to recent times. Meadows were left alone through most of the year, kept free of stock and only scythed back for hay towards the end of each summer; the hay, of course, vital to feed animals in barns through winters. Meadows have similarities to that other great feature of rural life of England and France – hedgerows. Hedgerows and meadows gradually evolve to eventually host tremendously diverse communities of plants. In fact, the antiquity of both can be estimated by the variety of plants comprising them – so many species for a meadow or hedgerow 100 years old, after 200 years so many more will have settled in and so on. The flowery meads inspiring the background of medieval tapestries (behind a milky skinned lady in blue conical hat, a unicorn lolling on her lap) were already certainly many hundreds, perhaps thousands of years old, even then in the Middle Ages. Jim Woolrich began slashing his bulb beds every summer at least from the 1960s, thus only another several hundred and fifty years for us to see what our soil and climate will allow naturalising. Still, with a half-century of slashing, our meadows are outstanding features of Cloudehill from mid-winter to high summer. Following a summer cut back they quickly green to a passable, rough grass look and two years ago we introduced mauve colchicums to the edges of paths, their March flowering coinciding with a smattering of flesh pink easter lilies. And a friend has a magnificent collection of autumn flowering nerines, surely these might thrive in sunnier niches? Another job for another season!

Opposite, clockwise from top left: *Holcus mollis* flowering; montbretia with mid-summer grasses; *Alstroemeria* and *Ranunculus repens*.

The photo was snapped by my sister Jenny. A family joke revolved around the closing of the school in 1958. It was always tiny, only a handful of pupils, and the Francis family leaving the district that year supposedly killed the Moulyinning School stone dead. Seeing the vacant building almost 50 years later was startling; I had no memory of the place being so absurdly tall. A tiny squarish structure, the ceiling seemed considerably higher than the length of any wall and the interior positively gothic. I attended for only two years, when five and six, and a memory lapse over its eccentricity and spookiness is understandable. On the other hand, I clearly remember the teacher, Mr Mycock, telling children to bring any war medals our fathers or grandfathers might have to class as part of Anzac day commemorations. When asked, Cam said he didn't have any. Next morning we trooped in and sat at our desks and my class mates spread out their family's ribbons and medals. Without exception everyone had a few and most brought along medals enough to overflow the long desk tops. I was astonished; and envious. All those vivid ribbons and starry medals were too enticing for words and I was the only child without any. That afternoon I asked my father why he had no medals and I swear I recall in photographic detail his startled, bemused look of reply. Years later it dawned on me that Moulyinning was largely settled by soldiers returning from World War One. Several Tenth

The old Moulyinning School, September 2007

Light Horse veterans lived nearby and the majority of farms were pioneered by survivors of those innumerable Gallipoli and Western Front battles. And it was some forty years for me to appreciate Cam's feelings at being denied the chance to fly.

From a bench against the holly hedge on the south boundary visitors may enjoy the meadows and a view down between two rows of copper beech. The beech avenue projects between the upper and lower meadows from an area of trees and shrubs in the centre of the garden. These copper beech were planted in the winter of 1962, after the bush fires of that summer and were intended for commercial cut foliage production. This was all too apparent as we commenced making the garden in 1992. The upper row was magnificent, approaching early maturity and growing with vigour. However, the lower row had been butchered by a gung-ho foliage gatherer, perhaps in the early 1980s. Important branches were lopped almost to the trunk. No doubt, it is none too easy climbing trees, slithering onto whippy, precarious branches and nipping off twigs; much less tedious and more profitable to use a chainsaw and take down large sections of tree. The lower row of beech looked irredeemably disfigured in the first year or two of our gardening and we contemplated removing them altogether, but eventually thought better of it – two rows of trees suggested all sorts of landscape treatments and we went to some effort to rehabilitate the forlorn beech.

A broad path now leads from the holly hedge bench across the slope and between our rows of beech, also two narrow paths radiate from the same bench to the upper and lower meadows. I have planted a collection of larger ornamental grasses and dry climate perennials to each side of the confluence of the paths to provide an element of mystery to those who happen to enter the meadows from central parts of the garden. Walking from either of the meadows towards the bench there will be a feeling of strolling into shoulder high banks of billowing green; adjoining paths, which fork awkwardly for those walking this way, will be concealed until one reaches the bench. On the other hand, for those who explore the garden anticlockwise, the proper way, one walks down narrow shady steps under the dense dark overhanging holly hedge, around the long weeping green fronds of a *Chamaecyparis nootkatensis* 'Pendula' and, stepping into sunshine, one turns to see the dramatic left to right slope of the meadows. Also revealed is that intriguing choice of three paths, clearly leading to different parts of the garden. A narrowish path is cut into the slope to the left towards the green theatre, the next, broad and straight and more or less level, tempting visitors across the hillside into the copper beech, and a final narrow curving path falling away to the right towards Rangeview, our neighbour's garden.

The beech walk in spring looking towards the bench under the holly hedge

Above: Spring
Right: Autumn

Visiting my grandparents' house with Jenny to take photographs in spring 2007, we found the roof off and the place a ruin. It was not unexpected. I knew the house had not been lived in since my grandfather's death in the early 1960s. As we walked across the paddock to the old place, Jenny pointed out the remnants of their corrugated iron and hessian shack from the 1930s and 40s. It seemed miniscule. I was also startled by how long they were there. Arriving at Lake Camm in 1928, my grandparents, my four uncles and my mother lived in tents with the shack in the middle as kitchen and living room, for a bit, while grandfather, in spare time from land clearing, built their first house nearby. This house burnt before completion in the big fire, around 1932 or 33, then they were reduced to making do with the shack. My uncles helped build a final house after the war, pouring the concrete blocks themselves and my grandparents finally took up residence in 1949.

With astonishment I realised that this house, which they struggled for so long to build, was only lived in for 15 years before it was abandoned. Yet the place seemed ageless to me as a small boy. I remember Christmases in the late 1950s, the house booming with my boisterous uncles and their families, my grandmother presiding with lively aplomb and my grandfather sitting quietly. "They were all snobs", Jenny told me as we picked our way through debris.

After a moment she qualified this saying, "But in a nice way". How their high-mindedness survived all of them living nearly 20 years in a hessian and tin shack a few paces square I have no idea. As was the case with most farmhouses built by that generation, their final home was smallish – a tiny bathroom in one corner, lounge and kitchen on the north side, enclosed sleepout on the south and two bedrooms. I remember the place almost revolved around my grandmother's bedroom, right smack in the middle; it was tempting to take a short cut through my Nanny's room as one walked about the house. I rarely did though, due, more than anything, to her collection of perfumes on the dressing table. The room throbbed formidably with every fashionable scent ever dispensed by the eager shop assistants of the

Remaining fragment of my grandfather's wall

Boans and Aherns and Bon Marche stores of 1950s Perth. Not much was left of my Nan's room – the ceiling part-collapsed, floorboards missing; and in place of her treasured perfumes there was half a truck load of opened 20-litre weedicide drums, empty but still with an acrid stink to them, left stacked against a wall to stop them blowing around the paddock I suppose. Jenny recollected our grandfather, 'Grandy', never slept in the marital bed. His place was not even the second bedroom but the far corner of the sleepout, an arrangement of long standing, Jenny told me. I'm not positive how old my grandmother was when she married, but after bearing four boys and a girl she was still not yet 22 apparently. Naturally, this hinted strongly at a good football team's worth yet to come. My Nan had plans for her life however, so, on the arrival of her fifth, my mother Jan, Florence put her foot down. She tipped my grandfather out of their bed, in fact out of the bedroom, and for the next 40 years he was relegated to anywhere with a bit of distance to it, at least a room or two away, if not a tent in the garden, or out in the paddock round the back of a tree.

After driving hours to see it, I was dismayed to find my grandfather's stone wall gone. Dismantled and trucked away by a local farmer I suppose; a small section still intact was very beautiful. A tamarisk tree, planted as a cutting 50 years ago was buckling the front of the house and the only other sign of my grandmother's garden was a pale blue statice flowering barely 10 centimetres high, some sort of dwarf limonium I have never seen anywhere else. The tiny plants had leapt the remnants of the wall and a few wind-blown colonies had moved into the paddock and were scattered for some distance beside the nearby wheat crop.

Statice collected from my grandmother's garden

Attending a sculpture exhibition in the mid-1990s, Valerie and I were taken with a bronze sculpture by Leopoldine Mimovich. Leopoldine's piece represented the seasons: spring, summer, autumn, winter, by female faces of a child, a teenager, an older woman and finally, a veiled face. The mood of Leopoldine's sculpture instantly reminded me of a series of translations in the *Oxford Book of Verse in English Translation* comparing generations of men to the falling of leaves. The translations were versions of the same several lines from the *Illiad*, by Chapman, Johnson and Pope, and also, mysteriously, cropping up in Ecclesiasticus. Something about the conjunction of Leopoldine's four figures in one sculpture and the four fragments of poetry made me wonder if an installation incorporating all these elements might not be interesting under our two rows of copper beech. The idea certainly provided an excuse to go along and meet Leopoldine in her garden, where she showed Valerie and me the original of the 'Seasons', marvellously carved from a block of exceedingly valuable huon pine. We were then taken to Leopoldine's holy of holies: her workshop. A lifetime's collection of wood-carving instruments were neatly laid out, sharp and

'Seasons' by Leopoldine Mimovich

gleaming. I could not help noticing though, her garage nearby, stuffed end to end with slabs and blocks and tree trunks of huon pine and every type of rare wood. I was impressed. Leopoldine was a few years past ordinary retirement age but seemed to have sufficient timber laid in to keep the speediest wood carver busy for decades. Her car was out in the sun and rain.

Without further ado, Valerie and I paid for Leopoldine's sculpture and placed it on a brick plinth at the northern end of the beech walk. We have been experimenting with the pieces of Homer since, finding the best way of carving the lines into plaques. There is yet work to do here. Still, leaves accumulate every May and if one is happy to have time's passing drawn to one's attention, then it is good to stroll the beech walk in this season, coppery leaves crisp underfoot.

THE PEONY PAVILION
AND ITS SURROUNDS

Tristisque lupini sustuleris fragilis calamos silvamque sosantem.

And you will pick off the fragile stalks of the sad lupin with its tangle of rattling seed pods.

Virgil, *Georgics* 1, 75.

The crinkle-crankle box hedge

Jim Woolrich grew his collection of deciduous azaleas in the extreme lower corner of the property, rowed out, two or three varieties in each row, a dozen rows and perhaps 150 plants in all. The specimen of *Rhododendron schlippenbachii* the Woolrich brothers ordered from Japan was planted near the top of the group. However, through the 1980s honeysuckle swarmed across the azaleas and weakened and strangled many, and where there wasn't honeysuckle there was blackberry. I took some time in spring 1992 to label different colours as the plants flowered. I remembered Jim talking of the breeding strains: mollis, ghents and double-flowered rusticas. A few varieties of each seemed to have survived, and plants free of honeysuckle and blackberry were awe-inspiring, 3, 4, up to 5 metres high.

We moved the azaleas worth rescuing in autumn 1993 and placed them on each side of the grassy strip between the rows of beech growing below the theatre lawn. Each bank of azaleas was tucked just under the drip line of their respective row of beech. A shallow flight of bluestone steps was then constructed between the azaleas with strips of grass to each side. Finally, crinkle-crankle box hedges were planted in 2000 to conceal the bony ankles and knobbly knees of the azaleas.

I remember winters of my childhood were filled with rain. Droughts were unheard of, almost unimaginable in those years and for months in winter the Moore River brimmed with muddy water sliding around Pat Kelly's hill. Every valley, every tiny ditch on Merrie-Lea chattered with water pouring off sodden slopes. Vehicles driven away from farm tracks onto uncompacted

The crinkle-crankle hedge. *Buxus sempervirens* is at home in the Dandenongs. From cuttings to a hedge takes just three years and it's always tempting to use yet more box to give instant, crisp edges to every extension to the garden. I use it in as many ways as I can think. One hedge is formally clipped on one side and rounded and undulating on the other for example, while the maple court parterres are planted to emphasise the horizontal plane. Keeping in mind the azalea walk has a view terminating in a grove of 60-metre-high mountain ash, hedges to each side seemed a cue for drama. Here our box is rounded and 'crinkle-crankled', the rate of the hedge's to-ing and fro-ing accelerating from the top to bottom, like an oscillating whiplash accumulating energy on its way down the hillside.

soil were likely to bog and the little depression running across the track behind the house hill collected water enough to flood a shelf of iron stone further down the slope so every tiny hole on its exposed lower face bubbled and jetted with an intricate melody of tinkling water. Mike and I spent half of every winter playing around the stream under the rock face, rearranging stones, digging the pool ever bigger and filling it with hapless tadpoles collected from the Digger's Hill Gully stream. The pond under the waterfall was part encircled by the overhanging iron stone wall, myriad holes riddled the rock and water squeezed through most of its lower half, leaving just a few watery threads spilling from the upper lip falling cleanly 2 metres into the pool.

Nineteen sixty nine was the first drought year in more than a generation. In late June there was still but the slightest tinge of green on the hills. I think of Cam agonising all one week over whether to ship 1200 sheep off on the railway or hire in a fleet of trucks, at considerable extra expense, to reduce grazing pressure on our non-existent pasture. The stock agent suggested we truck them the following Monday and so beat the Tuesday rush on the rail network. Every agent in WA clearly recommended the same thing as the market crashed on Monday and our good wethers were sold for less than the 25 cents per head we were charged to cart them to the Midland sale yards. My father drove down to watch the sale; Jan and I heard the grim news on the ABC Radio Country Hour at lunch time and mother warned me not to say a word to Cam when he arrived home that afternoon – we ate our evening meal without mention of the day's events. He had lost $3000 through not accepting a private bid from the agent the previous week. This was a very large part of a year's income in those days and it was some time before he could bring himself to speak of it. By winter's end we had quit most of our stock, but the wheat crop came through, our harvest respectable.

Winters were thoroughly spoilt for me after 1969. Every dry spell was reason to look to the west for a hint of rain. The autumn break seemed to shift further and further from mid-April into May and sometimes June. This meant the few weeks of reliable rainfall coincided with short days and the coolest part of winter and the only time of strong pasture and crop growth were those few brief days of early spring; then came October with summer closing in. By the 1980s I found myself storing more and more grain from the harvest to provide supplementary autumn stock feed, the unused grain sold a few weeks after the autumn break with a sigh of relief. And dams, at best, only ever half-filled, dried up in the first weeks of summer.

The year we bought Clover Downs, 1973, three of the previous four seasons drought-stricken, our dams empty and windmills sucking dry, we were reduced to pumping from our neighbour's brackish bore to water our breeding cows. The day we took possession of our new farm, around mid-March, Jan and Cam and I celebrated by droving the cattle from the northwest corner of Merrie-Lea, the Sherwood paddock, up over the hills to the springs on the *southern end of Clover Downs. It was a drive approaching 15 kilometres and hot, very slow, the bellowing cattle stopping to rest in every scrap of shade and detouring to investigate every dry dam and empty water trough they passed in their misery at weeks of drinking salt-polluted water. It took most of the day and the herd breasted the slope above the springs with a late afternoon sea breeze arriving through the big redgums. The lead cows caught the smell of moisture on the wind and they roared in a kind of agony and rage and stampeded down to the water. By the time we pushed weaker calves and stragglers along to join them, the pools were stuffed solid with cattle, standing jammed together in the shallow water, dripping bellies wall to wall, gobbling up bucketfuls, the entire herd bellowing in an ear-splitting bovine ecstasy.*

During the 1990s meteorologists began commenting that the dry winters seemed more than just an anomalous temporary cycle. Twenty-five and 30 years of low rainfall suggested trends of a scale beyond the thinking of only West Australia, and that a 30 per cent drop in annual rainfall and erratic seasons was the shape of the things to come.

Deciduous azaleas in October

Our azalea steps lead to a little apricot-coloured brick pavilion with a coppery green pointed roof at the top of the slope. We also needed something similarly imposing at the foot of the steps to encourage visitors down. Though easily substantial enough, Jim's old favourite, the *Rhododendron schlippenbachii*, seemed a little amorphous for this duty, but it looked too silly for words out on its own in the corner of the spring meadow. So, after moving the ghents, the loader gently picked up the elderly plant and carried it gingerly across the slope and we planted it in line with and just below the lowest bluestone step. I left space in front of the rhododendron to allow a copy of an urn from the Villa D'Este gardens, near Rome, to be placed onto a brick plinth and make a decisive focal point for this minor axis. The urn has been painted faded terracotta to contrast with the ethereal pink flowers of the R. *schlippenbachii* acting as backdrop. The flowers open early October, fortunately some days ahead of the deciduous azaleas, the ghents and mollis; many of these bloom in raucous mustard yellows and rusty flames. The lovely perfume of azaleas fills this place for most of October and some of November. During summer, lilies rear out from between the ranks of the azaleas and in the spring of 2003 I planted a *Clematis viticella* 'Royal Velours', to grow into the schlippenbachii, draping it with molten crimson and purple blooms through the warmer weeks of summer.

Rhododendron schlippenbachii is rare in Australia. It demands mountain soil and conditions to thrive and is almost always unhappy grown elsewhere. Even in the Dandenongs it can be tricky. I remember Jim chuckling, "Rhododendron schlippenbachii – always schlippenbach!"

Rhododendron schlippenbachii

Below the Villa D'Este urn and Jim's *R. schlippenbachii* is a grove of 80-year-old *Kalmia latifolia*, the American mountain laurel. These produce exquisitely intricate urn-shaped pink flowers during the last days of spring. Kalmias are related to rhododendrons and are slow to build with a twiggy growth habit. As their common name implies, they are yet another plant difficult to grow away from the Dandenongs. Ours approach 3 metres high, the tallest I'm aware of in Australia. A couple of new kalmia selections are planted nearby: *Kalmia* 'Clementine Churchill' has pink flowers several shades richer than the type and we also have the deliciously named *Kalmia* 'Bullseye' with circular, zigzag-patterned flowers. These two are placed beside the earth steps leading past the *R. schlippenbachii* and down under a huge *Magnolia denudata*. Denudata is the famous Yulan tree of China. I wish we had the history for this specimen. Denudatas in Melbourne are usually large shrub size, 3 to 5 metres. Ours is closer to 15, again the biggest we know of in these parts, and it covers itself with thousands of creamy goblets in August.

On the lee side of the *M. denudata*, I have a 'wedding cake' tree: *Cornus controversa* 'Variegata'. This small tree, growing 7 to 10 metres, radiates horizontal twiggy branches supporting level tiers of creamy white variegated foliage. It spreads wider than high and is an absolute show stopper of a plant. Ours is positioned to attract visitors along the path across the lower spring meadow from the holly hedge.

I trust as they climb the steps between the deciduous azaleas, visitors appreciate we are clipping the rows of beech to each side. We aim to have them neat and dense and their flanks in line with the axis. This is a precarious exercise, as trees at the lower end approach 20 metres high. For the past few years an arborist and dealer in flowers and foliage, Paul Cantlay, has climbed our rows of beech carefully reducing their height and spread and increasing the sun shining into the garden. Foliage gathered is sold and covers part of the effort involved and in this way a link is maintained with Jim's original business. For those having lunch in Jim's old house, now our restaurant, we also preserve a view of the Southern Alps above the trees. I was initially very hesitant to clip our rows of beech, remembering the many we originally found disfigured by rough and ready lopping. However, after experimentation we see careful pruning can be wonderful. With a little bit of pruning every three to four years the height of trees in each row is now uniform, their tops level and shoulders and flanks thickened and improved. The big 'named' beeches the brothers brought in from Fred Streeter's nursery 80 years ago we leave alone and wait to find just how large they may grow.

The 'wedding cake' tree, *Cornus controversa* 'Variegata', from the far end of the meadow. Milestone ceramic sculptures by Madeline Meyer.

View from the peony pavilion towards our neighbours' mountain ash grove

I was scarifying the southwest paddock on Clover Downs all through one night in the mid-1980s, the machinery hurling up a cloud of dust that the strengthening wind carried away to the west; hour by hour I was becoming more infuriated. After studying research on topsoil lost by wind erosion during cultivation, I had avoided 'working back' powder dry soil for years. Paddocks were only ever scarified (to kill regrowth weeds) when sufficiently moist so as little dust (soil nutrients) was disturbed into the air as possible. Once in the air it seemed, most dust and nutrients came down a long way off; with an east wind blowing, almost certainly settling onto the Indian Ocean. When conditions were good for cultivation and soil moisture just right, the scarifier wrenched weeds up to die with no dust at all billowing behind. That night, the soil bone dry and the following wind was swirling dust so thick I could barely see to steer; circumstances I had been avoiding for ages. After dry weather for weeks though, weeds surviving the initial cultivation were growing away strongly; they would soon be impossible to kill, no rain was forecast and that night was the last chance to salvage the original ploughing.

While driving the tractor I attempted to calculate the pros and cons of a good weed kill, thus a high-yielding crop versus the damage to the soil I was inflicting. The 140 acres would likely return $200 of wheat per acre while nutrients lost in the dust swirling to the west, I guessed, might depress future yields one percent, something approaching this at least. Whatever the figure from the negative side of the ledger, that reduction in yield would be a problem for a very long time; the advantage of a weed-free crop would inevitably be negated by the reduction in yields accumulating into the future. Just how long it would take for accumulating lower yields to outweigh the $28,000 in my pocket at Christmas time was the puzzle. I guessed at least 30 crops, maybe 50, possibly 80, several generations down the track. Once set in train though, that annual loss will continue accumulating, not just for a few generations, more probably thousands of years. Eventually, the soil will recover, the earth will heal itself. The activity of micro fauna and flora that created the vital topsoil from bedrock and subsoil in the first place will repair the damage of that night; but slowly, immensely slowly, at glacial speed, over geological periods of time. The final line of my imaginary balance sheet was the question mark representing damage likely to be inflicted by the sowing of future crops, this figure accumulating exponentially, catastrophically, for so long as the paddock is farmed.

I wondered about the soils of the Mediterranean, the deep alluvial soils in the valley of the Po, cultivated for millennia; ancient farms, surveyed after the Roman civil wars by centurions under Caesar Augustus and still existing, on their original boundaries, and still productive 2000 years later. I pondered that hoary chestnut, 'Live as though you may die tomorrow, farm as though you will live forever'. Yet these thoughts were absurd. For me, with responsibilities to my family and my bank manager, there was no choice in the matter. There was not a penny to be gained by considering generations to come and all of $28,000 to be lost. My duty was to me and mine; future generations would have to fend for themselves. Helplessness at the absurdity of it though, left me aching with rage.

Years later I was talking to a nephew who works on soil reclamation projects around the world and who had studied the logic of such moments as head of a United Nations team. He laughed and explained the concept of 'market failure', times when 'pricing signals' that should govern decisions seem irrelevant, times when it seems reasonable, inevitable, to accept damage to soil and other parts of the environment because predictable, end-of-year returns will always outweigh long-term theoretical losses; the latter spread immensely too far away from the present day to contemplate inclusion in any annual balance sheet. In darker moments I began to feel much of farming hovers along this fault line in the rhetoric of our times.

PEONIES

Tree peonies deserve several chapters in their own right. Suffice to say I began growing them almost by accident. Ronnie Boekel, a local nurseryman, mentioned that he was collecting and propagating tree peonies and maybe I might like to take a look at them flowering. Nearly 10 years later, they have become an important part of the calendar for us. Their season fills the three or four weeks' gap between the last of the spring bulbs and rhododendrons and colour filling the summer borders.

Chinese tree peonies are famous for sumptuous flowers in colours from white to pink to scarlet and purple. Catalogues, some very ancient, also list plants flowering gold and blue; these were almost certainly mythological, never existing in the first place. There is still no blue peony but we do now have good numbers of yellows; they are latecomers to our gardens, however. Despite effort over thousands of years to achieve this colour in China, the first nurseryman to actually hybridise the classic suffruticosa peony with the single yellow-flowered species, *Paeonia lutea*, was a Frenchman, Victor Lemoine. He displayed P. 'L'Esperance', the original example of this very difficult cross, in 1909. P. 'L'Esperance' is still grown for its lovely semi-double, soft yellow flowers, crimson flares erupting from their heart. Over subsequent years Lemoine released Chromatella, with soft yellow double flowers, Flambeau, with faded crimson double blooms and Souvenir de Maxime Cornu in yellow, orange and pink tints and flowers so doubled and colossal they frequently nod. Lemoine was a great friend of Monet and some of the first examples of these selections are still to be seen thriving at Giverny. Professor A.P. Saunders succeeded in repeating the painstakingly difficult lutea–suffruticosa cross in the USA in the

Aurea pavonum ridenti imbuta lepore
  saecla

The golden generations of peacocks,
  steeped in smiling charm

Lucretius, *De Rerum Natura*, II–501

A herbaceous peony, given to me as *Paeonia peregrina*.
A good plant, but I suspect wrongly named.

Left: *Paeonia* 'Leda'
Right: *Paeonia* 'Rose Flame'

1920s and went on to introduce further outstanding plants. And William Gratwick and Louis Smirnow have carried on Saunder's work to present times. The lutea hybrid peonies in raised beds above our ghent azalea steps are the fabulous progeny of these gentlemen. Lutea hybrids inherit the elegant dissected foliage of *P. lutea* and all possess some of its vigour. They are more disease resistant, more robust and adaptable than most Chinese and Japanese peonies and blooms are generally in flame colours: lemons, yolky yellows, tangerines and mahogany reds. Pinks are achieved by back-crossing with a suffruticosa peony; the progeny still have good vigour and we have three or four. The pinks contain complicated mixtures of colours, giving an overall pinkish effect. For instance, *Paeonia* 'Marie Laurencin', with substantial semi-double flowers in dusky cyclamen pink and *P.* 'Rose Flame', deep rosy pink to wine red, suffused with lavender tints. *Paeonia* 'Rose Flame' displays full, semi-double flowers over outstanding finely dissected foliage. It is one of the best of all these hybrids. I grow a number of older yellow and burgundy luteas including several exquisitely suffused with both these colours in varying proportions. Happy Days is a pale yellow variety with a hint of red, Gaugin is flame red with hints of yellow, and Marchioness is an extraordinary mix of these tints in equal proportions, its colour deepening as one looks to the heart of the flower.

The mystique of tree peonies is underlined by the resounding names breeders have put on them. In our collection for instance, Argosy and Artemis, both excellent yellows, and likewise *P.* 'Golden Vanitie'. Boreas, named for the north wind, is a superb wine red semi-double; burning bright with orange flame we have *P.* 'Tiger Tiger', and finally, towards the centre, *P.* 'Heart of Darkness', the deepest of burgundy reds.

Paeonia 'Thunderbolt'

Older houses of the Mogumber and Gillingarra districts were made from mud brick. The Merrie-Lea homestead overlooked one of these, sited in a cosy spot near where the Moore River looped towards the railway just across the road from our hay paddock. Built around the turn of the last century, 'Stanwell's' was abandoned years before Cam and Jan bought Merrie-Lea. Despite its dilapidation, an Aboriginal family lived there for a bit in the 1960s but it was really only used for storing bags of seed wheat. The corrugated iron roof was allowed to blow off in the 1970s and its mud walls quickly dissolved in the weather.

Further north was Pat Kelly's house, again mud brick. Old Pat and his wife Dolores lived there with the two younger children, Joan and Gerard, who Mike and I played with as we waited for the Gillingarra School bus. There was also a teenage brother, Peter, with his bed in the verandah sleepout and one tiny room was reserved for Pat Kelly's sister, known to all as Aunty Lena. The old 'Wicklow' house was really just a cottage, much the same as any to be found in Ireland, its thick earth walls white washed, just five tiny rooms, no ceilings, wide gaps between the walls and the tin roof and little fireplaces built into three rooms in an attempt to warm the place on wintry nights. The bath was a tin basin on the back verandah and the toilet was down towards the river. There was no electric lighting. At night Dolores' kerosene lamp glowed through a small piece of glass embedded in the stone chimney above the kitchen fireplace. We could just make out its orange warmth in the shadows of gum trees at the distant end of the valley to us, where the river plunged between our 'Sherwood paddock' hills and 'Pat Kelly's' hill to the west.

Pat Kelly's house, 'Wicklow'

When Jan and Cam first came to Merrie-Lea in 1959 our cattle broke out of a railway wagon beside the Gillingarra siding and disappeared into the sandplain. Cam and Pat Kelly went out on horseback to fetch them back and over several weeks tracked them to where the river cut into the sand hills towards the Moore River Settlement. I remember my father coming home each evening walking stiffly and complaining of his sore bottom. On the other hand, Pat Kelly seemed born in the saddle. He was wiry, lanky, sunburned, as ramrod straight and taciturn as a Banjo Patterson character, and handy with a stock whip. I'm sure he enjoyed the challenge of mustering our lost cattle but he didn't let on. Pat kept several horses on his few acres of river flat, and a milking cow with a bell hanging from a leather strap around its throat.

The first farms of the area were all made hard along the rivers. A few hundred acres of good silt soil were fenced off and cleared by the settlers and a shack thrown up in one corner, generally close to one of the river pools. Even now it is possible to see those tiny farms, their awkward paddocks clogging up cropping programs of their present owners. From the air, for anyone who happened to be flying over in the years around the First World War, they would have appeared as a mosaic strip of clearing in the midst of the bush; a tightly angled boomerang incised throughout its length with half-timbered, half-pastured pioneer blocks, running for miles, hugging the banks of the two rivers. A couple of the old farms were incorporated into Merrie-Lea at various times. Just to our north, Jan and Cam owned the Jilgil farm itself for a while, the 400-acre block immediately around the Jilgil river pool, for a good dozen years from 1962. During the 1970s they also bought the MacDonalds' block. This was a nice patch of some 130 acres of excellent wheat-growing soils near the southwest corner of Merrie-Lea. A shallow spring was excavated out into a 'soak' in the middle and a slab hut built under a nearby tree sheltering a long disused horse-drawn seed drill. Another slab hut was sited beside a stream running down from our hills. This one room building was just sufficient for two people it seems; in fact, the MacDonalds themselves were apparently still residing there those first few months of 1959 as our family were moving in a few paddocks away. The MacDonalds were very quiet, Cam told me, and extraordinarily tall, both husband and wife. I can't say I remember them but walked into the faint remains of their tiny house imagining them forever silently banging their heads on the low rafters.

In the old days there were many mud brick houses along the Moore River, up to Koojan and beyond. And several on the eastern branch of the river, at least 12 and perhaps 20, all built four generations ago. I can only think of one that is still in reasonable order. The corrugated iron of their roofs was generally attached to rafters made from eucalyptus saplings. As the wood inexorably shrank away from the nails, sheets of tin were pulled off by the wind. Once exposed to winter squalls, mud walls melted back into the soil and termites polished off the bush timber remains. By the mid-1980s all I remember of Stanwell's was a few rocks marking *the fireplace, a rose bush that happened to have just enough prickles to keep the sheep, try as they might, from eating all its leaves and killing it, and several almond, olive, fig and two big mulberry trees.*

*   *   *

Kaye Kelly tells me the Stanwell's rose is famous, among the Kellys of Gillingarra at least, planted to commemorate the boys returning to their farms from the Great War.

Traditionally, peonies are grown in raised beds; in China often in beds retained by wonderfully carved stone, almost altars. Raised beds serve to emphasise the plants and to bring the flowers to something like head-height. It is poetic licence to call them trees; a metre-high specimen has a few years behind it. They can achieve 2.5, perhaps 3 metres, but often require two or three generations of gardeners to do so. Not that they require much effort. Once established, they famously battle on, come what may, and become ever bigger and better. Older plants flowering with many blooms become legendary wherever tree peonies are grown. The cool dryish soils of Victoria's goldfields are home to several outstanding specimens. One handsome peony grows in the Melbourne suburb of Footscray and blooms with more than 100 flowers each spring I understand. I am told that the largest tree peony in Australia grows on a farm in Tasmania and flowers with close to 1000 blooms. Raised beds ensure sharp drainage, a crucial requirement of tree peonies. They enjoy neutral, even alkaline soils and we lime our mildly acidic loams to suit, but otherwise these ravishing plants are not fussy. Tree peonies thrive in full sun through to two thirds shade and, unlike their herbaceous cousins, do not require chilling to flower and grow well in sight of the sea.

Paeonia 'Age of Gold'

The tree peony pavilion overlooks our lutea hybrid tree peony collection. In the corners of the peony beds, nearest the pavilion, we have two golden fastigiate beeches, *Fagus sylvatica* 'Dawyck Gold'. These are young, some 12 metres high and 3 metres across and still growing rapidly. I suspect they will easily reach twice their present size. Their leaves are buttery lime in spring, turning pale green in summer. The golden beeches are placed each side of the steps just below the pavilion and serve nicely to frame the view to the Villa D'Este urn and the kalmias, and on to a glimpse of the spring meadow. In the mid distance, across our south boundary in fact, we borrow, so to speak, a small stand of our neighbour's mountain ash. The grove of *Eucalyptus regnans* happens to be perfectly in line with this minor axis and their upright trunks and narrow, vertical canopies echo the dawyck beech. As mentioned previously, I understand our neighbour's was a bare hillside before 1950. The eucalypts

The legendary Rock's peony, taken a few minutes before a storm shattered every flower

can only be a little over 50 years old, perhaps closer to 40 and most approach 60 metres high. They are just the right distance away to be dramatic without being overbearing.

I am looking at photographs of two country cricket teams. One shows the 1949 Lakes District Cricket Team, either about to begin or having just completed a tournament of 'country week' cricket in Perth. An unselfconsciously cheerful and nuggety group gathered before a backdrop of gum trees and date palms, for me their faces epitomise that generation. They are in their best whites for the commemorative photo, wearing open-necked shirts and their oiled hair is swept back over their foreheads in a style my father kept up all his life. These men exude toughness; I imagine the majority had a few years' service in the forces under their belt. My father stands in the back row, second from left, and my mother's brother, Stanley McPhee, is on the far end of the same row. He was always known as 'Brick', in fact I only became aware he was really Stanley some time after he died, more than 35 years ago. I asked Cam how my uncle came by his nickname. Cam replied it was because everyone thought he was 'a brick': friendly, outgoing and liked by all. The expression has fallen from favour so much that I felt a flicker of nostalgia in having this pointed out.

The second photo is from 1894 and shows the Nelson Cricket Club, all men from the volcanic, high-rainfall farmland of the extreme southeast corner of South Australia. I guess they are also in their finery. Their mood is very different to the relaxed and grinning players of 1949. These men are unsmiling, still, waiting out the slow shutter speed 1890s camera. One is bearded

and the rest, bar one, wear heavy moustaches. Ties lend an air of formality. My grandfather, Mark Francis, tallest of the back row, stands next to centre, arms folded, chest thrown out. His brother, Charlie, stands at his right beside him, and another brother, or perhaps cousin, Walter Francis, is sitting on the left end of the front row.

At first glance, the Nelson side looks a little more prosperous than the Lakes District team, ties suggesting a middle class English team about to play on a village green somewhere in the home counties. Then one notices two or three are wearing work trousers, cricket pads are worn and stained and rather than the tennis shoes of the 1940s team (and all of that team were keen tennis players), the 1894 team wear work boots.

One curious parallel between the photos is that I have members of both sides of my family in each team. My father and one of my mother's brothers figure in the 1949 team, and from 1894, my grandfather Mark and his brothers but also two of my grandmother's cousins: Harry Pick in the middle of the front row and James at the right-hand end with his arm resting on a cricket bat. Cam had been in love with Jan for more than eight years by 1949. In the case of my grandparents, I can only guess at the chronology. They married some 15 years past the date of the photograph though. Another parallel between the generations not to be seen in the images is that one relative from both sides of the family married an Aboriginal woman. Uncle Hec's wife, Aunty Eid, was part-Aboriginal. She was tall and athletic, adept at constructing makeshift toys for her many nieces and nephews. Those were days when toys were not too easy to be had – Aunty Eid was most popular with small nieces and nephews. Further back, Cam's Uncle Charlie married an Aboriginal woman sometime in the 1890s and together they moved to somewhere in the northwest of WA and in the way of these things they lost touch with the rest of the family.

*   *   *

After the five minutes' driving around required to enjoy the sights of Lake Varley in 2007, Jenny and I noticed a small sign directing attention to 'the Lake Varley Sporting Complex'. With time on our hands we took the track due east towards 'the fence' and soon came to another tiny sign pointing off into the scrub. Some moments further a golf course could be glimpsed through the mallee to our right; a bush golf course, rough grass fairways and sand covered 'greens' all with rake left propped conveniently close to smooth the odd player's approach to the hole. Passing the club house, an Australian Rules football oval appeared, then rows of tennis and netball courts and flood lighting towers, and a couple of hockey fields and several bowling greens, all with the latest artificial turf and more lighting. And in the midst of all these was a hall big enough to accommodate the entire population of the Lakes District to the last man, woman and child with ample room left for several opposition teams and their entourages. My sister and I walked around the deserted complex absolutely

The peony pavilion, *Hosta fluctuans* 'Sagae' below the window on the left

flabbergasted. It was a Thursday afternoon. Judging by how neatly everything was left we imagined weekends were busy. That evening I asked my cousin, Aubrey McPhee, how it was the district possessed sports facilities surely more appropriate to a town with 100, perhaps several hundred times the population. "Oh, they get used," he said, "and it's been the thing for ages. We all take turns to put a paddock in with a bit of wheat for the sports clubs."

The shady sloping beds to each side of the peony pavilion are planted to woodlanders, hostas, arisemas, kirengeshomas and the like. This is also a good spot for hostas, the slope faces south and two maples along the lip of the slope cast almost constant shade. From the seat in the pavilion it is possible to maintain a vigilant watch for snails and for that reason I have placed one of my more precious hostas to be admired through one of the vertical oval windows in each side of this structure. *Hosta* 'Sagae' (*syn. H. fluctuans* 'Sagae') forms a large mound, 60 centimetres by 1 metre. Large pleated leaves are glaucous blue-green with a thick yellow margin and the two colours bleed into each other with intriguing celadon streaks. This is a famous plant in Japan but difficult to find in Australia. *H.* 'Sagae' has been very slow for me; the one precious piece I was given some years back has increased to only four crowns this season, still these are strong and very handsome.

I am growing a couple of recently introduced American hostas in a milky turquoise glazed pot under the shady eaves of the peony pavilion. *Hosta* 'Patriot' and *H.* 'Loyalist' are smaller growing varieties with green leaves heavily variegated creamy white. Patriot is green with a wide cream margin, and loyalist precisely the reverse. Placing them in the same pot was simply too much to resist. To underscore the combination, I have trailing from under them *Ajuga* 'Arctic Fox', with small green leaves heavily mottled, again with creamy white. All these plants, naturally, enjoy this shady, bright position.

A collection of shade lovers. *Hosta* 'Hadspen Blue' on the left, *H.* 'Loyalist' and *H.* 'Patriot' in the turquoise urn, *H.* 'Frances Williams' on the right and *H.* 'Big Daddy' at the rear.

Near our *Hosta* 'Sagae' we have a clump of that most aristocratic of woodlanders, *Paris polyphylla*. It is slowly building up into a good colony from the three bulbs we planted a few years back. *Paris polyphylla*, or the 'no more gaps plant', as one gardener dubbed it, is a plant that particularly appeals to botanic artists; it is supremely architectural in its demeanour. *Paris polyphylla* produces bare stems to 75 centimetres topped with what appears to be a ruff, more correctly a whorl, of 10 or more leaves surrounding the stem; immediately above is a further ruff formed by the emerald green sepals and on top of this arrangement thread-like yellow stamen grow also in a radiating circle with, at their centre, a knobbly, violet-stained stigma. It is a puzzle for the average visitor to know where the foliage ends and the flower begins. Because we have only one self-infertile clone, the flowering is persistent for three or more months and we never see the plant's red berries.

We were given our first Paris bulbs a few years back by Eric Genet, a flower grower from Gembrook at the eastern end of the Dandenongs. Eric received seed from the North American Rock Garden Society in the early 1990s. He tinkered a bit to germinate it and the plants took a further five years to grow to flowering size. Paris may be stately in its growth, but it's actually easy in the volcanic soils of the Dandenongs and that original clump is now very strong.

It was always fun visiting Eric and Ethel, his wife, for a chat over a cup of tea and a stroll around their remarkable garden. In 1942 Eric was with Victorian battalions that, with almost no training, were thrown against the, until then, victorious and seemingly unstoppable Japanese forces in the Owen Stanley Ranges. Most old diggers have unhappy memories of the mud and vertical slopes of that vital campaign, but the New Guinea mountain tops delighted Eric. Why, they were covered in dwarf rhododendrons and warm climate blueberries and tropical violets and exquisite dwarf tree ferns and every sort of mind-boggling equatorial alpine. On several occasions I heard Eric talk at length and with intense enthusiasm on the flora of those rain-drenched mountains. He never mentioned why he was there, never raised the issue of an entire Japanese army doing their level best to spoil his botanising of the Kokoda Track, and who was I to remind him.

Eric's family now grow an astonishing variety of cool-climate plants in their Gembrook garden, with most harvested flowers and foliage going to one of Melbourne's more exclusive florists. I suspect the Genet's business is almost identical to Jim Woolrich's flower farm as it was 50 and 80 years ago; the Genets are almost the last commercial flower growers in the Dandenongs whose love of flowers has won out over the pressure to specialise. The family have generously donated many rarities growing in Cloudehill.

Opposite: A stong colony of *Arisaema candidissimum* beside the peony pavilion

The Sunshine harvester, spring 2007

Australian agricultural soils are prone to numerous forms of degradation. These include the obvious: salination and wind and water erosion, but there are other, subtler processes such as compaction, acidification and the depletion of soil micro-organisms, these last perhaps more difficult to counter than the first. Still, despite the array of problems I am sure solutions will be found. Farmers are highly innovative; they always have been, always will be. In fact, staggering advances have been made in the time since I was farming. Sowing rates of wheat crops are now computer-calibrated; the application rate of both fertiliser and seed altered continuously under the direction of global positioning satellite technology to accord with the precise soil type for that part of the paddock the machinery is passing over. This has dramatically improved yields, at negligible cost. Combine drills now use 'knife points' to cause minimal soil disturbance as seed is sown, almost eliminating wind erosion and to minimise soil compaction. Tractors are programmed to steer themselves on 'tramlines' and stay precisely on the same wheel track with an accuracy of a couple of centimetres every time the paddock is worked. The tractor is now a robot, its 'driver' merely supervising – farmers may sit in their tractor cabs watching movies all night. This technology simply was not dreamed of in 1989. With climate change the rural landscape will change and change again. Already I see it as I drive past the old place. Trees have been planted, the Mogumber hills are greener than they were. All is change and the changes of the next 50 years will, I'm sure, outpace those of the previous half century over and over. New technology has merely speeded that constant seasonal and millennial and eonic flux. A tiny 'sunshine harvester', abandoned and rusting, always reminded me as I walked past that modern dryland farming was, to a fair degree, invented by Australian farmers. The Sunshine harvester, the stump jump plough, the breathtaking, revolutionary idea that one or two people, by themselves, might farm and care for many thousands of acres as one single farm – this was the result of the sweat and determination of those fairly desperate pioneers two and three generations ago.

West Australian farmers have led the world in dryland farming for a long time. In the 1970s a number of WA farmers travelled to Libya as part of an aid scheme to demonstrate West Australian dryland agricultural techniques to Libyan farmers. Yet in classical times Libya was the breadbasket of Rome, her farmers the finest of the Mediterranean. Of course, the Sunshine factory has long closed. Trade globalisation means little farm machinery is made in this country. There are too few remaining on the land to provide a home market for manufacturers and Australian farmers harvest their crops with magnificent, state-of-the-art equipment which, as likely as not, comes from Italy. It intrigues me, though, that almost all these machines from every part of the world are still designed to the exact pattern of that little horse-drawn Sunshine harvester, made of wood and leather and cast iron and sheet tin.

We have several bonsais in pots on the terrace in front of the peony pavilion; they are all cheats, all actually grow as very dwarf plants with minimal attention. The collection includes *Tsuga* 'Minuta', the miniature hemlock and an extremely dwarf form of the common Japanese maple, *Acer palmatum* 'Komachi Hime', with tiny growth habit and miniscule leaves. We also have a naturally dwarf form of the European beech. I am not aware of a name for this neat little plant. It certainly deserves one. It came to us, prosaically, as *Fagus sylvatica* dwarf form. Conversely, the collection includes the resounding *Ulmus davidiana* 'Nire-keyaki', a miniature form of Pere David's elm. Nire-keyaki is an exquisite thing with tiny fringed leaves and very compact habit and for years was known mainly to aficionados for a magnificent specimen in the Emperor of Japan's private collection. I really have no patience for proper bonsais and am perfectly content to enjoy the handiwork of others. Our dwarf trees give the appearance of a bonsai collection with not much more than a sprinkle of fertiliser in the spring and a splash of water each day as I do my rounds of the pots. This is only 15 minutes of relaxation, really, and gives me a chance to look the garden over.

Ted Secombe's urn, planted with an *Acer palmatum* 'Komachi Hime'

The shrub walk connects the peony pavilion terrace with the water garden, so leading back to the beginning of our tour. A brick plinth constructed to one side of the peony pavilion provides a raised position to display a superb Ted Secombe urn. The ceramic urn is big, dramatic enough to serve as an eye catcher. The plinth was constructed in direct line with the path between the shrub borders with this in mind. Ted's piece has an intriguing, pale blue crystalline glaze and the form of the urn is oriental in mood, appropriate to the pavilion and nearby peonies. I have planted our specimen of the minature Japanese maple, *Acer pal*. 'Komachi Hime', with tiny reddish green leaves and dense habit, in Ted's urn while below *Hedera helix* 'Buttercup', with buttery yellow leaves, is planted to entwine around the plinth and suits the milky sky-blue of the urn nicely.

We are fortunate in having a few of Ted Secombe's pieces scattered strategically through Cloudehill. These are souvenirs of several exhibitions of his works mounted through the gardens over past years. A magnificent porcelain Japanese lantern, also by Ted, is placed under one of our big weeping maples. The lantern is glazed with a layer of cobalt blue overlaid with copper oxide red. During firing, the cobalt blue has burnt through the copper oxide to give various patterns of red and blue, and every colour between. The colours merge frequently to a purple very similar to the purples of the maples in mid summer foliage which, I hope, our visitors ponder as they admire. The lantern did not sell at the opening of the exhibition and it was a day or two before it occurred to me how I might use it and a little while

Viburnum plicatum 'Molly Schroeder'

Eriogonum giganteum, the giant buckwheat from the Santa Catalina islands off the coast from Southern California; the lovely *Rosa chinensis* 'Mutabilis' in autumn flower and below, the pleated silver gold foliage of *Strobilanthes gossypinus*

Golden pampas grass, *Cortaderia selloana* 'Aureolineata', a maroon form of the pineapple flower, *Eucomis bicolor* (possibly *Eucomis punctata*) and some *Stachys* 'Big Ears' in the lower right corner

Delphiniums, orange spire of *Isoplexis canariensis* (a shrub related to foxgloves), yellow foliage of *Physocarpus* 'Dart's Gold' and the fresh crimson growth of the copper beech hedge catching the light

negotiating with Valerie as to how we might afford it. Ted's pieces have drama enough to dominate any garden, the sheer vibrancy of his glazes means careful thought must be given to how best the surrounding planting may salute his work. I have planted chartreuse and sea-green hostas and the purple-crimson leaved *Heuchera* 'Plum Pudding' around Ted's red and blue lantern.

Eucalyptus macrocarpa

On the southern boundary of Merrie-lea, the western edge of the Darling escarpment rises dramatically out of the wheat paddocks to a ridge a little higher than any other in the vicinity. Older litho maps show the hills stretching away to northeast across Merrie-Lea as the Babillion ranges. One map Mike and I unearthed in Cam's office when we were young also mentioned a Mount Babillion. However, the position of the 'mountain' on this map made no sense; Mount Babillion seemed to correspond to a mere foothill below our airstrip. The handsome western ridge on our south boundary seemed a much better candidate to have attracted the attention of a map maker intent on elevating one of our hills into a mountain. The slopes surrounding our 'Babillion' ridge were all rocky and rugged, it was the last hilltop on the list for clearing and at some point in the 1970s Cam decided, maybe, he just wouldn't bother and the 100 odd acres could stay as a reserve, a souvenir of the original bush.

As kids and teenagers, Mike and I regularly explored the scrub on the slopes of our Babillion paddock. Stunted white gums, wandoos, grew along the ridge, also several clumps of the dramatic and rare Eucalyptus macrocarpa, a type of mallee with giant crimson flowers and powdery white leaves with the unlikely common name 'Rose of the West'. Once or twice we spotted wallabies dodging through the thick scrub; this was exciting because wallabies are extremely rare around Mogumber. Emus were common, as were kangaroos. Western grey kangaroos and even inland red kangaroos camped in reasonable numbers on the middle slopes of the big hill.

Over the years, climbing through the scrub became progressively more difficult. The bush became ever more congested with a handful of vigorous species, mainly dryandra and tammar scrub, the smaller woody shrubs and herbs were gradually shaded out. By the 1980s it was clear a high percentage of original flora would soon vanish unless there was a fire to expose fallen seeds of smaller shrubs to sun and the chance of germination. However, such a fire would destroy the surrounding fence line and the terrain was too rough to construct effective firebreaks. We sat back and did nothing, half thinking a stray lightning strike from a summer storm might decide the thing for us. It was a good idea except, despite its height, lightning always missed the big hill and the process of gradual deterioration continued. We sold that section of the farm in 1982 and the next owner continued with the same hands-off policy. In fact, driving past several years into the new millennium I can see the same tangled mass of scrub still clogging the hilltop. By now, I suppose nearly all original

The gnamma hole paddock with Cam's nature reserve atop 'Mt Babillion' on the skyline

Opposite, clockwise from top:
Fuchsia magellanica 'Versicolor, the moptop hydrangea 'Heinrich Seidel' planted in a half-barrel, with the complementary trunks of magnolias and *Hydrangea quercifolia*; a few metres along the bank, *Cornus alternifolia* 'Argentea', the wedding cake shrub; 'Heinrich Seidel' and the fuchsia eight weeks later

flora is gone, along with our hopes of preserving a reasonable selection of smaller plants. All that is left are memories from nearly 50 years back.

While writing these past months I have tried over and over to imagine how the Mogumber bush looked prior to the arrival of the shepherds. All guesswork really, but an essential clue was to notice the Scotch shepherds could actually drove their sheep through that original bush. I know from experience merino sheep prefer open country – they are jumpy in dense vegetation and avoid it. The landscape cultivated lovingly by the Yuad people and first entered by the shepherds in the 1840s must have been much more open than the bush we found on hilltops and road verges in 1959. This line of thought leads me to ponder how the hills may have looked before the time of firestick agriculture, before the coming of the Yuad people, 30,000, perhaps 50,000 years back; the days of megafauna and giant marsupials: enormous kangaroos and colossal wombats and probably tree kangaroos all living in dense forest. I try to grasp the concept of geological 'deep time', puzzle at the Merrie-Lea streams flowing perennially, right through the heat of summer, edged with plants that now grow in Tasmania. Those hills are immensely old; once much higher, cooler, greener, the world a different place with all of Australia, to its northern coasts, washed by the southern ocean. These thoughts slip from my mind and I turn to the changing patterns of the last generations. October 1959, my first spring at Merrie-Lea, seven years old and I remember climbing the steep rocky slope above the homestead. The air fairly shimmered with the strange, rich and resinous perfumes of the pastel flowering bush. All was mysterious and extraordinary and its memory intense. That slope is turned to pasture now and today's rye grass and clover have an entirely different beauty.

THE SHRUB BORDERS

Opposite: View from the gateway cut through the hornbeam hedge beside the water garden. The gate is by Don Nixon, after a similar design in an Irish garden. Our Monet haystack hedge and archway beyond.

A low flight of steps leads from the peony pavilion terrace to the shrub borders. At present, we have panels of a small leaved, silvery green pittosporum flanking the steps. *Pittosporum tenuifolium* 'Silver Sheen' is one of the James Stirling group. All possess similar foliage and, unfortunately, all have the serious fault of growing far too quickly to clip into good formal hedges. Our panels need shearing six to eight times a year; far too many hours of clipping for me. A good hedge should only need clipping annually, or a midsummer trim plus autumn tidy. Watching Silver Sheen over the seasons, however, I noticed its growth is concentrated more heavily than many plants to the top of the hedge; the sides are often perfectly dense with the top metre irritatingly loose and open. Keeping this peculiarity in mind, I am now experimenting with allowing the top of the hedge to grow informally, clipping only occasionally while keeping the lower two thirds rigorously trimmed to give something of the look of one of Monet's haystacks from his paintings of the 1880s; in other words, a hedge with dense, vertical sides and shaggy overhanging roof. Now, this runs counter to how most hedges should be clipped, ideally, with a batter sloping 15 degrees into the light keeping lower parts of the hedge growing healthily. In the instance of our reasonably shade-tolerant pittosporum, so far this unorthodox treatment is working; the maintenance involved has been reduced by more than half and the part of the hedge rising above the shrubs has assumed an interesting, top heavy, rather fluffy appearance. The hedge gives not a bad impression of a haystack somewhere near the Seine. So far, so good, now we need only to find how well this regime works over a few seasons.

Delphiniums, purple flowers of *Rosa rugosa* 'Scabrosa', purple and pink *Berberis thunbergii* 'Rose Glow' and our golden pampas grass, *Cortaderia selloana* 'Aureolineata', the copper beech hedge behind

Walking over the Merrie-Lea hills with my camera in 2007 was unexpectedly tiring. Despite 17 years living in the Dandenongs on a – albeit small – mountain, the Mogumber hills seemed much more steep and rugged than I remembered; in fact, a very much more difficult hike than I allowed for. The reason was clear: the pasture is quite different now, much longer and coarser – and the sheep pads no longer exist. Although the sheep paths were narrow, 4 to 6 inches wide, we used them whenever we were in the hills. They were so convenient. They braided the earth everywhere, swooping around slopes, their weaving logic covering every possible permutation of wandering across the landscape with the least possible effort. Their design was impeccable, beyond the capabilities of the finest of two-legged landscape architects.

Changes to the look of the Merrie-Lea hills are due to the collapse in the wool market of the early 1990s. Losing money hand over fist with sheep in his first years on the farm, Paul Linke, the present owner, had no choice but to swing over to cattle and there has not been a sheep

on the place in more than 15 years. Cattle have a very different style of exploring their paddocks and choosing their grazing. Although I know only too well sheep are not kind to the soil, to drive around in 2007 and see barely one merino in the entire Mogumber/Gillingarra district was profoundly disturbing.

The shrub borders were originally planted with a high percentage of roses. These are gradually being replaced with more interesting plants, shrubs with better foliage, perennials with longer seasons of flower, anything not quite so spotty in its effect and needing a strict schedule of spraying for every disease under the sun. Then again, we will persevere with a few roses. I like the old Scotch briars, which flower cheerfully in mid-spring with masses of little blooms over excellent ferny foliage and intriguing black hips are produced in autumn with the leaves colouring to rusty tints. *Rosa chinensis* 'Mutabilis' is also excellent, reasonably vigorous and very long flowering with always a good number of single blooms opening soft apricot and fading to crimson over several days. I have a couple of autumn flowering agastaches to each side, one with crimson flowers, the other with apricot, and the combination is too cunning for words.

Above: A Scotch briar rose, I think 'Mary Queen of Scots' developing autumn tints. Notice its handsome prickles!

Left: *Rosa* 'Mary Queen of Scots', *Berberis thunbergii* 'Rose Glow', *Agapanthus* 'Guilfoyle', a few blooms on the David Austin rose, 'Sharifa Asma' and, at far left, a pollarded specimen of *Salix alba* 'Sericea'

I have a little collection of *amoena* forms of tall
bearded iris. They appear and disappear amongst the
shrubbery which, with luck, conceals their untidy
foliage during the second half of summer but still
with enough sunshine to bake their crowns and keep
them happy and flowering.

On the lower side of this walk, in fact growing along the top lip of the bank to the
side of the theatre lawn, we have several trees. Their canopies make an interesting
backdrop to the shrubs along the walk and they also screen the theatre. A couple of
trees have always grown here, or at least for the past 40 or 50 years: a specimen of
the American tulip tree, *Liriodendron tulipifera*, swiftly approaching 15 metres in the
lower corner of this area for instance. It has thrown up a dense tower of large,
lobed, pale-green leaves and the textual effect of its foliage is good. However, its
green leaves precisely match the pale green tulip-like flowers it famously produces.
They do have orange markings within the bowl of each bloom and I'm sure rosellas
enjoy the show peering down from its top twigs in early summer, but I have to
remember to look for the flowers and only more observant visitors notice.

Other trees on this bank include two or three maples and an ancient, increasingly
decrepit Japanese silver bell, *Styrax japonicus*. The silver bell is so old it produces its
tiny bell flowers only the occasional spring and I have prepared for its demise by
planting a *Malus tschonoskii* close by. This spectacular crabapple is grown for silvery
green summer leaves turning scarlet in autumn, the undersides creamy pink. The
combination is startling, especially as its growth is vigorous and columnar, the pale
pink felted lower surface of the foliage prominent from below. Nearby we have an
upright small tree with smooth grey bark punctuated by narrow creamy horizontal
ridges, its tiny evergreen leaves are indented giving a lacy appearance, which, in
addition to the elegant branch structure, makes for a noteworthy tree. But what
on earth is it? We wondered for at least 10 years and posed the question to many
people with an arboreal bent until the mystery was solved by Ken Allen, who
identified it at a glance as *Nothofagus microphylla*. Ken did have the advantage of his
years as superintendent of the Melbourne Royal Botanic Gardens with a nice
specimen of this tree in his charge. *Nothofagus microphylla* is a South American
southern beech and rather rare. We also have a couple of the New Zealand species,
Nothofagus fusca and *N. solandri*, the red and black beech, and one of our local species
Nothofagus cunninghamii, the myrtle beech. Our myrtle beech grows beside the nursery
car park, by coincidence, at the end of a row of northern beech, *Fagus sylvatica*. Lovely
stands of myrtle beech can be found on the higher mountain slopes above
Warburton, just across the valley from us. These gnarled trees with their dark lacy
canopies seem like a Shakespearean *Midsummer Night's Dream* woodland, perhaps
wrenched from forests of New Zealand or Chile. They certainly appear out of context
with their gum tree surrounds. Southern beech and northern beech are loosely

Our wedding marquee with the *Pittosporum* 'Irene Patterson' hedge. *Echium* 'Cobalt Giant' in flower on the right.

The quadrangle, bench by Graham Foote

Holly topiary, archway through hornbeam hedge, early autumn

related. However, southern beech are quintessentially Gondwanna Land relics, evolving when South America, Antarctica, New Zealand, Australia and India were locked into one land mass. Before the advent of the theory of continental drift it was impossible to see why closely related trees should grow isolated along distant shores of the world's greatest ocean. With our understanding of plate tectonics, the gradual reshuffling of the world's continents over the earth's surface, we puzzle no longer.

The araucarias are another example of a Gondwanna plant. *Araucaria araucana*, or the monkey puzzle tree, forms immense forests in Chile while, on the opposite side of the Pacific, the Norfolk Island pine comprises the one big tree of that particular island. A little to the northeast of Norfolk Island, several species of araucaria survive as a present-day Jurassic forest on the islands of New Caledonia. The bunya bunya pine of Queensland, *Araucaria bidwillii*, is Australia's most famous member of this family. Our neighbours have a spectacular example of bidwillii growing in the Rangeview woods below Cloudehill.

27 April 2005

A cool, bright autumn day, no cloud, the sky milky blue. The Yarra Valley buried below mist earlier, but we in our pale sunshine. The past two weeks without rain has been good for seasonal colour. Jim's big weeping maples are flaring to a warm red, close to the colour of the setting sun. They are almost at their best for this season. The two big Enkianthus perulatus above the summer house have softened to a dull purple and will probably flush crimson next week. By our restaurant, the Senkaki maple is now a mass of lemon, with orange-pink tints bleeding over the upper canopy.

Five pm, the air still and pale with suspended water. Colour in the trees across the garden fades minute by minute and cooling air is made visible with its thick burden of water. Evening air thickens from transparency to a mere grey translucency with gathering dew.

Japanese tree peonies
Top: *P.* 'Hana-kisoi', Floral Rivalry
Above: *P.* 'Renkaku', Flight of Cranes

Most of the plantings in the shrub borders are still experimental and I am changing them, year by year. Shrubs, however, are meant to dominate, making up two thirds of the planting. Perennials, annuals and biennials, even climbers such as clematis are used in frontal positions and to extend the season. We aim to have shrubs flowering from mid spring to early summer and perennials providing interest to late summer. Shrubs provide winter structure, helping define and screen the borders from the quadrangle lawn to be found up the little flight of steps towards the row of European beech along our north boundary.

The quadrangle lawn connects with a further small enclosure in which we have erected an ornamental marquee. Cloudehill hosts the occasional wedding ceremony,

Top to bottom: *P.* 'Hana-daijin', Minister of Flowers;
P. 'Taiyo', Great Emperor; a good plum form
of *Helleborus x hybridus (orientalis)*

and on showery days the wedding parties may need shelter, or ordinary garden visitors for that matter. The marquee has a pointed roof and is a rather tizzy affair so we have planted a rather tizzy hedge around it made from the creamy white variegated *Pittosporum tenuifolium* 'Irene Patterson'. This is a slower-growing pittosporum, requiring around three clips annually to maintain and I think it can make an excellent hedge, if one can find a way to incorporate its tizzy look.

Above the quadrangle lawn and in the lee of the boundary row of beech, we have a raised bed devoted to a small collection of Japanese tree peonies. Peonies in the 'botan' group are trickier to grow than the lutea hybrids, also depressingly difficult to propagate. However, they are unearthly when growing and flowering happily. Their blooms may be all of 20 and 30 centimetres in diameter, larger still than chinese peonies, those in the 'mouton' group, but in similar colours: lustrous whites and rosy pinks and crimsons and purples. Flowers usually form in bowl shapes with a boss of golden stamens and colossal, almost translucent, very delicate petals. It does not take much of a shower to collapse and destroy one of these ravishing flowers. The Japanese place umbrellas over the finest blooms – a bizarre thought, but with our spring rainfall I suspect we might need to do likewise. When one sees *Paeonia* 'Renkaku', Flight of Cranes, with magnificent, luminous white semi-double blooms however, or *P.* 'Taiyo', the Great Emperor, displaying extraordinary goblets of scarlet and ruby red, then the reason for taking the care required to flower Japanese peonies well is self-evident. I am still adding to my collection, and we have room for perhaps a dozen of these aristocratic beauties in this bed. They still need a few years to show why they deserve so much mollycoddling.

The flowering of Japanese peonies is as short as it is ravishing, so to provide a warm up act to their display I am under-planting them with hand-pollinated hellebores. *Helleborus orientalis* grows easily in shady places throughout the garden. We found any number of plants of this variable species with interesting and not so interesting flowers, growing from Jim and Bessie's time. These were the old whites and pinks and murky purples, sometimes spotted, sometimes not. However, we now have hellebores available in vibrant plums and coal blacks and mauve slate greys and limey primrose, also doubles in many of these colours. Hand pollination ensures that seedlings produce blooms with similar colour and form to their parents. Ordinary seedling hellebores are much of a lucky dip, there are always a high percentage of murky flowered specimens. It is worthwhile hunting down hand-pollinated hellebores; they are such useful plants, they adapt to most gardens in southern Australia, any garden in fact with shade from a tree where little else will grow. Their blooms are a leading feature of the cooler months when every flower is valuable.

As we drove along the entrance track together into the old Bletchley house to take photographs in the spring of 2007, the first time either of us had seen the place since January 1959, my sister Jenny remembered meeting Cam walking in a rainstorm along the very same track in the early 1950s. He was sheltering under a jute wheat bag slit down one side with the intact bottom over his head as a hood, striding through the storm grinning from ear to ear, exultant at the rain.

To our dismay the house itself had not been lived in for nearly 40 years and was ruined. Despite the poor season the farm itself seemed in good heart, apart from a few hundred acres swallowed by salt over the past half century. Crops seemed as good as the season would allow, still, I am glad Cam never saw the Bletchley house with part of its roof missing, its verandah peeled away by the wind and crumpled corrugated iron and tumbleweed everywhere. He spoke to me of it only months before he died and was sure it was still lived in and cared for. Bletchley was a very happy place for Jan and Cam.

The Bletchley homestead, a windy day,
September 2007

Commemorative plaques,
Lake Varley

Two days later, Jenny and I went to see the Francis family's old Holt Rock farm. It was the first time for me and to our amazement we found Cam's 1938 mud brick house in tiptop order with a sparkling new corrugated iron roof and looking good for the next 100 years. A promising wheat crop stretched away in what was their original 50-acre paddock, except now that same paddock seems to extend on and on to the boundaries of the old farm, 1200 acres (480 hectares), and perhaps beyond. And the farm, as it is now, has grown to 14,000 acres (5600 hectares); every acre of it cropped each year. Individual paddocks were so immense as to make an estimation of size impossible; impossible to guess if a wheat field was 200 or 400 or 800 hectares. Paddocks were all treeless, yet divided by broad strips of the healthiest eucalypts I have seen for ages. Despite colossal paddocks, every view was dominated by trees.

As it happens the present owner is another Cam, short for Cameron this time around: Cameron Mudge. Cameron's family took over the property from my father's family around 1970 and he now has a business with a capital value of several million dollars plus a million or two in machinery and using world leading technology at every point in his operation.

I was also astonished to find the homestead was so close to the 'Number One Rabbit Proof Fence', a few minutes' drive – fewer than 10 kilometres, with pastoral country stretching away to arid zone mining towns of Norseman and Kalgoorlie off to the east. However, despite sitting wedged firmly against the edge of the wheatbelt the eastern lakes district is well regarded – in a drought-blighted season the crops of Lake Camm and Lake Varley and Holt Rock were as promising as any I saw anywhere in Australia that season. Cameron was looking forward to a respectable harvest with rainfall for the year of just 170 millimetres (around seven inches); desert rainfall really, by the standards of ordinary cereal growers around the world. The district is tightly held, descendents of pioneers are still prominent.

Looking back, I think my father's life in so many ways was blessed. Certainly he suffered privation as a child, yet this was offset by extraordinary good fortune: robust health and his Hollywood good looks, the support of my mother for all those years and their passion for each other; also that they commenced married life during that golden age of Australian farming, the 1950s. The first years of my parents' marriage at Moulyinning coincided exactly with reliable seasons and the best prices for Australian agricultural products for generations. At no other time has it been possible to establish a farming business from scratch within a mere seven years.

Except for a handful of stories, all brief in the telling, his pioneer taxi driver anecdote for one, and listening to 'synthetic' test cricket matches from England featuring Don Bradman on a crystal radio in the small hours, my father never spoke of Holt Rock until near the end of his life. For example, I had no idea I had two aunties on my father's side of my family until Cam *announced brightly one day he was visiting his big sisters and, after asking if I might like to come, drove me around to their house and introduced me to Dorothy and Ruth. This was just before Valerie and I moved to Victoria. Jan was most unhappy and would not come but she accepted my going with Cam. Dorothy and Ruth were naturally elderly, in fact both widows by then; intrigued at a first meeting with a middle-aged nephew. It was a curious afternoon, the atmosphere tentative, calm, no hint of the bitterness of 40 years earlier. It was good to meet them; both died very soon afterwards.*

I have long suspected Jan's influence on my father was pivotal. She was several years his senior. I have photographs of each of them taken, by coincidence, on the same piece of pavement by a street photographer outside the old Commonwealth Bank building in Murray Street in Perth, the two shots taken in the late 1930s I'd guess, certainly within yards and possibly within weeks of each other. My mother is strolling along dressed to the nines in the latest fashion, shoulders straight, head thrown back, smiling airily and oozing joie de vivre. On the other hand, Cam in his photo is with a couple of gangly mates, all three giving appearance of boys just down from the bush, in the big smoke for a day or two and out for a bit of a spree. He is wearing no more than might be expected at any Lake District occasion. The second photo left me nonplussed; whenever he was away from the farm, I myself remember Cam very smartly turned out.

Water catchment wall and storage tanks, Holt Rock, the Francis family farm beyond the trees

Fallen Gimlets

For a man with a childhood most might see as austere, my father went on to varied achievements, apart from 50 years in agriculture and three times building up properties from scratch. He was a Victoria Plains Shire councillor, was instrumental in the establishment of the New Norcia branch of the St John's Ambulance Brigade, sat on the WA Agriculture Protection Board, served as a justice of the peace, was even a delegate to an Anglican synod. None of the latter were easy for him – he had a dread of speaking in public. On several occasions I heard him stumble into anguished silence, once in a relaxed gathering as he proposed a toast at a neighbour's wedding; after long uneasy moments I turned away, deeply embarrassed and a little angry. The image springing to mind as I puzzle on it, is the view from the summit of the Holt Rock, just a ten-minute stroll from the family's 1929 camp: the crumbling, sun-blasted surface of the rock itself, rolling away in strange little rounded hills and valleys, oddly reminiscent of a scaled-down English downland district; stunted mallee and sheoak struggling in its eroded gullies, and beyond, open wheat fields and dry climate eucalypts spread endlessly over the slow undulations of that voiceless landscape.

Mind you, on ordinary social occasions the qualities everyone saw in my father were his affability and good humour. A female friend remembers him from the 1980s as the most charming man she had ever met, and had an unspoken "crush on him for years", – she less than half his age. Any inadequacy he felt over his background was outweighed by his confidence – in his own physicality, I suppose – and his sense of fun. He never forgot a face

and remembered names with ease (a shame he so carelessly neglected to hand those sterling virtues down!), he made friends wherever he went and kept his wits about him to the end. It was not a matter of chance that the saving grace of Cam's final years were his friends; there were many to keep an eye on him, especially when frailty and illness suggested he should not be living at home on his own. At the close of my father's funeral, as the casket glided away into the rear of the crematorium, a girl, one of his carers of those last months, darted from the congregation and threw a red rose down beside the sheaf of sunflowers resting on the polished wood.

Gimlets beside the road a few minutes' north of Holt Rock, September 2007

THE EMPTY THEATRE

In her book, Italian Gardens[8], Helen Atlee describes an 'entertainment' staged in the gardens of Flavio Chigi's villa outside Rome in the summer of 1668, the evening brief, yet so memorable it is described in letters and essays by several participants; even a set of engravings commissioned by one as an aide memoir. Guests to a twilight banquet find flaming torches illuminating a darkening garden and an elderly gardener apologising: they are too early, tables not laid, nothing ready. Only, the gardener, long known to every visitor, is apologising in verse! Guests, puzzled, embarrassed, notice the gardens seem strangely unfamiliar, things shifted and changed, large trees and a little fountain in what was always a bare courtyard; but were they, in fact, in place when all arrived? And from gathering shadows gods and deities now emerge: actors in costume. Guests exclaim in confusion, how is it these smiling gods, Pomona, Flora, Bacchus, are strolling among them without anyone noticing their entering the garden? And in the torch light several tables can now be seen: one piled high with extraordinary dishes carved wondrously from sugar, another with curious drinks and a wine fountain, a third with crystal goblets and silver cutlery; all appearing in the midst of guests, it seems, as by magic. People gather round their phantasmagorical feast and a tremendous clap of thunder sounds. Fading echoes are accompanied by a storm of rose water and confetti and, the air clearing, astonishingly, all see not only are the deities suddenly melted away, but the laden tables also. The gods and the feast are vanished, conjured back into the shadows; the garden deserted now, but for the guests themselves. It becomes clear there will be no banquet this night. All are left to find their way to carriages and return home, bewildered, delighted; still hungry.

not a mouse
Shall disturb this hallowed house,
I am sent with broom before
To sweep the dust behind the door.

Shakespeare, *A Midsummer's Night's Dream*

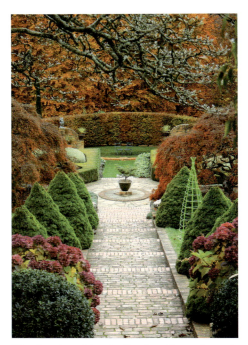

View from top of steps leading from the maple court to the restaurant

Looking from the Japanese tree peony bed, a flight of stone steps leads the eye down to the heart of the garden, the theatre lawn. Our green theatre is the central component of this axis. From the quadrangle lawn looking to the south, one's gaze flows from the uncluttered circular space of the theatre out through a gap in the surrounding beech hedge into the spring meadow. The turf and clipped hedges of the green theatre also form the denouement of the east–west axis as one stands and looks down the slope from between our weeping maples. After exploring the maple court, visitors may descend formal brick steps between the parterres to the gently sloping circular lawn. In the context of the garden, the lawn is meant to be reasonably generous, some 25 metres in diameter. At the bottom of the lawn and enclosed by brick walls a small crescent-shaped piece of grass forms the stage. The tops of the brick walls, curved into a quarter segments of circles, echo walls in other parts of the garden. The walls serve as wings to the stage.

30 April 2005

A mild, overcast day. Very still earlier, but this evening wind is rising, rain expected tonight. The air cool and I take the chance to warm myself stoking an autumn fire of seedling chestnut and blackberry. Walking through the car park I watch wind gather beech leaves into a corner. They scatter and regather against the low stone walls. An echo in my mind of dry leaves flicking stone pavement, sailing in and out of the light from street lamps. Kew Gardens in London, an evening ten days into October, 1973. Coppery bat wing leaves from street side London planes skittering and whispering at my feet, last days of a perfect summer.

Both the circular lawn and the stage area are surrounded by hedges of green beech. Most are clipped to 2 metres; however, the hedge behind the stage is cut into an arc with its highest part over 3 metres and in direct line with the axis from the maple court. Standing on the stage, one looks up the slope of the auditorium to red brick formal steps between the heavy stone walls retaining the maple court. The ivy-covered walls are capped with a strip of deep green box (actually the edge of the maple court parterres). From the maple court further steps lead on to Jim Woolrich's old house, recently converted into Cloudehill's restaurant. A final flight of wooden steps, enclosed with curving, rusted steel balustrades, welcomes the weary visitor up onto a deck beside the restaurant where we have lemonade and cake at the ready.

Looking at a plan of Cloudehill, the garden consists of four more-or-less parallel axes intersecting a further four more-or-less parallel axes more-or-less at right angles, and several minor axes are to be found lurking. Along with straight lines and squares and rectangles there are several circles. Also, the symmetry in the upper parts of the garden falls away gradually to the informality of meadows and wooded areas below.

The beauty of working with these ingredients is they allow the rooms within a house, in our case the restaurant, to flow out into garden compartments. The creation of compartments – garden rooms – allows a gardener to play tricks with perspective from one part of the garden to the next. Also, it is easy to use a variety of themes, whether colour, texture or structure. A generous assortment of themes can be squeezed into a much smaller space than any other style of garden might require. Cloudehill has 24 and more individual gardens within its bounds.

Structure thrown up by garden compartments also provides the best possible backdrop for shrubs and perennials. Despite the current enthusiasm for naturalistic and prairie-style planting in Europe and the US, I think herbaceous perennials are at their finest displayed against hedges and walls. Architecture is also a vital element in winter, during the period herbaceous plants retreat underground. Mind you, grasses and massed herbaceous plants in an open setting can be good and I am experimenting between the upper and lower meadows with this in mind.

Two final family photographs: the first of my mother taken as a young woman in the early 1930s, gazing past the left shoulder of the photographer, thinking heaven knows what thoughts. The second is a family group staged in a way that photographs are never staged today, I guess from 1922 or 23. It shows my mother's family when she was young. My grandparents sit at each end of a handsome table set out in a garden, laid with a lace table cloth and a vase of flowers. The family are resplendent in their Sunday best, suits and ties, mother in a lacy little-girl outfit of the period. Behind the table stand the boys, my Uncle Ronnie and Uncle Stanley when they were around 10 and 12, flanked by the two older brothers, my Uncles Hector and Aubrey. My mother sits carefully on the ground in front of the table. Jan was Elinor Jean in those days. She changed her name to Elinor Janet and began using the second name, I think, because she always distrusted the anomalous spelling of 'Elinor', then thought if she was to be known by her second name she would really prefer to choose it herself. She became 'Janet' only in her 20s. And she was always Jan later in life, I never once heard her called Janet.

The most astonishing thing for me is my Uncle Aubrey, standing to one side. He died of kidney disease more than 10 years before I was born. It was thought for a very long time no photograph of him survived and this, certainly, is the only existing image. Aubrey was by reputation the most promising of the family and he was the brother Jan loved the best. He had time to research the disease that killed him; my mother vividly remembered Aubrey telling her that the shame of it was, he had been born just a few years early; machines for cleansing the blood were just around the corner and with them his disease would no longer be fatal. Jan also remembered Aubrey, Hector also, admonishing the younger brothers: they

*"must never be unkind to their sister". I suspect my mother was raised in a household of,
at times, almost 19th-century courtesy and gravitas, at least in the relations of the family
members; and also perhaps, as the youngest, and a girl in a family of brothers, with more than
a hint that, ultimately, little would be denied her. It made for a kind of serene, self-contained
certainty in everything she did – in how she set about winning and loving Cam. It was evident
also in how she faced up to the disease that blighted her last years. She suffered it for a long
time, quietly, with no word to any in the family except, I suppose, my father. At first it was
diagnosed as a rare form of Parkinson's. There were no tremors and other symptoms for
a long time not obvious. I had no idea she was ill when Valerie and I moved to Victoria.*

*The photograph might easily commemorate the McPhee family setting off to the Lakes District
to settle their farm. It was certainly taken within a little while leading to that date but there
is no way of knowing for sure now. The photo was lost to the family for nearly 60 years, burnt
in the fire that destroyed their Lake Camm farm in the 1930s. However, perhaps because the
family portrait was a grand occasion, my grandparents sent a copy to relatives in Victoria,
and it seems they put it away and forgot about it. The photo turned up again in the late 1980s
and was sent on to my sister, then living in inner Melbourne. Jenny framed it nicely and put
it on her mantel. Jan and Cam came to visit for Christmas in 1990 and my sister thought it wise
to mention the photograph to Jan as she arrived and directed her to the room. As it happened,
Jenny was right to be prudent. Jan was momentarily lost in wonderment and distress. Seeing
the photograph, mother said only, "But they are all ghosts".*

'Why dost thou so explore,'
Said Glaucus, 'of what race I am, when like the race
of leaves
The race of man is, that deserves no question? Nor
receives
My being any other breath. The wind in Autumne
strowes
The earth with old leaves; then the Spring the woods
with new endowes—
And so death scatters men on earth, so life puts out
againe
Man's leavie issue.

From Homer, *The Iliad*, book IV,
translated by George Chapman

All flesh waxeth old as a garment: for the covenant
from the beginning is, thou shalt die the death.
As of the greene leaves on a thicke tree, some fall,
and some grow; so is the generation of flesh and blood,
one commeth to an end, and another is born.

Ecclesiasticus 14: 17–18

One project of recent years has been to find places for a series of small pieces of text. These were displayed originally in the garden back on Clover Downs. My sister-in-law, Trish Stewart, inscribed several lines onto terracotta plaques, which I hung on the piers of a pergola. The lines were by Harold Nicolson, the co-creator of Sissinghurst, and were translations of favourite pieces of Virgil[9]. Wrenched out of context, these fragments have a quality reminiscent of haiku. The plaques came with us over the Nullabor and I use them now to suggest a mood to parts of Cloudehill. Over the years I have collected scraps of poetry from anywhere and everywhere, from Shakespeare all the way to the *Oxford English Dictionary* (in which I found the lovely Chaucer fragment: "the hous is krynkeled two and fro..."). Earlier I mentioned ceramic plaques inscribed with several translations of Homer comparing generations of men to the falling of leaves, and a passage from the Bible with a similar theme. These were placed into the copper beech walk several years back. Round the same time I began experimenting with Trish Stewart's terracotta plaques on the brick walls and arches along the main terrace. Placing a piece of text in the garden makes for conundrums. As hedges grow and areas mature the mood to part of the garden will change, consequently plaques have tended to shift about. Eventually they will be fixed into place as I become confident of various themes in parts of the garden.

Like Leaves on Trees, the Race of Man is found
Now green in Youth, now with'ring on the Ground,
Another Race the following Spring supplies,
They fall successive, and successive rise;
So Generations in their Course decay,
So flourish these, when those are past away.

From Homer, *The Iliad*, book IV,
translated by Alexander Pope

In 1988 I found a monograph by Yves Abrioux on the garden made by Ian Hamilton Finlay: Little Sparta or Stonypath[10]. I think the alternative names are very appropriate to this inspirational place. Stoneypath is one of the great gardens of the last 50 years.

Frail as the leaves that quiver on the sprays,
Like them man flourishes, like them decays.

From Homer, *The Iliad*, book IV,
translated by Samuel Johnson

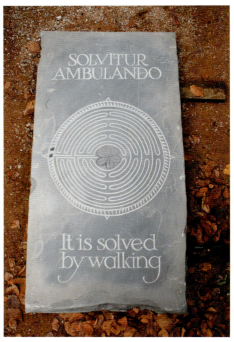

Top: Ian Marr in action letter cutting

Above: Piece by Ian Marr, now installed into the paving between the water garden and the steps down to the warm borders

Made from a few acres around an abandoned farmhouse in the Pentland Hills, south of Edinburgh in Scotland, the garden is full of poetry, either composed or collected by Hamilton Finlay. Poetry is inserted into the fabric of his garden as carvings on wood or stone, even cast into bronze. I was already thinking about poetry in the garden at the time I discovered Hamilton Finlay. Studying Stonypath certainly added impetus to my own experimenting. Reading Sheeler's monograph[11], I was astonished to find that one of my 'collected' pieces, a poem titled *The Middle of Life*, by Friedrich Holderlin and translated from the German by James Blair Leishman, has also caught the attention of Hamilton Finlay. Or rather, Hamilton Finlay incorporates the first stanza into Little Sparta while I, so to speak, had had my eye on the second:

> With yellow pears leans over,
> And full of run-wild roses,
> The land into the lake,
> You gracious swans,
> And, drunk with kisses,
> You dip your heads
> In the sacredly-sober water
>
> Where shall I gather though,
> When winter comes, the flowers, and where
> The dappling shine
> And shadow of earth?
> The walls will stand
> Speechless and cold, the wind-swung
> Weather-vanes clatter.
>
> Friedrich Holderlin, *The Middle of Life*
> translation by James Blair Leishman

Using text in gardens has a long tradition. Perhaps at its height in the 18th century with the making of Stowe, and Pope's composing lines specifically for the grotto at Stourhead in Wiltshire, it is something I hope to explore further for the possibilities it provides of incorporating mood in the landscape. So long as the grating clichés of the makers of concrete garden ornaments are avoided, I think the use of inscriptions is to the good.

Walking past the collapsed and disintegrating outbuildings of the Bletchley homestead I remembered it was exactly this place, at age four, perhaps five, I experienced some sort of epiphany: the thought I could be the only real person in the universe. Everyone else, including my own mum and dad, might be simulcras (I might call them now); put on earth to test my – honesty I think it was. This train of thought sprang from a talk on 'cupboard love', at school, or was it bible classes? I have no clear recollection now; all I remember is the question put to us: did we love our parents, really and truly, or were we just making a show of affection in order to beg lollies and treats? The proposition floored me. The very question seemed unfair. How could I be sure of my motives? It was all too easy not to notice slipping from love to guile – 'If I'm good I might be given an ice cream'. It followed – surely there must be someone keeping tabs on such moments. And then, who was it doing this – in fact, how could I ever be sure that even my own mum and dad were not part of some immense experiment checking on my character. Perhaps they were angels in disguise whose job it was to find me out. I stood that morning, these thoughts windmilling, thinking my head might explode with the wonder of it. The moment certainly made an impression. The same spot on the sandy path stood out as I strolled past 50 years later.

Bletchley landscape. The exposed foreground sand is the fire break that farmers in Western Australia are required to maintain around their farm boundaries.

On another point though, my memory let me down utterly. Astonishingly, I could easily see while driving most of the way around the outer fence line to speak to a neighbour, Bletchey's soil from boundary to boundary was all sand – not much better than the sandhills of the Dandaragan Plateau. I had spent 50 years of my life until that morning thinking it was goodish loam, from memories as a six-year-old, one paddock in the southwest corner I would have sworn was red clay. However, we were warned by the neighbour the track leading in was likely impassable due to the dry season; we could expect our vehicle to bog in loose sand. I was almost disbelieving, except – the district was clearly mainly sand. Ten minutes later I found the clearing around the ruins of the house was entirely sand. Drifting sand entirely concealed the paving near the back door, was mounding over the disintegrating verandah and blowing through the house. And now, I am thinking of the sandy, salt-laden paddocks of Holt Rock and Lake Camm and only as I write do I see why Cam was so happy to take on the rough old rock-strewn soils of the Gillingarra hills. And abrasive, were those Gillingarra soils abrasive! There are soils in farming districts so smooth that the hardened points attached to scarifier tynes can be left in place for years, for the life of the machine in places; when ploughing the earth slips past like rustling silk. In fact, the paddocks of Moulyinning and Holt Rock were not far from this, though the ease of working those soils was outweighed many times over by their lack of nutrition, their tricky rainfall, their consequent knife-edge profitability. Ploughing Merrie-Lea, on the other hand, the gritty, quartz raddled soil hammered case hardened points back to misshapen useless lumps in less than 18 or 20 hours of good solid work on average. Every few hours through every night, the tractor would be stopped with me under the 33-tyne scarifier swapping points over; usually unbolting half a dozen each time, hammering every fresh point to shape against its tyne, bolting it firmly home. Still, in among the rock and rubble, the soils of Gillingarra and Mogumber had guts. A glance at a tree making growth, a stroll through any pasture, the good green of the clover, the strength of the rye – all were confirmation. I reckon Cam, doing his inspection way back in the winter of 1958, standing, listening to the water from the cloudburst just passed over crashing through rocks above, swivelling his boot heel through the capeweed to see the colour of the soil, could not believe the chances of it, couldn't credit his luck at finding this place.

It astonishes me to think, now, how fortunate we were to find that Jim Woolrich's life's work led so seamlessly into the creation of a garden that I had been contemplating for many years. Jim's hillside, as it was in 1992, with its air of a biggish, between the wars, cottage garden let go for 25 years, seemed to cry out for 'restoration' and the addition of structure. We were also fortunate that within the context of the high rate of exotic planting in the Dandenongs, part of the history of these hills ever since Ted Woolrich opened his nursery for business nearly four generations ago, our garden is reasonably at home. A Cloudehill made in the surrounds of pristine bush would, I grant, be ridiculous.

What might I have done if we were still living on the farm at Mogumber? I have wondered often how a garden like Cloudehill might be made in a bush landscape. It could not be done literally; indigenous plants filling compartments would be absurd. However, I suspect the introduction of structure and mass into native gardens can be good. How splendid it could be for walls to provide a sense of demarcation and scale to natural rock formations for instance, perhaps on an arid hillside, and to use plants with a degree of discrimination. Walls made from the earth itself perhaps, as a backdrop to our unworldly and subtle indigenous flora; an excellent project for a future lifetime!

I find myself drawn to the window seat on flights back to Western Australia. Read a little, or close my eyes and doze over the Great Australian Bight, but I take notice as we cross the coast and commence passing over the wheat belt. I look down on the huge grey paddocks of the Esperance sandplain and Ravensthorpe and consider the salt lakes. Everywhere small and large lakes cascade from district to district; their edges are forever on the move, expanding and coalescing with seeming organic vigour, reminiscent, perhaps, of bacterial blotches on their way to overwhelming a colossal petri dish. From 10,000 metres their colours are breathtaking, pale pewter pinks and cloudy greys and sandy browns with wind shifts of colour from shoreline to shoreline. Winter cumulus clouds echo the land forms, shadows tethered beneath, and reflected sunlight semaphores from lake to lake as we fly overhead. And I can never help but ponder, from my window seat, anyone with an interest in contemporary 'land art' should surely approve of the view: circles and ovals and swirling oddities of lakes scattered with studied ease across innumerable intersecting straight lines; the strictly linear ground plan grid of farmland.

Great constellations of lakes lay scattered from end to end of the wheat belt, from the outer edges of the Lakes District right across the Great Southern. Lakes Grace, Kukerin, Moulyinning, Dumbleyung, Wagin; all are hemmed with salt lakes. Lakes rim the gentle slopes of the Avon Valley and the inner wheat belt and lap insistently against the thin grey forests of the Darling Ranges. Ten thousand rectilinear paddocks are interspersed everywhere with luminous, crushed mother-of-pearl lakes; ocean archipelagos, indifferent and serene, stranded through the green-gold wheat.

Hydrangea 'Heinrich Seidel' with *Phalaris arundinacea* 'Mervyn Feesey'

Steps from theatre to quadrangle lawn

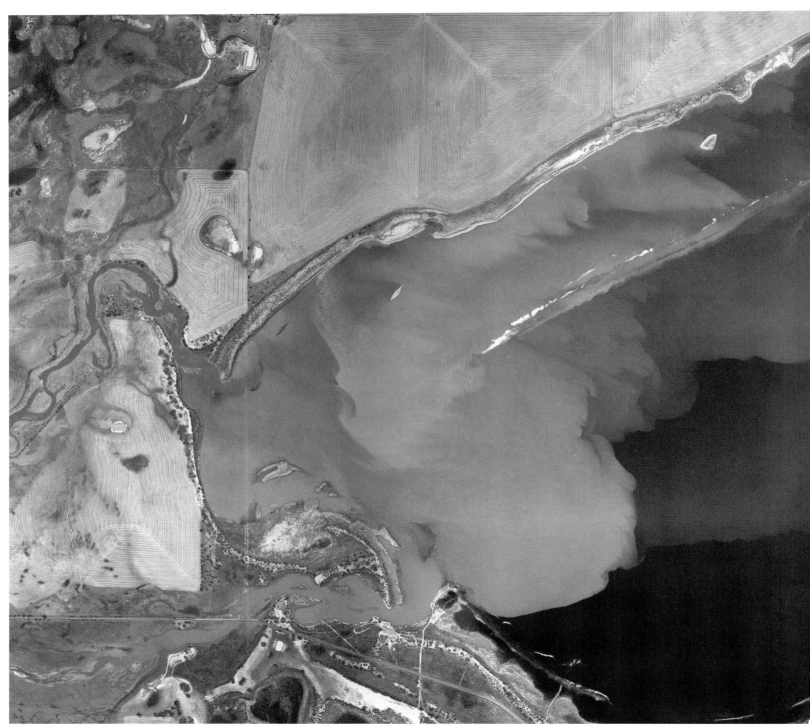

This extract of *Drifting Narembeen* (Kondinin Lake, WA) is part of the 'Earth is Art' series, www.landgate.wa.gov/earthisart.
Image provided courtesy of and reproduced with permission of Western Australian Land Information Authority, 2010.

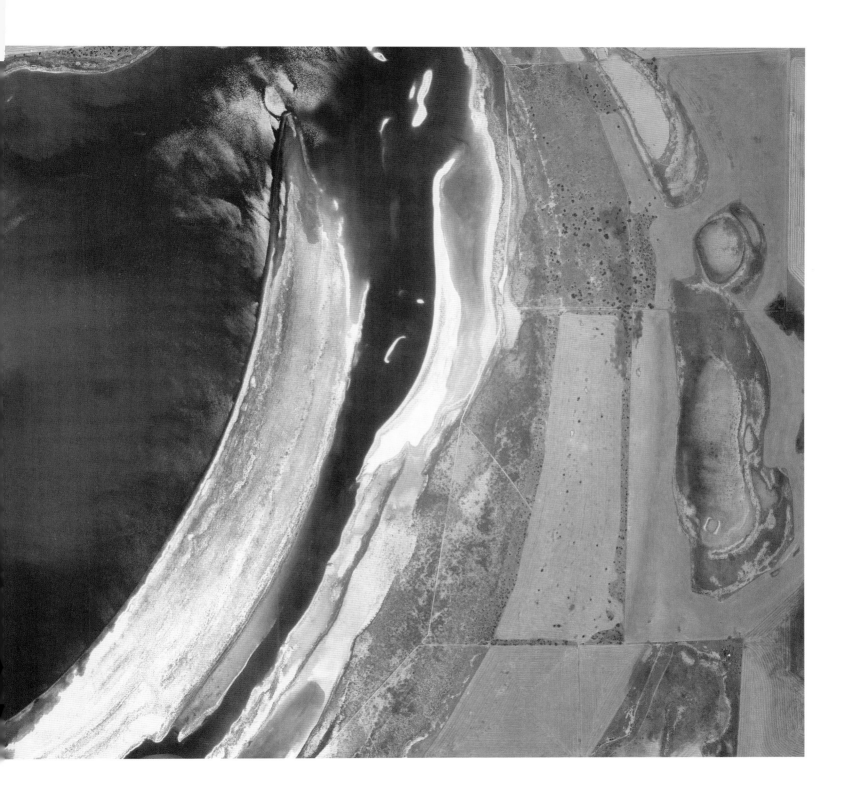

Outdoor theatres go back to classical times; they were the focus of the Greek city states and the cities and towns of the Roman Empire. If we contemplate the nexus between religious ritual and performance, perhaps theatrical themes in the landscape can be traced to the stone circles of megalithic Europe, of the Wiltshire plains, French Atlantic coast and Hebridean islands. However, the green theatre, the *teatro verde*, as a component of a conventional garden, originated with the renaissance and baroque gardens of 16th- and 17th-century Italy. A number survive. The gardens of Villa Gori and Villa Geggiano, for instance, both have theatres, and the lovely theatre of the Villa Reale di Marlia, near Lucca, was famous for its outdoor court performances for hundreds of years; even today terracotta Commedia del' Arte figures glance out of niches in old walls and hedges. In 1550, Eleanor of Toledo, wife of Duke Cosimo the First, excavated on heroic scale to turn the entire

Boboli Hill beside the city of Florence into an amphitheatre. A substantial part of the well-to-do population of Florence could be accommodated to enjoy the family's weddings and pageantry and theatrical performances within these stupendous gardens. Even water theatres were incorporated into the grounds of several gardens, for instance, the Farnese Palace at Caprarola, and a sense of performance seem to be the essential theme in the very structure of the famous gardens of Villa D' Este and Villa Lante. How far can this idea be taken? Perhaps the making of every garden with the thought of a visitor is at some level an act of performance. Or, at the least, every garden includes an element of stage design.

A number of English gardens of the past 120 years have a green theatre within their layout. One of the finest is in Hidcote. Adjoining Hidcote's main axis is a large rectangle of lawn enclosed by hornbeam hedges. Towards one end, a circular dais has been raised above the lawn as a stage; visitors are invited to notice the stage is the highest part of this hilltop garden. The circular stage is three quarters enclosed with more hornbeam hedge, the broken circle of hedge lying open to the body of the rectangle. The stage is bare except for three beech trees. These elements make a fine theatre, atmospheric and intriguing. The idea of incorporating a theatre into Cloudehill came from my thinking of garden making traditions of both Italy and England.

Part of the logic behind Cloudehill's theatre is to provide a calming blank space as contrast to the surrounding garden. Contrast, especially, to the song and dance of the herbaceous borders on the terrace above. The circle of grass enclosed by its 2-metre-high green beech hedge is primarily meant as a place to settle the mind. One may look above the sweeping line of the clipped hedge to the taller beech behind the stage, the row of trees planted back in the winter of 1962. The latter rise some 10 metres above the arc of the formal hedge and although several copper beeches are intermingled with the greens, the colour and texture of the low hedge is, on the whole, repeated in the trees beyond. The tall beech, naturally, are more open than the formal hedge and in leaf they respond to wind with vertical waves of moving foliage while the leaves in the lower hedge barely flutter. The massive 1928 riversii copper beech to the right of the lawn is much closer to maturity than the 1962 trees, old enough to have developed considerable stiffness in its growth. Although the riversii no longer possesses the elegance of the younger trees; it is full of character, monumental even. We prune its lower foliage to keep a view of multiple grey trunks rearing majestically into its canopy.

Much Ado about Nothing, courtesy of the Great Southern Shakespeare Company

View from the theatre to the upper meadow

In autumn, beech leaves darken to a strange grey-green, then turn and fall coppery gold. Conversely, the formal beech hedge retains its foliage through the cold months and the warm brown tonings of dry leaves harmonise wonderfully with the terracotta and apricot brick wing walls to each side of the stage. Otherwise, in the twiggy canopy of bigger trees, all is grey and silver. I have planted a *Salix acutifolia* 'Blue Streak' to lean over the beech hedge at the top of the auditorium. This willow's varietal name refers to the silvery blue new wood produced as it grows swiftly into a pendulous mound of around 8 by 8 metres. Blue streak's narrow leaves hang through summer to give a thoroughly willowy look to the thing, they turn lemon while falling in autumn and in May the previous season's wood produces narrowly pointed, intensely silver catkins. These expand and are handsome through winter, and fluff into creamy yellow little powderpuff flowers come spring. In colder months, our blue streak willow is the loveliest plant in the garden. Studded with silver catkins, its long pale twigs catch the faintest movement of air elegantly and thrash in the most violent storm without breaking.

Perhaps though, winter in the theatre, the best time is a morning with no wind. A morning with sunshine through mist, beech leaves in the encircling hedge darkened to chestnut with dew, leaves glistening and the enclosing tracery of trunks and branches and twigs of taller trees now silhouetted against, now lost within an ever-changing blue silver sky.

Saturday, 28 May

ENDNOTES

1　Ted Jordan Merideth, *Bamboo for Gardens*, Timber Press, Inc., 2001

2　Jane Brown, *The English Garden in our time*, Antique Collectors' Club, 1986

3　Marina Schinz and Gabrielle van Zuylen, *The Gardens of Russell Page*, Stewart, Tabori & Chang, Inc., 1991

4　Anne Scott-James, *Sissinghurst: The Making of a Garden*, Michael Joseph, 1974

5　Roger Grounds, *Ornamental Grasses*, Timber Press, Inc., 2003

6　Graham Stuart Thomas, *Perennial Garden Plants*, Frances Lincoln Ltd, 2006

7　E.A. Bowles, *My Garden in Spring; My Garden in Summer; My Garden in Autumn and Winter*, Timber Press, 1997

8　Helena Attlee, *Italian Gardens*, Frances Lincoln Ltd, 2006

9　Vita Sackville West and Harold Nicholson, *Another World Than This*, Michael Joseph Ltd, 1945

10　Yves Abrioux, *Ian Hamilton Finlay, a visual primer*, Reaktion Books, 1985

11　Jessie Sheeler, *Little Sparta: The garden of Ian Hamilton Finlay*, Frances Lincoln Ltd, 2003

Note: The historical information in the essays on pages 17–19 and page 21 is sourced from Rica Erikson's book, *The Victoria Plains* (Lamb Paterson, Perth, 1971).

INDEX OF PLANT NAMES

PHOTOGRAPHY AND DRAWING CREDITS

Unless otherwise noted, photographs are from the Francis family archives, or have been taken by the author.

Photographs by Paul Cantlay
87 top right, bottom right

Photographs by Graeme Chapman
(www.graemechapman.com.au)
44, 45

Photograph of *Darwinia carnea* (a 19859)
© M. Fagg, Australian National
Botanic Gardens 46

Photographs by David Glenn
66, 67

Drawings by Ian Marr
8, 19, 22, 25, 158, 238, 240

Map of Cloudehill by Ross McLeod
132

Photographs by Marcus Ryan
178, 179

Photographs by Claire Takacs
6, 104, 111, 112 bottom, 137, 138, 143, 149 top left, 151 top, 167 bottom, 168 top, 172, 174–75, 182, 189, 190, 191, 192, 197, 198, 202, 203, 227, 232 top, 256

Extract of *Drifting Narembeen* (Kondinin Lake, WA) provided courtesy of and reproduced with permission of Western Australian Land Information Authority, 2010
254–55